STORM WARRIOR

First printed 1991

STORM WARRIOR
By Ian Minter and Ray Shill

Copyright:
Ian Minter and Ray Shill 1991.
No part of this publication may be
reproduced, stored in a retrieval
system or be transmitted in any form
or by any means, electronic, mechanical
photocopying, recording or otherwise, without
prior permission in writing of the publisher.

Produced and printed by
Amber Valley Print Centre, 388 Boldmere Road,
Sutton Coldfield, West Midlands
for the publisher.

ISBN 0 9517755 0 2

STORM WARRIOR

by

Ian Minter and Ray Shill

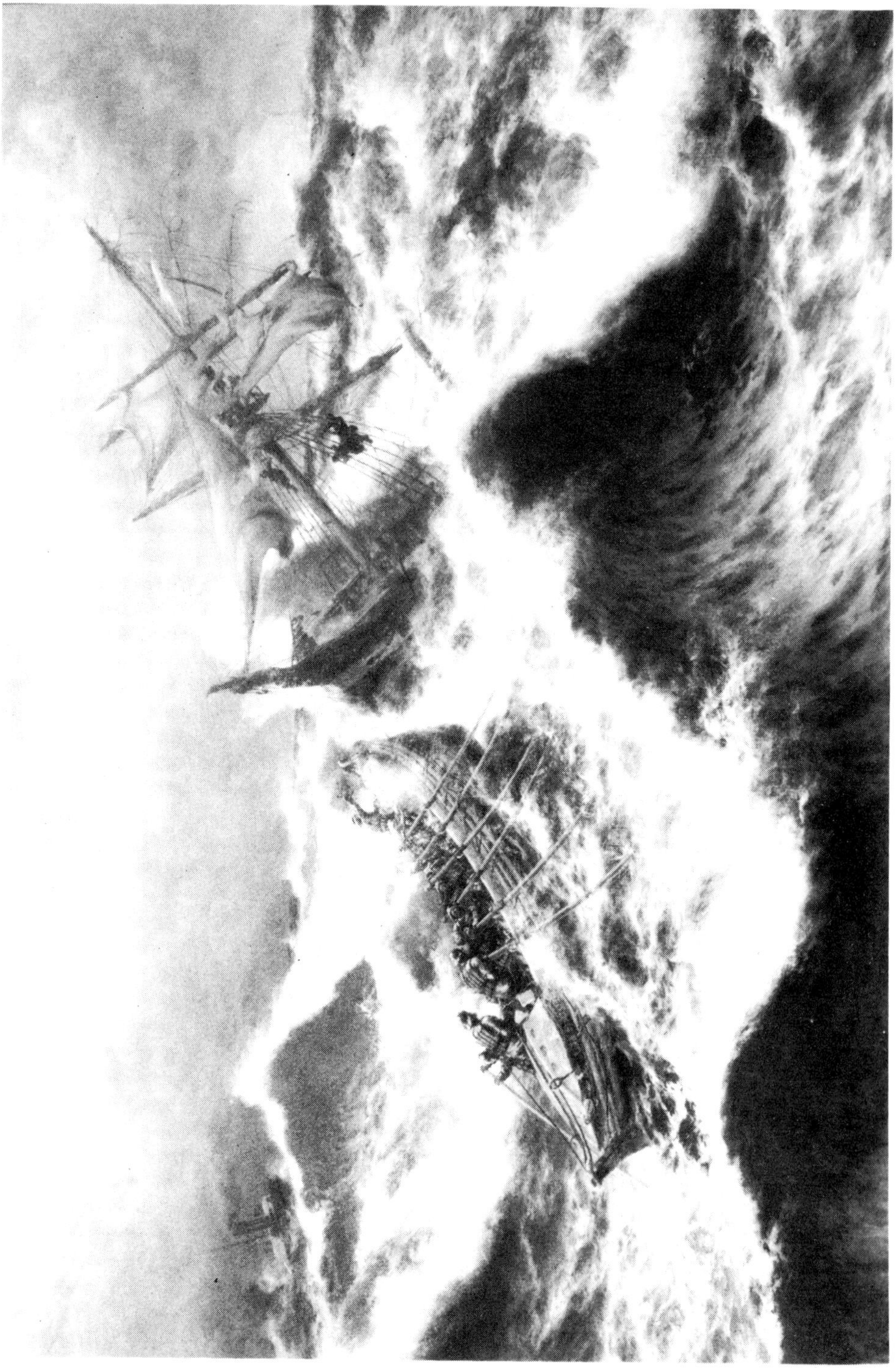

CONTENTS

Chapter		Page Numbers
1	The Initiation	6
2	The Early Years of Henry Freeman, Whitby Fisherman	15
3	The Busfield Family	31
4	Henry Freeman and the Lifeboat Years 1861-1866	50
5	Henry Freeman, Fisherman	58
6	Coxswain of the Lifeboat	77
7	The Wreck of the Visiter 1881	96
8	Calm Before the Storm	117
9	Before the Magistrates	122
10	The Troubled Years 1883-1891	140
11	Henry Freeman Ambassador and Spokesman	154
12	The Freemans in Whitby	169
13	The Watson Family	188
14	Henry Freeman, Veteran Lifeboatman	199
15	A Question of Legality	211
16	A Peaceful End	217
	Postscript	224

Appendix 1	The Family Tree of Henry Freeman	228
Appendix 2	Henry Freeman's Fishing Cobles	229
Appendix 3	The Rescues in which Henry Freeman participated	230

Bibliography and Acknowledgments 232

Index 236

"STORM WARRIORS' Painted by Thomas Rose Miles (1869-1888). Reproduced by kind permission of David Oliver May, Esq. FRINA of Lymington Marina.

CHAPTER 1

THE INITIATION

The gale had blown all night. With each passing hour it had gained in strength. Finally with the dawn, a ferocious storm broke. The seas went wild unleashing all the fury at their command.

Many vessels were off the Yorkshire coast on that stormy Saturday morning, the 9th. February 1861. Colliers mostly, they had set sail from ports near and far, from the North and the South: from faraway Dundee, from Newcastle, from Sunderland, from London, Portsmouth, Folkestone and Brixham. Whatever its port of origin, or its destination, every vessel found itself locked in the same desperate struggle for survival, compelled to run the gauntlet of the most violent storm for years.

On the evening of Friday 8th February, the first assault was launched by abnormally strong winds from the North-East. The battering went on through the hours of darkness as the mounting force of the gale drove the ships off course. At daybreak, the punishment became savage and cruel, with a redoubled onslaught from both wind and sea.

Among this huge fleet of hapless vessels was a brig from Sunderland, the *John and Ann*. Its crew of five men had fought bravely to hold their course, but they were powerless against the storm. Not long after dawn, the brig was driven on shore at Sandsend, a short distance along the coast from Whitby.

An eyewitness to this first casualty of the storm was the look-out at Whitby itself. He spotted the vessel in distress at about 8 a.m. But there were seven more witnesses to the plight of the *John and Ann* who were closer to the scene.

Walking along the beach from Whitby towards Sandsend was a group of fishermen. Confined to the port by the violent seas, they had resolved the night before to set out at first light to search the beach for wreckage. Items useful to fishermen such as yards and ropes could often be found on the shore in the wake of a storm.

Six of these men were lifeboatmen. John Storr, Robert Leadley, George Martin, William Tyreman, John Dixon and William Dryden were all accustomed to saving lives at sea.

The seventh man, however, Henry Freeman, was younger than most of them and lacked their experience. Until recently he had been a brickmaker by trade, and he had only lately turned to fishing as a livelihood.

Portrait of Henry Freeman *(By Alfons Ludyk)*

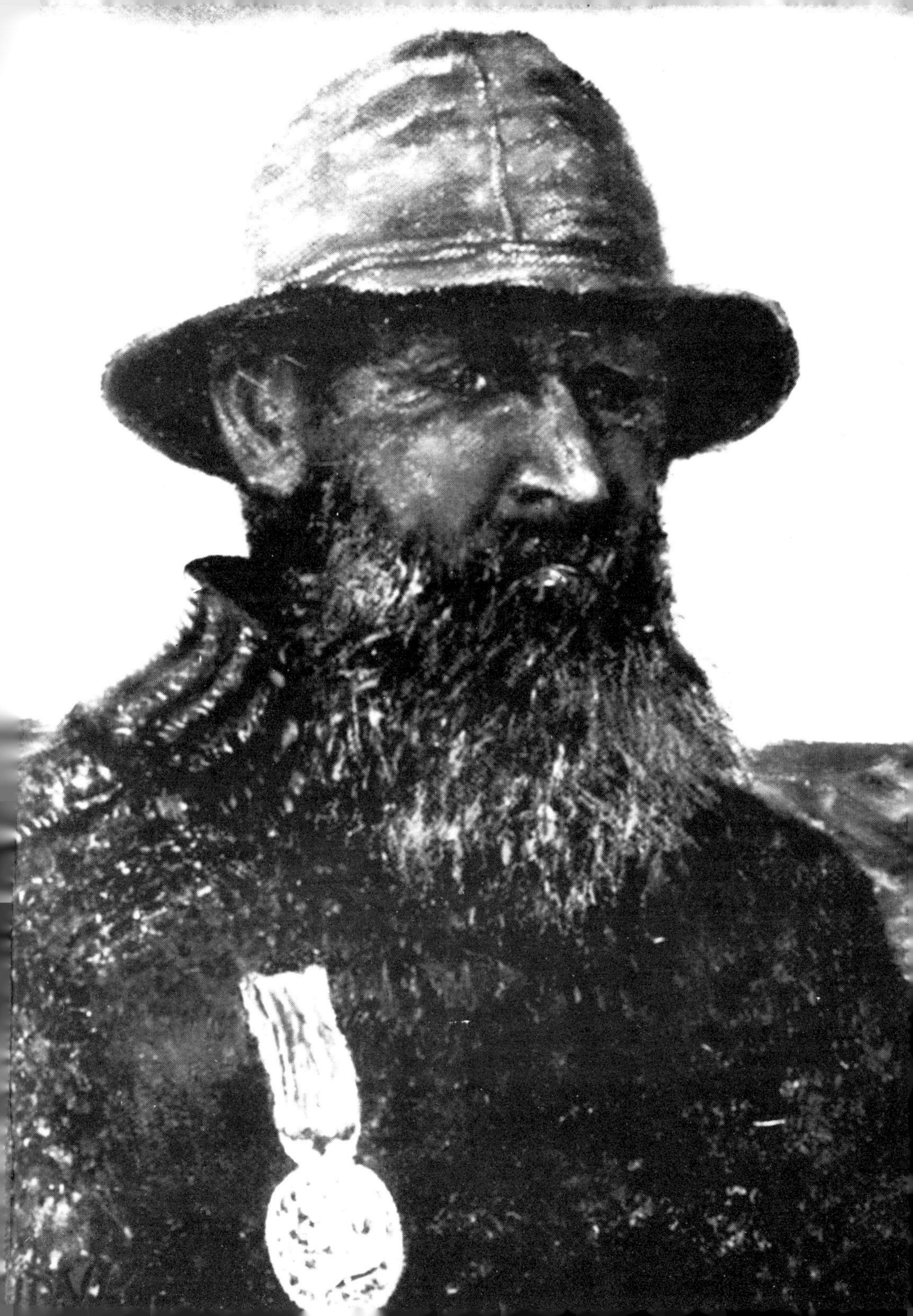

The fishermen knew there was no time to waste if the crew of the *John and Ann* were to be saved. The tide would be turning soon, and the gale was still gathering force. All seven manned a Sandsend coble and put to sea in her.

The rescue was a difficult and hazardous venture. At any moment the waves might have capsized the coble. But dismissing the risk to their own lives, the Whitby men saved all the brig's crew.

The rescue successfully completed, the lifeboatmen returned with Henry Freeman to the town. They got back to Whitby about ten o'clock and found the people were getting out the lifeboat to go to a vessel that was coming for the beach. They fell to and helped to get her out and the lifeboat and its carriage were hauled by a team of horses to the water's edge, not far from the pier.

Into the lifeboat, under John Storr's command went all the men who had been with him at Sandsend, except Dryden. In addition, there were Christopher Collins, Matthew Leadley, John Philpot, R.Stainthorp, and John Storr's two brothers, Thomas and William. Of the twelve men only Henry Freeman had never been in a lifeboat before.

The vessel in distress was the schooner *Gamma* of Newcastle, bound for London with a cargo of coals. She had come to the beach only three or four hundred yards from the pier and run aground. Her crew of four men were in grave danger, and to avoid being swept overboard had taken at once to the rigging.

The lifeboat was pulled off by her crew. The four men on board the schooner were rescued and landed safely on the sand. Once on the shore the lifeboat was replaced on its carriage, and hauled back up the beach to await further service.

After getting the boat up, the lifeboatmen went and had a glass of grog each. Some were wet through to the skin and all were cold. They badly needed the hot rum drink to restore them. Freeman joined them, but John Storr remained behind with a few other men and anxiously awaited the next emergency.

It was not long in coming. When Freeman and the others returned to the pier, they saw a barque heading for the shore. It was the Prussian barque *Clara* bound for Madeira from Newcastle with coals. She came ashore at 11.30 a.m. a little to the north of the *Gamma*.

Immediately an attempt was made to get a line to the wreck. Captain Butler's men dragged the rocket apparatus from the Coast Guard station along the sands to bring it up close. But no contact could be made, for the line broke as soon as the rocket was fired.

The lifeboat was launched again, with only one change in her crew: William Walker replaced Stainthorp. After a hard pull and being repeatedly driven back, they managed to reach the vessel. The *Clara* was taking a dreadful battering from the waves and was close to destruction.

In spite of the danger, a full fifteen minutes had to be spent alongside the wreck, as it was feared that one of the crew had not been accounted for. The fear proved groundless, and the lifeboat left the ship with all eleven of her crew safe on board. Not long after they touched the sand, the barque broke up, and disappeared beneath the tremendous seas.

The lifeboat was replaced upon its carriage and again hauled up the beach. This done, her crew went for another glass of grog. John Storr remained behind in conversation with William Tose, the Harbour Master. Tose had noticed that something seemed to be troubling him.

The lifeboat was new and Storr had not been out in her before. "Well John", inquired Tose, "how do you like the boat?" Storr's frown deepened: "The boat is alright, but too narrow" he replied; "there is not enough leverage to pull the oars. If we have to pull off with a heavy sea, it would tire any man to get her off."

Only half an hour later, about one o'clock, the brig *Utility* from Folkestone, and the schooner *Roe*, from Dundee, hit the shore almost together, both of them close to the Coast Guard Station.

The lifeboat was manned again, but not before an argument had broken out among the lifeboatmen as to who should replace Thomas Storr. He had been called away to look after his father's fishing boat, which had suddenly been placed in jeopardy by the storm. At once, two men climbed into the boat to take his place, Isaac Dobson and Robert Harland. None was willing to give up his place in favour of another, so finally she was launched with a crew of thirteen men, instead of her normal twelve.

After another battle against the furious seas, they reached the schooner, and rescued the crew. Then they passed onto the brig, and took her men on board. They brought them all safe to land, four from one vessel, and six from the other. Hearty cheers greeted the lifeboatmen on their return, for by now a huge crowd of anxious spectators had gathered.

By two o'clock, the tide was well up. The sea now covered the lifeboat slipway. Huge waves were breaking over the pier and flooding the road leading to it. Mr Tose and John Storr, the men's leader, had already agreed after they landed the two crews that the lifeboat would have to be suspended from service until after high water. Any launch before then would be extremely dangerous.

The men were returning down the pier after finishing another glass of grog when they saw a schooner coming for the beach. Another schooner, the *Flora* of London, from Portsmouth, had already responded to Mr Tose's signal to make for the harbour, and had successfully completed the risky manoevre. Her crew was safe, and the vessel not too seriously damaged after its collision with Tate Hill Pier.

The schooner upon which the men had fixed their attention had not been so lucky. Named the *Merchant* and bound for Maldon from Sunderland, with coals, she had tried to follow the *Flora*, but her sails had given way before she could reach the safety of the harbour. At once the storm drove her, helpless, towards the beach. She ran aground between the *Utility* and the *Roe* where she began to take a dreadful battering from the violent waves.

The lifeboat crew were weary after their labours during the day. Freeman and his fellows had not consumed anything since breakfast in the morning apart from the grog. Yet exhausted and hungry as they were, the men could not forget that the lives of the stricken crew were in their hands.

Attached by a rope to the pier, the boat was launched for the fourth time, in spite of the earlier decision that she be suspended from duty. The schooner *Roe* lay in the path between them and the *Merchant*. The intention was that with the help of the rope, the lifeboat could pass safely between the pier and the *Roe* without colliding with either one.

The crew in the boat was the same as on the previous launch. John Storr remained as steersman, as he had been all along, and William Storr, his brother, assisted him on this occasion. The men wore lifebelts of the standard type, which fitted low on the body to allow free movement of the arms.

One man, however, had a belt of a more recent design. Henry Freeman was wearing an experimental cork life jacket which fitted over his shoulders. He had refused one of the conventional type when it had been offered to him earlier because he thought there was no danger. Later he changed his mind and took the new life jacket which happened to be in the boat.

The treacherous back and cross seas from the look-out and the pier soon placed the lifeboat in grave danger of being dashed against either the pier or the *Roe*, in spite of the securing rope. John Storr decided to cast off the rope and steer well away from both obstacles. He gave the order and his men immediately pulled hard to the north of the vessel.

Passing round the *Roe*, they succeeded in reaching the *Merchant* but only with the greatest difficulty. The lifeboat suddenly seemed strangely unequal to the conditions: the men could sense the difference in her, and were beginning to feel uneasy about it.

The *Merchant's* crew had no rope ready for them when they drew alongside her. While they were getting one, the lifeboat was swept astern. The lifeboatmen struggled to get in the lee of the *Merchant* but were driven back several times by a mighty cross sea.

Finally two enormous waves collided with a third on its rebound. They spurted up together like a mighty explosion right under the bottom of the lifeboat. The combined force of the waves threw the boat completely out of the water and turned her right over. Before they knew where they were, the entire crew were in the sea.

John Storr managed to climb onto the bottom of the upturned boat, while others were floating about with their lifebelts on, struggling for their lives. Watching their plight, barely sixty yards away, were thousands of horrified spectators, shrieking and crying in despair. This sudden cruel twist of fate was more than they could bear. Standing little more than a stone's throw away, they could do nothing to assist.

As soon as he saw the accident, Captain Butler fired the rocket to throw a line to John Storr, but it was to no avail. The rocket went off, but the line broke and blew away to leeward. John Storr had disappeared before another rocket could be fired.

Desperate to help, the crowd of onlookers frantically hurled life-buoys in a frenzied bid to save the dying men. Their efforts were futile, for the men lay outside their range. One after another the heads of the lifeboatmen were overwhelmed by the sea. When the wave had passed, only their backs could be seen, brought to the surface by the lifebelts they wore around their bodies. No help whatsoever reached the drowning men, some of whose wives and children stood, numb and disbelieving, amongst the weeping spectators.

One member of the lifeboat crew, however, had not succumbed. When the boat capsized, Henry Freeman found himself trapped under it. He tried to find the air pipes but could not, as the boat was full of water. Letting go he plunged under her side, and hauled himself out.

For a brief instant, as if in a dream, Freeman caught sight of John Storr upon the bottom of the boat, clinging to it desperately. That glimpse, lasting only seconds, was the last he saw of Storr alive. Suddenly Freeman lost his grip of the boat's landing and he was swept away. Next he saw John Philpot and Matthew Leadley, struggling in the water. He managed to shout some words of encouragement to Philpot. And then as before, they were gone, as the sea swept him on, this time towards the pier.

For an agonising moment, it seemed as if he would be crushed to death against the pier, for a vessel was being thrown against it repeatedly by the sea. But a huge wave swept Freeman out of danger, towards the slipway.

Freeman's cork jacket was easy to spot from a distance, and the crowd soon saw him. People rushed to the slipway to save him. Twice he was carried by the waves towards their outstretched hands, only to be dragged away again before they could seize him. At last, the third time, some men caught hold of him and pulled him from the water.

Brave efforts were made to rescue the bodies of Freeman's dead comrades. One man who went down with a line round him to recover Matthew Leadley's body received injuries and concussion after the battering he took from the waves. Other men risked their lives and sustained injuries to rescue the bodies of Tyreman and Dobson from beneath the boat when it was washed to the shore.

The loss of the lifeboat did not deter others from mounting a fresh attempt to save the *Merchant's* crew. All five men on board the schooner were rescued. When the rockets failed, Captain Butler had used the mortar, and succeeded in getting a line thrown across the ship. The rescue apparatus was passed to the vessel, and one after another, the crew of five were safely hauled to the pier in the cradle. Shortly afterwards, the *Merchant* yielded to the raging seas, and became a total wreck.

Henry Freeman was the sole survivor of the thirteen men who had gone to the aid of the *Merchant*. Eleven of the twelve men who died were married, and left families behind. Only Henry Freeman, and one other, Christopher Collins, were unmarried.

The final tragic rescue attempt had been launched at about 3 o'clock, and had culminated in disaster a matter of minutes later. It was over so swiftly that William Tose never saw the boat upset as he looked away momentarily to check that the cradle was ready for use.

The Lifeboat nears the wreck intent on saving lives

More rescues were to follow. The work of saving lives was not over until nightfall, the final rescue of the day being to the brig *Tribune* of Brixham, at seven o'clock that evening. All day long, shipping was destroyed in the storm. More than two hundred vessels were lost in the freak conditions. A number of ships sank at sea off the coast of Whitby, far beyond the reach of any help.

The following morning, the beach was strewn with wreckage. Many Whitby folk combed the shore for anything of value they could find, precisely as Henry Freeman and his dead colleagues had done on the morning before.

Just twenty-four hours earlier, Freeman had been a complete novice to lifeboat service, a raw recruit. In the most cruel initiation imaginable, he had gained a lifetime's experience in a day, narrowly cheating death, and seeing all his comrades perish in the storm. The tragedy would remain fixed in his memory for the rest of his life.

Only a cork life jacket had spared Henry Freeman from a certain death at the age of just 25 years.

THE LIFEBOATMEN LOST IN THE 1861 DISASTER

Name	Age	Abode
John Dixon	55	
William Walker	53	Church Street
John Storr	50	Church Street
William Storr	45	Church Street
John Philpot	44	Church Street
Robert Harland	42	Cragg
Robert Leadley	42	Church Street
Matthew Leadley	37	Church Street
Isaac Dobson	35	Cragg
William Tyreman	29	Haggersgate
Christopher Collins	28	
George Martin	25	Cragg

All save two were buried in St. Mary's Churchyard. The bodies of Christopher Collins and John Dixon were never recovered.

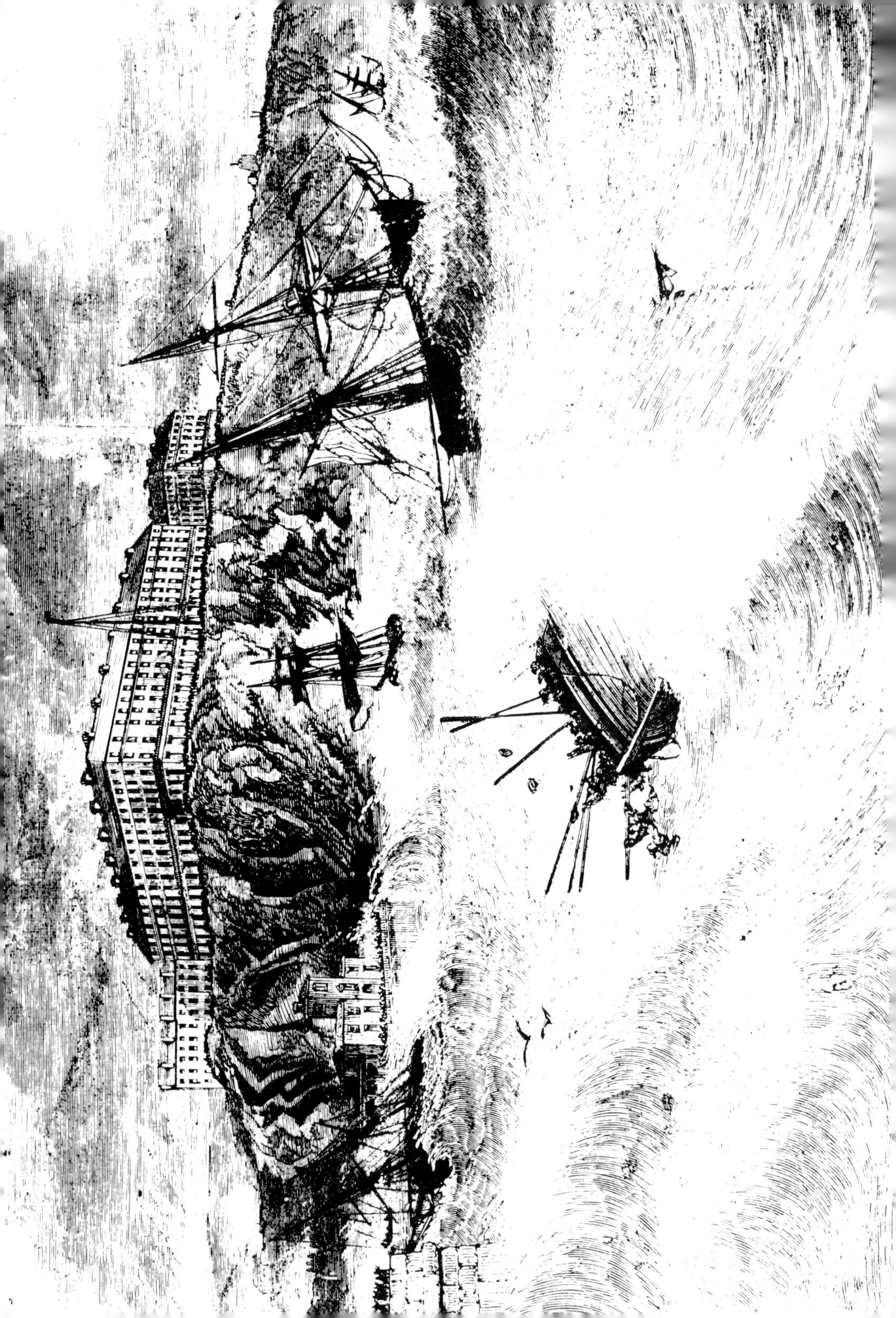

CHAPTER 2

THE EARLY YEARS OF HENRY FREEMAN, WHITBY FISHERMAN

No one could have foreseen that Freeman's induction into lifeboat work would be so traumatic. But it might reasonably have been predicted that after such a close brush with death, the man would abandon all his seagoing ambitions, in favour of a safer occupation. Few men, after all, except the foolhardy, the insane, or the very brave, willingly court death more than once.

Yet, so far from avoiding danger, Freeman positively embraced it. He persevered in his twin careers as fisherman and lifeboatman, and in time became greatly respected for his achievements in both.

To understand why Freeman continued his career as a fisherman requires an examination of the rather complex set of circumstances which brought him, from his native Bridlington to Whitby. A wide range of influences, including geographical considerations, economic and social factors and Freeman's own personality itself, all played a significant part in charting Freeman's course in life.

Yorkshire to many people's imagination is a county of stark beauty encompassing windswept moors, dark stone villages and breathtaking views of hills and dales. Yet, as a county, it is full of surprises and there are parts which more closely resemble the flat land of Holland than the rugged scenery usually associated with Yorkshire.

The Vale of York is a case in point, particularly that land which lies between Goole and Hull and borders on the rivers Humber and Ouse. There are many small villages here and the staple industry is agriculture. In the summer fields of wheat stretch for miles, often as far as the eye can see.

It was here that the Freeman family had its roots, deep in the farming community. There were Freemans recorded in the district in the sixteenth century and no doubt they were there earlier than that. They feature particularly in parish records belonging to the ancient minster of Howden.

Nearby at the hamlet of Portington Henry Freeman's father, William was born. Today it is a collection of a few farmhouses and some lie derelict. Large fields stretch into the distance indicating that agriculture remains the major industry there.

The 1861 Lifeboat Disaster   *(Photograph courtesy Illustrated London News)*

In William's time it was very different. There would have been more dwellings and more families living there then. For he was born when the Parliamentary Enclosure Acts were changing the Yorkshire farming landscape. The traditional method of working strips of land was giving way to the farms, fields and hedgerows, while new land was being reclaimed from the estuary and marsh. The whole area was undergoing a tremendous change.

The future which these changes created for the county's young people was far from promising. Reorganisation of the land offered fewer jobs for the agricultural worker. Here as in other parts of rural Britain the trend was to leave the land and take the more lucrative but tedious jobs provided by the Industrial Revolution.

William's brother John carried on the family tradition through farming at Gilberdyke. But William chose another course, that of brickmaking. There were several brickyards in the area especially near Gilberdyke where the Market Weighton Canal could carry the bricks down to the Humber. No doubt William found employment in one of these or another in the neighbourhood where he learnt the trade which was to fashion his future life.

One mile south of Portington lies the village of Eastrington whose old brick cottages mingle with the new around the stone church in much the same fashion as they did in William Freeman's time. William Freeman was brought to this church for christening on the 1st of March 1795, as had been his older sister and brother and three younger sisters later on.

View of Eastrington Parish Church. It was in this ancient Gothic building that Henry Freeman's father, William, was baptised and married. *(Photograph Ray Shill)*

THE VALE OF YORK AND NORTH LINCOLNSHIRE

It was in this region that the Freeman Family had its roots

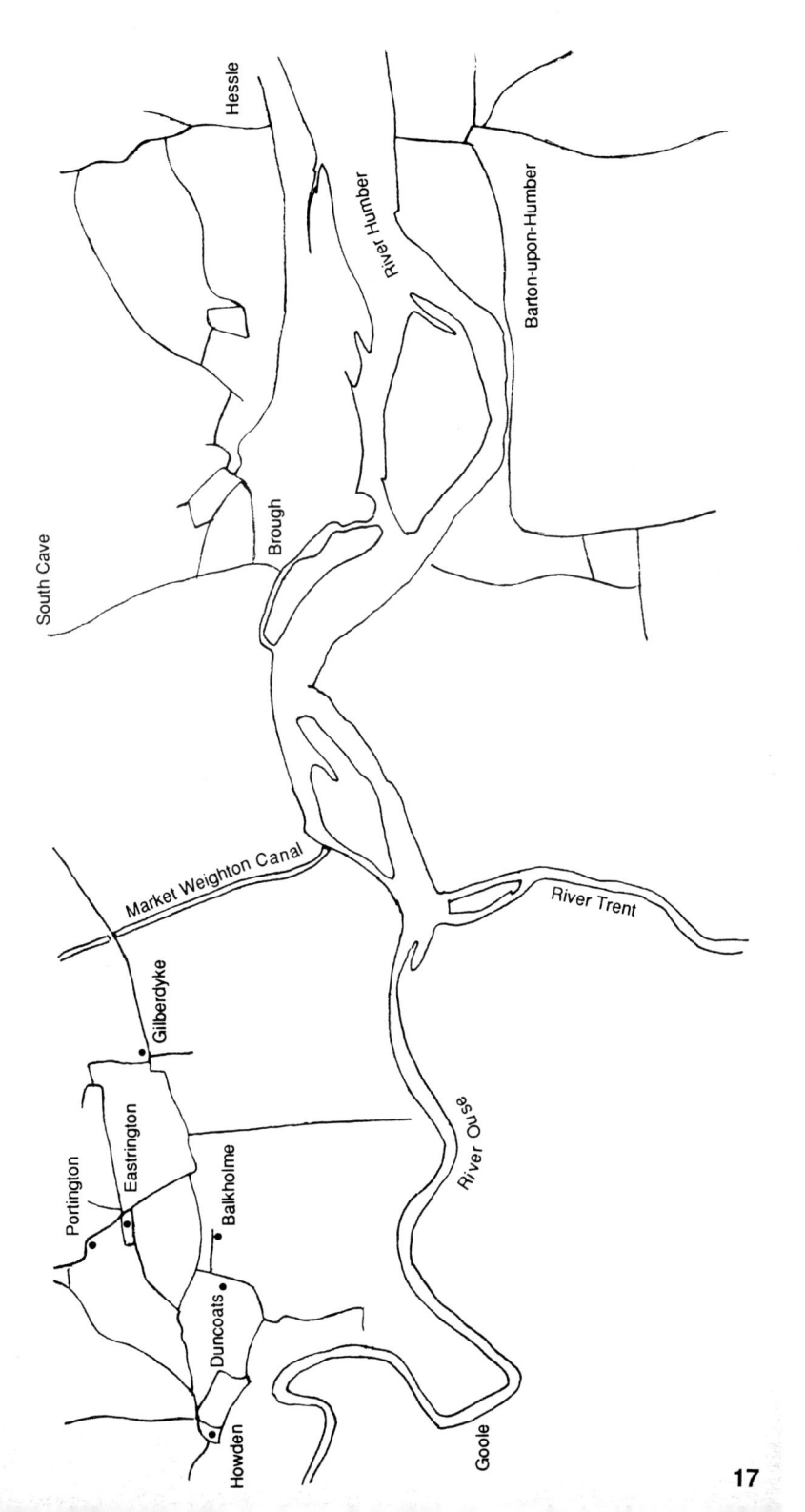

He married at the same Church in December 1820 a local girl called Margaret Priestley, a labourer's daughter. She had been born at Duncoats, a small hamlet of Balkholme, on the 12th August 1795. Their first child, Ann, was baptised at Eastrington on the 13th January 1822.

William Freeman's choice of work led to an itinerant life for himself and his family. In these early years he lived in the Howden area where Margaret bore him another daughter, Mary, then a son, John. By 1827 they had moved to the busy brickmaking town of Barton on Humber where a second son, William was born.

For Margaret, a brickmaker's wife, life could not have been an easy one. With a growing young family about her, and with nothing better than hovels in which to set up home for them, the going must have been hard. Home comforts were beyond her husband's means and she had to accommodate herself to hardship. Yet she was not alone: doubtless many other young wives shared her predicament.

Within two years William Freeman had moved his family yet again, this time further north to Bridlington. In those days the town was actually two towns, the old town (sometimes known as Burlington) and the new town of Bridlington Quay. It was at the Quay, a former fishing port, that the rich and well-to-do chose to settle first in their fashionable residences. But, gradually the Quay became a resort as visitors began to arrive in greater numbers. New residences, guest houses and hotels were needed to meet the demand. A tremendous building programme was embarked upon which drew skilled men such as William Freeman to Bridlington.

William Freeman settled in the Old Town, when the two places were completely separate. Bridlington Old Town was really one long street with side streets branching off it. Nearby was the Priory Church which was the surviving remnant of a monastery established during the reign of Henry I. It was a market town known for its trade in corn, cattle and malt. Yet during William's stay he would have witnessed quite a marked transformation as gas lighting and the railways came to serve the town. Everywhere new building flourished until the two towns merged into the one Bridlington known today.

Margaret bore William more children here. First Thomas who was baptised in the local Zionist chapel on St John's Street, then George and Charlotte. Unfortunately Charlotte died in infancy and was buried in Priory Churchyard on 6th January 1833.

Henry Freeman was born on the 29th April 1835. The baptism register of Bridlington Priory Church shows that Henry was baptised there four days later on May 3rd. 1835. The entry reads, quite simply: "1835, May 3rd. Henry, son of William and Margaret Freeman, Abode, Bridn. Father's trade, brickmaker."

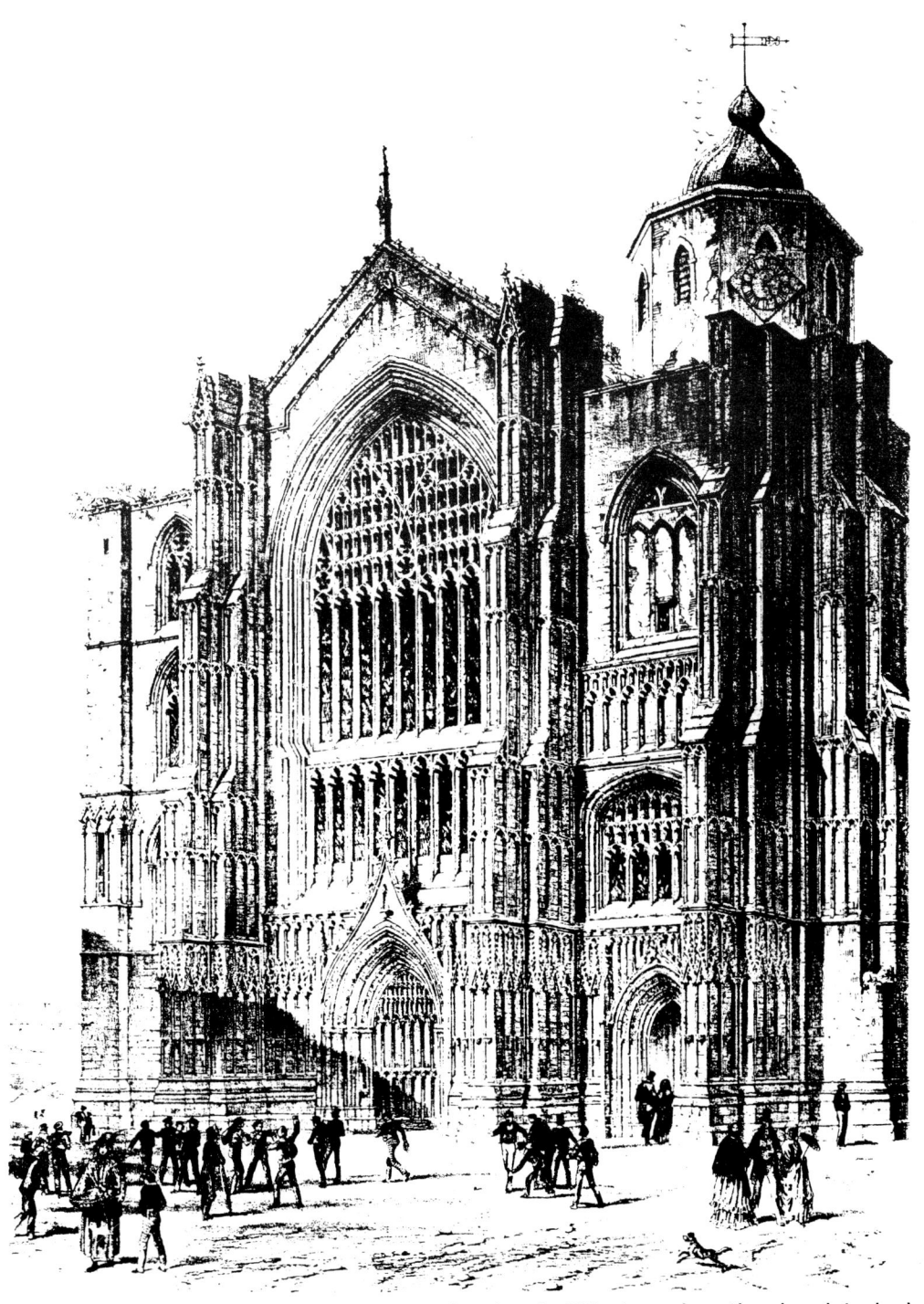

West front of Bridlington Priory. This print, dated 1835, shows how the church looked at the time of Freeman's birth.

Bridlington Priory Church as it appears today. The church records show that Henry Freeman was baptised here on May 3rd 1835. *(Photograph Ray Shill)*

At the time of his baptism, the Priory Church would probably have looked quite different from the structure which stands today. The two front towers were incomplete in 1835, and many of the stained glass windows which are visible today were absent then.

In 1837 the twins Jane and Sarah were born and it is known that the family was then living at St John's Street. At the time of their births, William was an Inn Keeper, but this was an occupation of which he apparently soon tired. For a few years later, he resumed his former trade as a brickmaker, and moved yet again to Flamborough, taking with him the younger members of his family.

Perched high on the cliffs, Flamborough was a fishing village which was situated inland. Its inhabitants knew intimately the sea's harshness: they witnessed its power, year by year, especially when the waves boiled around the jagged cliffs in the winter gales.

Only two safe havens were afforded to the small fishing boats owned by the Flamborough folk. These were the North and South Landings, each about a mile from the centre of the village. In Freeman's time, the boats, or cobles as they are known locally, would discharge their catches onto the beach to be sold there and then. The fish would be loaded into panniers and carried up the steep slopes of the landings to Flamborough by donkey.

The seasons of the year brought forth their own special harvest from the North Sea: crabs in the Spring, herrings in the Summer and deepwater fish such as cod in the Winter.

Henry Freeman spent his childhood in this environment. The experience must have had a profound effect upon the young boy and aroused his curiosity. During his formative years, Henry Freeman must have become well acquainted with the ways in which the fisherman adapts to nature's cycles in the search for the fish. Possibly, enthusiasm or excitement may even have stirred the lad to help the fishermen, either at the landings, or on the donkey trains.

Flamborough Head and Lighthouse.

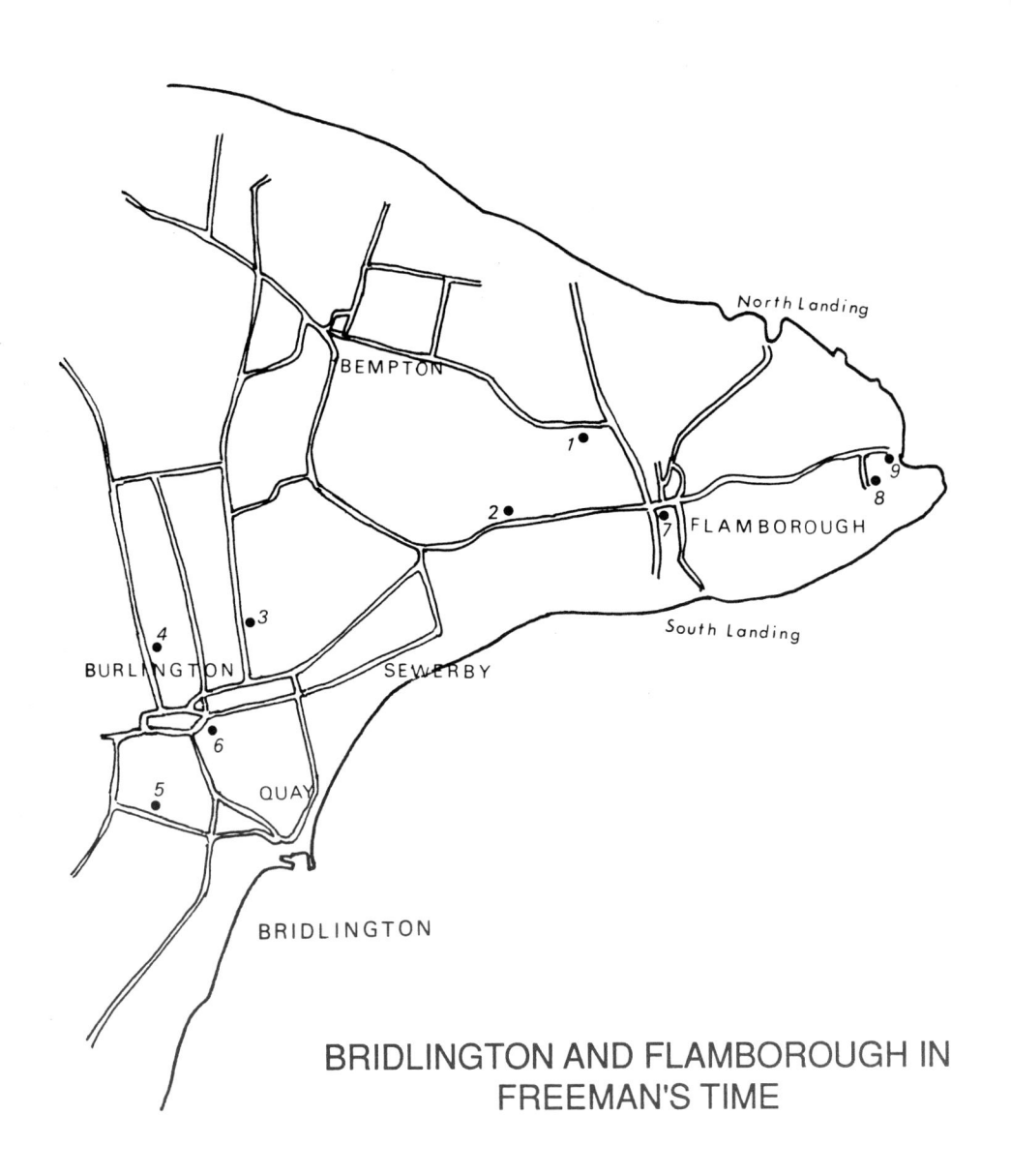

Map of Bridlington and Flamborough. Key: 1 Flamborough Brickyard. 2 Sewerby Brickyard. 3 Bempton Lane Brickyard. 4 Bridlington Brickyard. 5 Bessingby Brickyard. 6 Bridlington Priory Church. 7 St Oswald's Church, Flamborough. 8 Lighthouse Farm. 9 Flamborough Lighthouse.

It is unlikely that Henry had much schooling here for the National School was not opened until 1845, when he would have been ten years old. For both Henry and his brothers, their training for the future came from their father, William, who instructed them in the brickmaking trade.

The future for Henry's sisters depended less on any formal education or training than on how good a wife they would make. Few women in the Victorian times were able to break free from the narrow subservient role which society imposed on the female sex, and neither, it appears did they.

During the Freeman family's stay at Flamborough, Margaret Freeman gave birth to another son, on 26th. June 1841. This child, baptised as James Freeman four days later, was frail and lived only a short time. James died when he was just ten days old, after suffering from convulsions.

How long William Freeman remained in Flamborough is not certain. By 1851 he was back in Bridlington working as a brickmaker and living in Ings Lane. By this time his eldest son John had become a brickmaker in his own right and married a local girl Patience Gutherleys whose father was a labourer. John lived in a cottage beside the brickyard in Bempton Lane (a site near the present Hospital) where he worked and raised a large family.

Henry's brother, William, took to working on a farm. In 1841 at the age of 13 he is described in the Census as working for Christopher King, Farmer, at Boynton as an agricultural labourer. Later, he also took up brickmaking and lived in lodgings at the Old Town. He married Ann Langton, a girl who lived nearby.

George and Thomas may have spent time in their youth as farm labourers, too, but this is uncertain. The only evidence available points to their having stayed with their father.

Henry followed his brother William's example. By 1851 he was living in Flamborough working as a farm servant at Lighthouse Farm for the Woodcock Family. Their property, which is known today as Head Farm, still stands on the headland overlooking the sea from steep cliffs. Flamborough Lighthouse remains, as then, on adjacent land.

It was the custom in these parts to employ servants every November for a year's work for which they were paid a princely sum of between £12 and £15 annually. For Henry, the work must have been arduous, and as a brickmaker's son, he must have found some difficulty in adjusting to the agricultural life. Yet it is likely that it was on this farm that the seeds of his destiny were planted. For, all around him was the sea, and he was witness to all its moods and angry outbursts throughout the seasons.

Head Farm had both cattle and crops which would have presented a variety of work for the young Henry Freeman. The busiest time was in late August and early September when the Harvest was gathered. Bridlington was flooded with itinerant workers looking for the relatively well paid jobs as mowers, gatherers and binders. It was the time of the year, also, when the farmers prayed for good weather. In 1851, the weather proved favourable and the harvest was good all over the region.

The sea around Flamborough was part of a great highway used by many trading vessels which hugged the coast en route from the south of England to the north. In late September 1851 severe gales swept across the sea and land, placing many vessels in trouble. Two ships foundered and sank off Flamborough Head. One lost all hands while the other had its crew rescued. Henry should still have been on the farm then and may even have helped with the rescue. Certainly he must have heard about the event and perhaps it made him reflect upon the vulnerability of ships at sea, and upon the dangers faced by their crews. Reflections such as these could well have been an influence upon his future direction in life.

Eventually he did move back to Bridlington and took up the Brickmaking trade as his brothers had done before him. Not all the brothers worked for the same yard as there were then three in the town. George, for example, worked in a yard at Bessingby and for a short time even lived in a cottage beside that yard while brother Thomas earned a living as a labourer.

Thomas appears to have been somewhat of a tearaway. According to the *Hull Packet and East Riding Gazette*, Thomas Freeman was in the local Police Court during October 1854, together with Edwin Stephenson and Thomas Pool. All three were charged by Harriet Jackson with breaking her house door and shutters. The 'delinquents', as the newspaper describes them, were fined 21s each.

After George Freeman married Jane Stephenson, the daughter of a cattle jobber, in February 1855, the family began to split up and go its separate ways. They had been more or less together in the Bridlington district until then. First to go in 1855 was Henry Freeman, himself. By this time he had become a qualified brickmaker and perhaps because of the poor job prospects in Bridlington he moved to Whitby to work for a brickmaker called George Splayfoot whose health was then failing him. He was followed within a couple of years by brother William who settled in a yard behind Baxtergate with his family and also carried on the trade of brickmaker. Sister Sarah went along as well. Thomas moved to Filey during 1856 where he married a sailor's widow.

Henry Freeman's sisters appear to have fared badly in their adult lives. Few seem to have settled successfully into a lasting marriage, as their brothers did. In the cases of Ann and Mary, it would seem that their relationships with men were fleeting and unstable. Little can be discovered of them beyond that they came to live in Bridlington, and both had illegitimate children. No record has been found of a marriage for either of them. Mary was living in Bempton Lane in 1845 when her child was born. Of Ann, very little can be traced, but three children's names are written in the Bridlington Parish Church baptism register as daughters of Ann Freeman, between 1850 and 1855. It fell to the lot of their mother, Margaret Freeman, to look after their children.

Jane married mariner Henry Varley in Hull under what appears to be clandestine circumstances. The marriage certificate for 20th August 1856 which gives Jane's father as John rather than William and her age as 20 rather than 18 suggests this marriage went ahead without the father's consent.

Sarah Freeman was married on Christmas Day 1858 in Whitby. Her husband was William Wherrit, a butcher. They lived in Baxtergate and Sarah bore him a daughter who was christened Margaret Elizabeth. As the child was born on the 25th April 1859, it would seem that the marriage may have been forced on them by the impending birth of the child. What happened to Sarah after that is uncertain. No record can be found of her having died, so it is likely that she left her husband. In 1865 William Wherrit married Mary Thompson in Hartlepool where he continued to live with his daughter by Sarah, Margaret Elizabeth.

According to Sarah's marriage certificate William Freeman, the father, had become a well sinker. This occupation also appears on the 1861 census, when he was given as living in one of the yards behind Westgate, Bridlington. His age was then 69.

John and George settled in Bridlington and carried on the brickmaking trade. Both brothers had large families each with twelve children. John moved to a new brickyard at Sewerby about 1862. He lived there until his death, carrying on the business of brickyard proprietor, a role which fell later to Patience, his widow. George lived to a great age, finally dying in Bridlington in 1914. He had worked in various brickyards around Bridlington including one near the Union workhouse in the Old Town.

Henry Freeman's earliest days in Whitby were associated with the brickmaking trade and labouring jobs on the new buildings going up around the town. In those days supplies of bricks came from a variety of sources. Small brickyards existed at Hawsker, Lower Stakesby and Newholme; other bricks came in on ships from Holland used as ballast. Otherwise local clay was utilised to make bricks when the need arose. Clay was found at the base of the cliffs where it had fallen through erosion. From this, handmade bricks would be fashioned by the skills of a brickmaker.

Henry would have spent his time with Splayfoot making handmade bricks. George Splayfoot had contracted tuberculosis and died during November 1857 leaving Henry in charge of the business. Another worker at the yard was a man called Charles Jackson who shortly afterwards married Splayfoot's widow.

At this time a contractor called Freeman was involved with a small brickyard at Fishburn Park where new houses were under construction. This yard must have been only a temporary site where the clay was brought and made into bricks for the houses. It seems likely that the contractor was Henry Freeman, but it is just possible that it might have been Henry's brother, William Freeman. He may have been at Whitby by that time; conceivably both may have been involved in running the yard.

In 1856 the *Whitby Gazette* carried a statement that visitors were leaving the town through lack of accommodation. The demand was soon made for new buildings to be erected and builders such as George Vasey played a major part in their construction. A staunch Methodist and lay preacher, George Vasey had an established building firm in the town. By 1856 he was taking things easier and passed on many of the contracts he received to his eldest son George Vasey Junior. Between 1857 and 1859 George Vasey Junior built several houses on the West Cliff including properties in Belle View Terrace and New Crescent.

During April 1858 Henry Freeman was working at the West Cliff as a brickmaker for George Vasey Junior. One Saturday afternoon he was looking out to sea when he saw a coble upset between Upgang and Sandsend. At first it was believed Henry had been mistaken because they were a considerable distance away. Later, it was established that two young men had, in fact, taken a coble to sail to West Hartlepool, but it had capsized hurling them into the water and they had drowned. That Henry chose to spend his time looking out to sea when he should have been working suggests that he had become bored with his job. Perhaps he regarded the sea as a form of escape from the tedious and repetitious tasks involved in being a brickmaker.

At the end of 1858 George Vasey Junior was engaged in building a new house for John Wilson at Hanover Terrace. Whilst busy with this contract he fell ill with typhoid. It was a short illness and one which was to prove fatal. George Vasey Junior was buried in St Mary's Churchyard on the 26th of February 1859. He was only 37.

After George Vasey Junior's death his business affairs were managed by his father who by this time was in his sixty-seventh year. No doubt he had little enthusiasm for reassuming responsibility for the family business. Within six months the outstanding contracts were complete and there is no information available to suggest George Vasey took on any further commitments.

It is very likely that Henry Freeman remained in Vasey's employment until these contracts had ended but then would have been out of a job. At this point in his life, Henry must have been faced with a decision. He had to choose whether to continue to earn a living as a brickmaker or to follow his instincts and try an occupation which had a definite interest for him. He looked to the sea for his employment.

At that time the carriage of coal from the Northumberland and Durham coalfields was chiefly by ship. Railway companies such as the North Eastern Railway were only just getting a share of the market. Countless sailing vessels based at Hartlepool, Shields and Whitby regularly ran through these northern waters fully laden with coals for East Anglia, the Port of London, Southern England, France or the Baltic. Also some iron ore was carried from mines near Whitby.

Henry was known to have made a number of journeys to London by ship and it is likely that he worked as a seaman on one of the colliers. A search of many of the ship registers for the period has revealed inconclusive evidence. Fortunately there were few sailors called Henry Freeman, but crews lists are not particularly accurate. One possible ship Henry could have travelled on was the *Cruiser,* which was engaged in the coal trade from Hartlepool to London. A Henry Freeman aged 30 joined this vessel in London on the 14th September 1860, having previously been discharged from the *George Bentinck* two days earlier. The *George Bentinck* had come down with coals from Shields.

The Henry Freeman who sailed aboard the *Cruiser* and who was described in its crew list as London-born sailed back with the ship to Hartlepool as an Ordinary Seaman under the command of George Ord, Master. He was discharged at Hartlepool on the 30th September 1860, his pay for the voyage being the princely sum of £2.50.

Modern view of Boltons Buildings, Cliff Street. In 1861 these were divided into tenements, one of which was rented by Margaret Snowden. Freeman lodged with her at the time of the lifeboat disaster. *(Photograph Ray Shill)*

WHITBY IN FREEMAN'S TIME

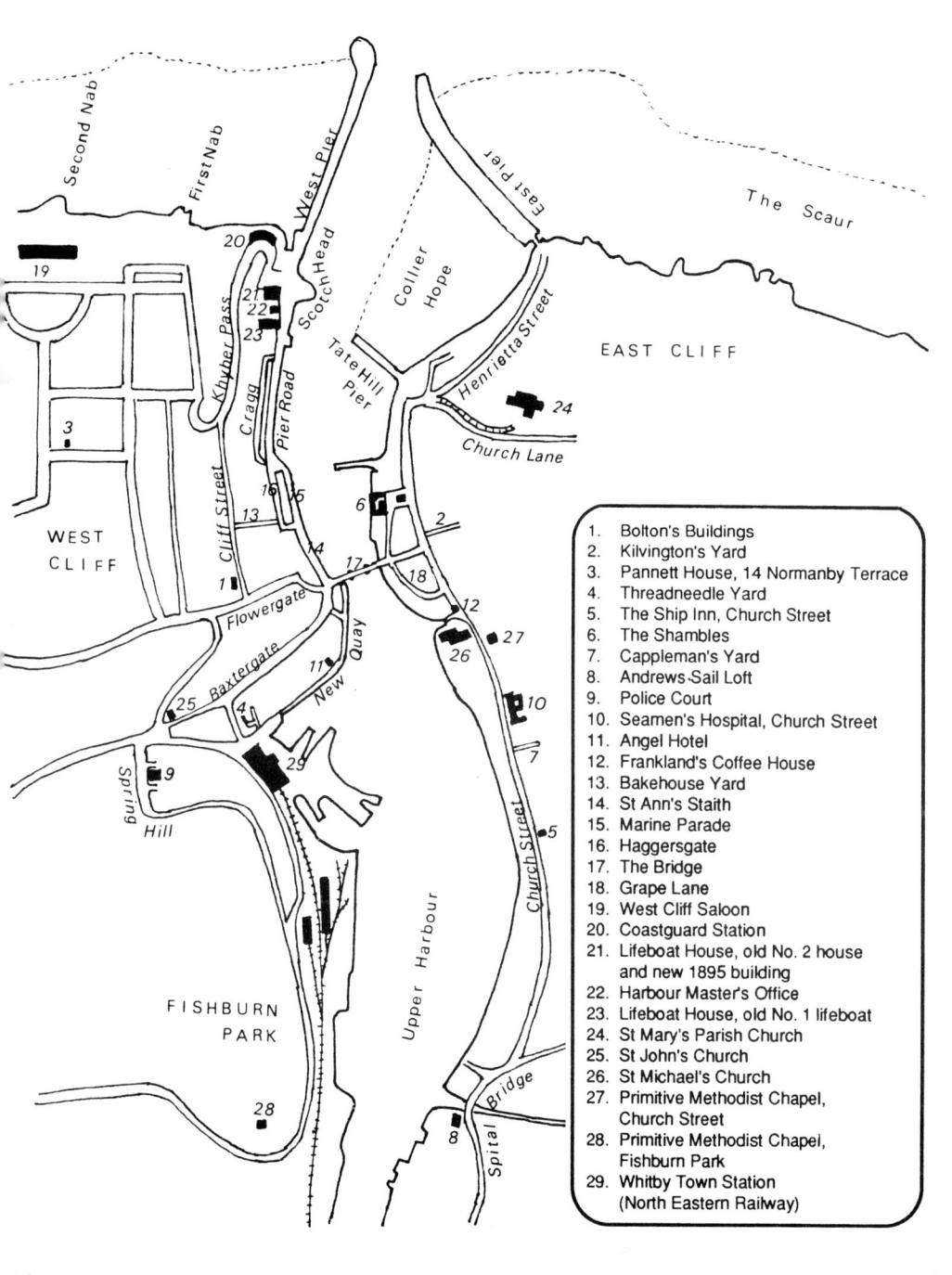

1. Bolton's Buildings
2. Kilvington's Yard
3. Pannett House, 14 Normanby Terrace
4. Threadneedle Yard
5. The Ship Inn, Church Street
6. The Shambles
7. Cappleman's Yard
8. Andrews Sail Loft
9. Police Court
10. Seamen's Hospital, Church Street
11. Angel Hotel
12. Frankland's Coffee House
13. Bakehouse Yard
14. St Ann's Staith
15. Marine Parade
16. Haggersgate
17. The Bridge
18. Grape Lane
19. West Cliff Saloon
20. Coastguard Station
21. Lifeboat House, old No. 2 house and new 1895 building
22. Harbour Master's Office
23. Lifeboat House, old No. 1 lifeboat
24. St Mary's Parish Church
25. St John's Church
26. St Michael's Church
27. Primitive Methodist Chapel, Church Street
28. Primitive Methodist Chapel, Fishburn Park
29. Whitby Town Station (North Eastern Railway)

Perhaps the ship's crew list was inaccurate, both about this crew member's place of birth and about his age also. There are several reasons why this seaman may not have been a Londoner at all, but in fact Henry Freeman of Whitby. It seems strange that a London-born man should spend so little time in his home port. This ship's destination was Hartlepool, and from there it would have been an easy matter to travel home. Henry may not have had the opportunity to take a Whitby-bound vessel. The Henry Freeman aboard the *Cruiser* was an ordinary seaman, too, not an able-bodied seaman. Brickmaker Henry had virtually no seagoing experience, and could only have signed on as an ordinary seaman.

Whatever ships he sailed on, Henry must have come to a decision that life as a mariner was not for him. At the start of 1861 Henry was back in Whitby as a fisherman. He had taken lodgings with Margaret Snowden a merchant seaman's widow who provided lodgings in Boltons Buildings, Cliff Street, for several men. In the winter, the fishermen would be long line fishing and Henry must have gained a place on one of the boats.

Barely two or three months later, Henry found himself risking his life at sea and suddenly a hero. Henry had scarcely begun as a fisherman when this calamity happened. He surely must have been a fit man to have survived this ordeal. No doubt his labouring and brickmaking days kept him in good shape. At the inquest he described his part in the rescues and in later years he would often be called on to recount his experiences. Strangely, the best description appears in his obituary published in the *Whitby Gazette* which repeated his words:

> "When the boat turned over I was underneath her with the Gun'ale across my chest. My body was under the boat and I was looking upwards through the water. A sea struck the boat and released me and I floated free. I was wearing a new kind of cork belt, which had been sent down for trial, like the ones now used. I was the only man wearing one in the boat. There was a ship wrecked alongside the pier, and every now and then this ship was being banged by the waves against the pier. The waves drove me along towards the wreck and I was afraid every second that I was going to be crushed between the ship and the pier. But a big sea came and carried me safely between the ship and the pierside and I was then washed towards the slipway. A wave carried me right up to the top and several men tried to get hold of me but the strong backwash took me out to sea again. Another sea then took me up the slipway again, and the people tried to save me but I was washed down again. Then a third time was carried up the slipway and this time some men got hold of me, and I was half carried up the pier, home, I was properly done up."

In spite of this dreadful experience, Henry remained in Whitby and carried on fishing. A chapter had closed in his life; the brickmaking trade had seen better days and was now in decline. It seems as if from his earliest years, Henry knew that there was something else he must do. From his boyhood he had developed a fascination for the sea, and it was now in his blood. His courage and his rugged single-minded determination fuelled his ambition. Not even the fear of death itself could deter him.

Through his ordeal, he had earned the respect of the people of Whitby, and Whitby was now his home. It might take time to win acceptance by Whitby folk as one of their own, but he would settle for their respect. The sea had given him his reputation among them, and he saw no reason why he should not remain.

How he was received by the fishing community is not clear. The deaths of members of the Storr family had obviously touched on the lives of all and Freeman's survival was an uncomfortable reminder of those who had perished. It appears that Henry may have had difficulty in winning acceptance in some quarters; even in years to come there was certainly friction between Freeman and his fellow fishermen.

Thus, Freeman had established a new life for himself in Whitby in quite a dramatic way. The brickmaker had become a fisherman, forsaking the tedious and back-breaking work of getting and firing the clay which comprises the brickmaker's art, for the challenge of the sea where no two days' work are the same.

While Freeman's choice of profession was perhaps surprising, his choice of location was not. Whitby was and is a picturesque port to work from. The red of the roof tiles and the whitewashed walls of the buildings contrast well with the green of the hills and the black stone of the ruined Abbey on a summer's day. While standing apart on the hill is the Church of St Mary's, seemingly as permanent as the sea lapping at the cliffs below. It is very easy to see why Henry would have wanted to remain here.

CHAPTER 3

THE BUSFIELD FAMILY

From its commanding location on Whitby's East Cliff, the 12th Century parish church of St Mary keeps watch over the narrow streets of the old town, over the huddle of red-roofed harbourside cottages, and over the harbour itself. With the ruins of the old abbey standing nearby, this cliff top edifice dominates the skyline for miles around and is an unmistakable landmark for the traveller.

There has been a church on the same site since Saxon times, but the present building dates from 1110A.D. All that remains of the original Norman construction, however, is the chancel and the south wall of the nave. The rest comprises a series of additions made over the years, including the North Annexe.

A unique feature of St Mary's Church is its approach from the narrow cobbled streets below. The churchyard is reached by ascending a total of 199 steps, an exhausting climb, yet one that is made well worth the effort by the rewarding panoramic views to be seen on the way up.

In the eighteenth century these steps were referred to as "the stairs" because they were constructed entirely of wood. It was by these stairs that a great many of Whitby's dead were conveyed to their final resting place in St Mary's churchyard by the coffin bearers. It could be particularly exacting for the bearers to make the long ascent with their heavy load, and so the steep climb had to be broken by suitably-spaced resting places, in the form of broad, level platforms. These resting places still remain today, but over the years the stairs were entirely converted into solid stone, paid for by money raised by the churchwardens.

It was in St.Mary's churchyard that the lifeboatmen who died in the disaster of 1861 were buried. Contemporary newspaper accounts of the funerals of the deceased give little description of these events beyond recording that very large numbers of people attended. The body of the church was full, the galleries held indeterminate numbers of mourners, while hundreds more filled the churchyard. Clearly in the aftermath of such a major tragedy, the townspeople were anxious to pay their last respects to the twelve men whose lives had been lost, and to share the burden of grief of the ten widows and forty-six fatherless children they left behind.

Only a little more than six months after these terrible events, Henry Freeman was married. The marriage took place at St Mary's on 24th October 1861. The service was conducted by the Revd Ralph Oldham, Curate.

Freeman's bride was Elizabeth Busfield, the eldest daughter of Thomas Busfield, a jet ornament manufacturer, residing in Church Street. Elizabeth was a 26

WHITBY.

Whitby's Upper Harbour in Freeman's time. St Mary's Church and the Abbey dominate the East Cliff.

year-old dressmaker. Unlike her husband, she had been born and raised in Whitby. One of the witnesses to the marriage was a local hairdresser, Joseph Brown Whitton, who in the following year was to marry Elizabeth's younger sister, Rebecca.

Elizabeth must have counted herself a very lucky woman on the day she married Henry. His gallant conduct had been acknowledged at a public meeting held in Whitby just a few days after the lifeboat had capsized; and in March, he had been awarded the Royal National Lifeboat Institution's Silver medal for his part in five successful rescues on February 9th 1861. Only a handful of Whitby men had been honoured by the Institution before him.

Henry too must have counted himself extremely fortunate. He had survived to marry the woman he loved. But St. Mary's must have evoked many vivid memories and inspired in him very mixed emotions. The happy memories of his sister Sarah's wedding three years before, and the prospect of married life with Elizabeth, must have been overshadowed by haunting images of his dead comrades, whose graves were just outside in the churchyard.

A view of St Mary's Parish Church. Part of the present building dates from the twelfth century. Inscriptions on the surrounding gravestones bear testimony to Whitby's maritime history. Henry Freeman was married in this church. *(Photograph Ray Shill)*

St Mary's Church is reached by 199 steps which wind from Church Street to the top of the East Cliff. A steeply graded cart road called Church Lane runs beside them. In this view, the Lower Harbour, Tate Hill Pier and Whitby's East Side are visible.
(Photograph Ray Shill)

Memorandum That on the Twentieth day of May 1816 Thomas Busfield Son of William Busfield of Whitby in the County of York Mariner was Bound an apprentice to me Henry Gibson of Whitby aforesaid Boot and Shoemaker for the Term of Seven Years to learn the Trade or Business of a Boot and Shoemaker which Term the said Thomas Busfield duly honestly and faithfully served to my satisfaction and I Do hereby Certify That the said Thomas Busfield is a good substantial workman Witness my Hand this 19th day of April One thousand eight hundred and twenty four —

Henry Gibson

Witness to Henry Gibson's Signing
John Fewster

Dated 1824, the above testimonial gives a favourable account of Thomas Busfield's seven year apprenticeship to Henry Gibson, Boot and Shoemaker.

(Courtesy of Mrs Ann Hill)

Elizabeth Busfield was the eldest in a family of five daughters and one son. Her father Thomas Busfield was a Whitby man by birth. Her mother, however, had been born in Melbourne, a small village to the south-east of York. Before her marriage to Thomas Busfield, she had been Elizabeth Craven: her maiden name was later to pass to her only son, Thomas Craven Busfield, the youngest child. All six Busfield children were born in Whitby.

Thomas Busfield had married Elizabeth Craven on 7th December 1834. Their first child, Elizabeth, had been born on 6th October 1835, to be followed by a further four sisters: Jane, born 17th November 1837; Rebecca born 9th April 1840, Elizabeth Mary born 10th November 1842 and finally Emma, born 12 June 1845. In 1851, the family's address was in Grape Lane, off Church Street, Whitby. Elizabeth was by then 15 years of age, and Emma the youngest daughter, just 5. The family were still living at this address when Thomas Craven Busfield was born two years later. Elizabeth gave birth to him when she was 41 and there were no further offspring after him.

Originally apprenticed to a boot and shoemaker, Thomas Busfield had taken up the trade of Jet Manufacturer by 1837. He is shown on the 1851 Census as a Master Jet Manufacturer.

A very hard, black form of natural carbon with a high lustre, jet lends itself perfectly to ornamental purposes, and has been used in this way for a very long time. Indeed, it was prehistoric man who first pioneered the difficult art of polishing jet during the Bronze Age. These primitive workers fashioned beads and other items of personal adornment with the most amazing skill.

The neighbourhood of Whitby has always been a rich source of the mineral. Jet seams were to be found not only in the cliffs, but also in places further inland, well away from the sea. The material was gathered in a variety of ways and locations. Many jet miners, for example, lived in coastal places such as Staithes, Runswick or Sandsend and they worked the "jet holes" near their homes. Others meanwhile patrolled the seashore on the lookout for falls of cliff, searching the debris and the sand for pieces of jet. These men found no difficulty in selling their finds to the jet masters.

When he became a jet craftsman in Whitby, Thomas Busfield was entering a small but long-established local trade which had seen little change in working practices until quite recently. The primitive methods of fashioning jet by knife, file and rubbing stone had only started to be replaced by mechanical methods of production at the turn of the century. Innovation, however, was a slow process. Jet workers accustomed to traditional ways saw no financial advantage in modernisation. In 1832, when Busfield was just learning the trade perhaps, two Whitby jet shops were employing some twenty-five people.

However, other developments in Victorian England created an unprecedented demand for jet products, and provided the ultimate spur to the industry's growth. The expansion of the railways brought new visitors to the seaside towns. Those who came to Whitby for their seaside holiday soon found that a piece of jet made an ideal souvenir. New fashions in jewellery appeared as a response to changing fashions in clothes. The lightweight clothes of the regency period were supplanted by heavier, darker, more ample dresses. The fuller styles called for much larger jewellery, and for this jet was the perfect material since it was naturally suited for the production of very large but lightweight pieces.

About 1850, there were at least seven firms of Jet manufacturers in Whitby, of which four were based in Church Street: Flintoff and Lister, John Kimmings, Wright and Slater and James Pennock. It seems therefore that the Busfields had taken up residence in the centre of the industry. One firm, that of Thomas Andrews, at New Quay, was advertising as a jet ornament manufacturer to Her Majesty Queen Victoria.

After jet was displayed at the Great Exhibition of 1851, orders began to be received from further afield, notably from the continent. In 1854 alone, Isaac Greenbury, a prominent manufacturer, received orders from the Queen of Bavaria and from the Empress of France.

Around the years 1840 to 1860 many jet workers sold their jewellery to families of deceased persons. When Albert, the Prince Consort, died in 1861, Queen Victoria entered a long period of mourning. Only jet jewellery was allowed to be worn at court, and Queen Victoria bought and wore a great deal of jet. The people followed court fashion. As a result the trade gained much publicity and grew.

When Henry married Elizabeth, therefore, the manufacture of jet was becoming a highly profitable business. The Busfield family no doubt shared in this new prosperity. The industry grew rapidly through the sixties, reaching its peak in 1872. In that year there were some two hundred shops employing fifteen hundred people, and a good craftsman could expect to earn up to £4 per week. Jet workers had premises in all parts of the town. Some were very large, capable of accommodating more than a hundred employees. Others were much smaller, sometimes being nothing more than an attic or a poky wooden outbuilding where one man might live and work.

Then came a decline, forcing many workers to seek alternative employment. By 1884, less than three hundred people were employed in the trade, and a man could only earn about one third of the weekly earnings enjoyed during the boom period.

Thomas Busfield was a jet manufacturer. He had at one time a jet shop at Morleys Yard, 73 Church Street. His was typical of the smaller workshop where only a few men produced jet ornaments. This picture, however, shows a large premises in Haggersgate, belonging to Mr William Wright, where many jet craftsmen were employed.

(Frank Meadow Sutcliffe)

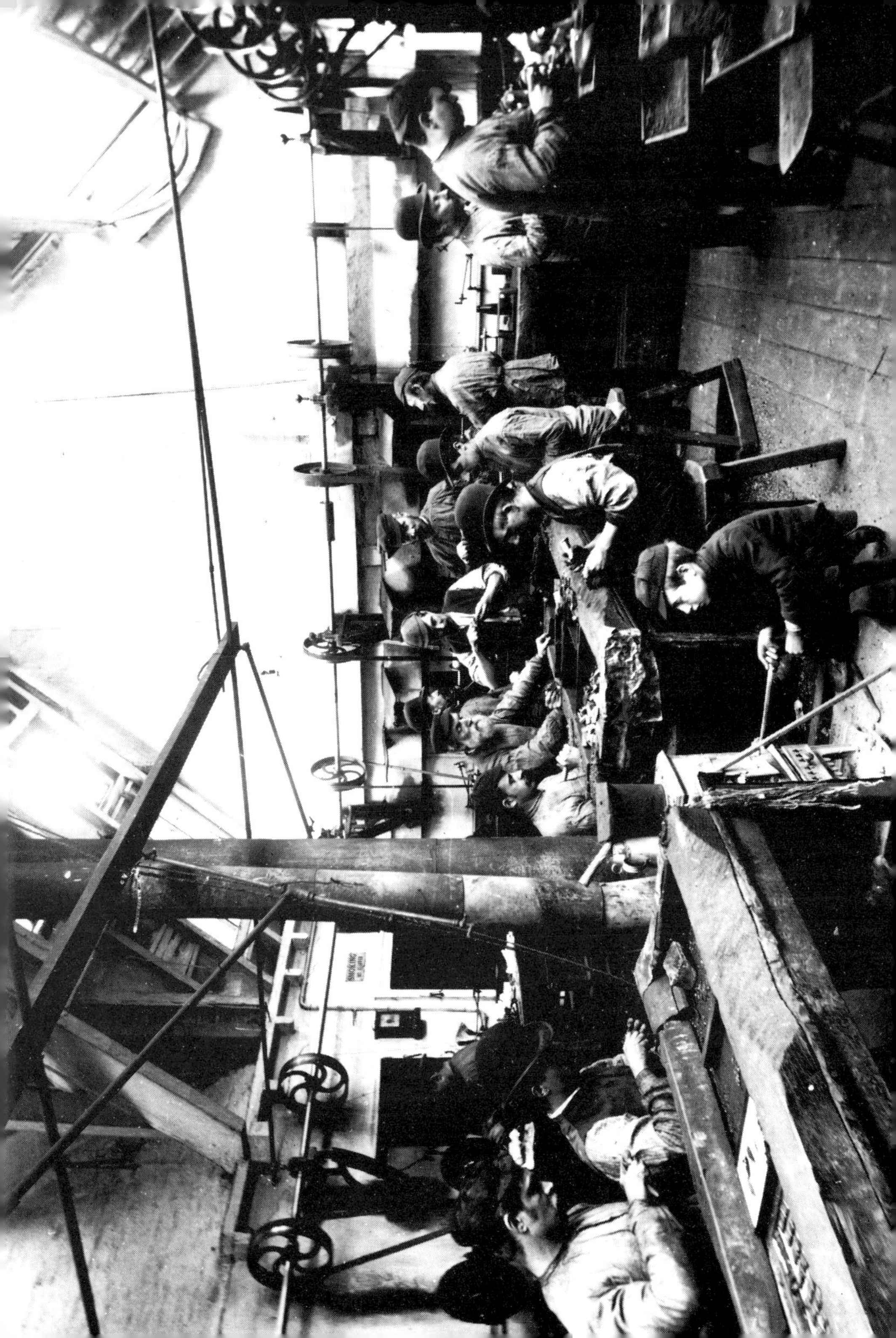

Jet workshops were once common in the port. John Reid owned this establishment on Marine Parade. *(Courtesy of Whitby Literary & Philosophical Society)*

      Thomas Busfield died just a few years after the decline began. At the end of his life he had contracted dysentry and had suffered for over two years with this illness before dying in November 1875, when he was seventy years of age. His widow Elizabeth survived him by six years. During his illness, it fell to Elizabeth to support

Whitby's jet industry has declined over the past century but traces of its former prosperity can still be seen, as is shown by this inscription on the wall above the Freeman Hardy Willis shoe shop in Baxtergate. *(Photograph Ray Shill)*

him as well as herself. It seems she earned her living through domestic service. This is shown by the 1881 census taken only a short time before her death. It records her occupation as housekeeper/domestic servant, and also shows that she had taken three lodgers into her home at Kilvington's Yard, off Church Street. She died on the 13th April that year, at the age of 69. Despite the prosperity which the jet trade had afforded to the best craftsmen, Thomas could not have left Elizabeth well provided for.

Living at close quarters to the Busfield household at that time were Henry Freeman and Elizabeth. They too lived in Kilvingtons Yard, and had done so since at least 1871. Clearly there was a close link between Elizabeth Freeman and her parents from the time of her marriage right up to their deaths.

Before Elizabeth Busfield died, she had seen all of her children married save the youngest, Thomas. His marriage was to follow some eighteen months later, in November 1882. The first daughter to marry was Jane Busfield. Her wedding to Matthew Groves took place at the Parish Church of Scarborough on 28th May 1860. He was a 23 year old joiner from Scarborough, and the son of a labourer, Robert Groves.

Much of Matthew Groves's work was involved with the building trade where carpenters and joiners were needed just as much as the brickmakers. But unlike the brickmaking Freeman family Matthew Groves apparently earned a respectable wage from his trade and was able to provide a decent standard of living for his own family.

The demands of his job were just as vigorous as that of a brickmaker, and Matthew moved from place to place following work. As can be seen from the baptism records of his children he and his wife, Jane, spent time in Scarborough and Whitby before finally settling in Hartlepool.

Jane and Matthew had at least nine children. By 1870 they were residing at West Hartlepool. They lived first at Union Place, then Roker Street and finally York Road. Jane Groves died in September 1901 at the age of 63. Matthew Groves was to live a little longer. He died in 1906 at the age of 69 and was one of the few people connected with the Busfield family to leave a will. Daughter Mary Jane, spinster, was the beneficiary of his estate which amounted to £204-10s.

Elizabeth was the next to marry. Unlike her sister Jane, she had no children even though her marriage to Henry Freeman lasted almost thirty-seven years. Henry clearly liked children, for his obituary written years after records that he was in the habit of patting children fondly on the head when they passed him by in the town. Perhaps this was how he compensated for the lack of any children of his own.

Rebecca Busfield, the third daughter, was married at St Mary's Parish Church, Whitby, by William Keane, Minister, on June 29th 1862. Her husband Joseph Brown Whitton was the son of Jonathan Whitton, a Whitby saddler. They had a large family including at least six girls and three boys all of them born in Whitby. Joseph and Rebecca lived their entire lives there, first in Cliff Street, then 3 Bakehouse Yard and later in Millers Yard. Joseph Brown Whitton died at the age of 62 years; he was buried on 28th December 1899. Rebecca outlived him by some eight years. She died at the age of 66 in February 1907.

The two youngest Busfield daughters, Elizabeth Mary and Emma were the least fortunate in their marriages. Both of them were widowed after just a few brief years of married life.

Emma Busfield was the fourth daughter to wed. She married on 22nd October 1863, when she was only eighteen years old. Her husband was Kirby Watson, a twenty-three year old Railway Porter from Pocklington, the son of a farmer, William Watson. The marriage was solemnized in the Primitive Methodist Chapel in Whitby, owing to the strong ties of the Watson family to the Primitive Methodist faith.

Clearly, Kirby's job on the railways must soon have necessitated a move from Whitby to West Hartlepool. Whitby was at the end of a North Eastern Railway branch line, while the Hartlepools had a rich supply of railway lines serving the docklands, nearby collieries and the expanding iron and steelworks complex. Certainly Hartlepool had much more to offer an ambitious young man such as Kirby Watson and by December of 1865, when their first child, William Thomas Watson was born, Kirby and Emma were living in Whitby Street, West Hartlepool. The birth took place on 29th December 1865.

When Emma's second child was born, she and Kirby had moved again, and Kirby had changed his occupation. Their second son, John Henry Watson, was born on 6th August 1867, at the new address of Gray Street, Ruswarp, not far from Whitby. By now Kirby Watson was an Insurance Agent.

Kirby Watson's commitment to Primitive Methodism was clearly a strong one. When the Fishburn Park Primitive Methodist Chapel was opened in Whitby in 1868, Kirby seems to have played an active role in its ministry.

One newspaper report dating from March 1868 describes a public meeting held at the Chapel where addresses were delivered on different subjects. At the top of the Agenda was the spreading of the Christian gospel in the community. Supporting the Minister on the platform were a number of lay-preachers who each spoke to the assembled gathering. Among the laity who spoke was Kirby Watson.

It was Kirby Watson's missionary zeal that led to the tragedy which befell him in the following year. On October 16th 1869, Kirby Watson sailed from England for America, and arrived at the home of his uncle in Bloomington, Illinois, on 30th October. He had gone to serve as Minister at the Pleasant Grove or Rodman Chapel, in McClean County, even though he does not appear to have been an ordained priest of any denomination.

Within a day or two of his arrival, he was invited to go hunting. He took a gun, and went out to shoot ducks, accompanied by a 9 year old nephew. While along the Kickapoo Creek, southwest of Holder, he found a polecat. This encounter with a strange animal evidently took him by surprise, because he seems to have acted upon a sudden impulse and used his gun as a club. As he struck out with the butt of the gun, the blow broke the breech, and the gun went off. He was severely wounded in the thigh by the blast. Dr William Hill, a veteran Civil War Surgeon, was called in after some delay, and with the assistance of a Dr.Elder, he amputated the limb near the hip joint. *The Bloomington Daily Leader* states that it was not until evening that the necessary operation was performed.

Although Kirby had left his family in England, it was his intention to bring them to America to join him. He was greatly distressed after the accident, being concerned for his wife and his mother, and this did not help his recovery. In the event, neither his wife, his mother, nor his children were ever to see Kirby Watson again. The amputation was successful, but a combination of shock and the painkiller that was used proved too much for him. After two or three days, his condition worsened. Those

Fishburn Park Primitive Methodist Chapel, opened in 1868. Kirby Watson was a lay preacher here. *(Photograph Ray Shill)*

who witnessed his death on Friday 5th November reported that he died triumphant in the faith of Christ.

Watson's funeral was attended by a large gathering of people from the township. Though a stranger, Kirby Watson had made a very favourable impression upon them. Today he lies in an unmarked grave in either the Pleasant Grove Cemetery or the Frankenberger Cemetery. No record of his burial has been found to date.

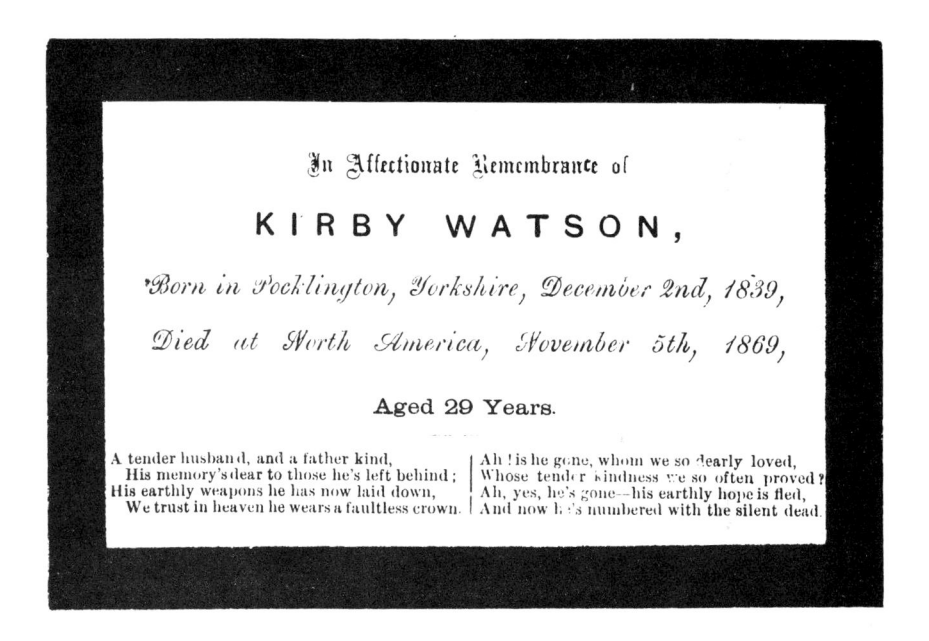

> In Affectionate Remembrance of
>
> **KIRBY WATSON,**
>
> *Born in Pocklington, Yorkshire, December 2nd, 1839,*
>
> *Died at North America, November 5th, 1869,*
>
> Aged 29 Years.
>
> A tender husband, and a father kind,
> His memory's dear to those he's left behind;
> His earthly weapons he has now laid down,
> We trust in heaven he wears a faultless crown.
>
> Ah! is he gone, whom we so dearly loved,
> Whose tender kindness we so often proved?
> Ah, yes, he's gone—his earthly hope is fled,
> And now he's numbered with the silent dead.

Thus it was that Emma Watson, at the age of just 24, was left a widow. Not only did she have two sons to look after, but there was another baby on the way. This child must have been conceived just before Kirby's departure for America. She gave birth to a third son on 1st July 1870, at Church Street, Whitby, and he was named Kirby after his deceased father.

After her husband's death, Emma found employment at the Angel Hotel in Whitby which was run at the time by William Piercy and his wife Mary. Emma served in the hotel as a nursemaid, one of just two widows among more than half a dozen other young unmarried servants.

Emma's children were looked after by family and friends. At just nine months, Kirby, her youngest son, is shown on the 1871 Whitby Census as being a boarder in the home of Thomas and Eliza Walker at 34 Church Street. Thomas Walker was a miller by trade. Emma's parents looked after their grandson John Henry Watson in their home in Kilvington's Yard. He had still not reached his fourth birthday.

Emma was to remain a widow for the next thirty years. In 1881 she was still in service, this time, however, to the distinguished solicitor and public servant, Robert Elliott Pannett. A life-long bachelor, he lived at 14 Normanby Terrace, Whitby. Robert was looked after by his mother until her death in 1873 and then by his sister Sarah until her death in 1879. Thereafter he was looked after by a succession of housekeepers. His first housekeeper probably began her duties in the summer of 1879 and may even have been Emma herself.

For how long she remained in his service is not known; certainly she was with him as housekeeper and domestic in April 1881, at the time of the Census. But nothing more can be found out about her until 1901 when she was living at 30 Roker Street, Hartlepool with her sister Jane and her husband Matthew.

The early married life of Eliza Mary Busfield bears some uncanny resemblances to that of her sister Emma. Eliza Mary was the last of the Busfield sisters to marry. Until this time she lived at home with her parents in Kilvington's Yard and worked as a milliner. Her wedding took place at the Parish Church at Sunderland on January 7th 1872 when she was 28. Her husband was Matthew Thistle, a 38 year old mariner from Sunderland, the son of Matthew Thistle, a labourer.

By 1876, Matthew Thistle had risen to the rank of Captain, and he and Eliza Mary were living at 6 Fishburn Road, Fishburn Park, Whitby. At this time they had no children. Matthew Thistle was master of a 280 ton brig called the *Trebizond* belonging to the Whitby shipowners Messrs. Marwood.

The *Trebizond* was employed on the Baltic sea route and on the 16th October 1876 Captain Thistle set sail from Kronstadt with a load of grain bound for the East coast of Great Britain.

The brig had been at sea for more than two weeks when disaster struck. On the 4th November, as the *Trebizond* was passing through the Kattegat off the North East coast of Denmark, the vessel was completely wrecked. Captain Thistle, aged 42, the ship's mate, James Marsh Rudder, aged 20, and all hands on board were lost.

A report from Fredrikshaven dated 8th December stated that the remains of a wreck supposed to be a grain-laden brig, had been found at sea in the neighbourhood of Laeso Island. Among the wreckage pieces of a nameboard were recovered bearing the letters ZOND, and supposed to have formed part of the word *Trebizond*.

A view of Dock End showing the Angel Vaults, a quayside hotel where Emma Freeman worked as a nursemaid after her first husband, Kirby Watson, died in America.
(Photograph Frank Meadow Sutcliffe)

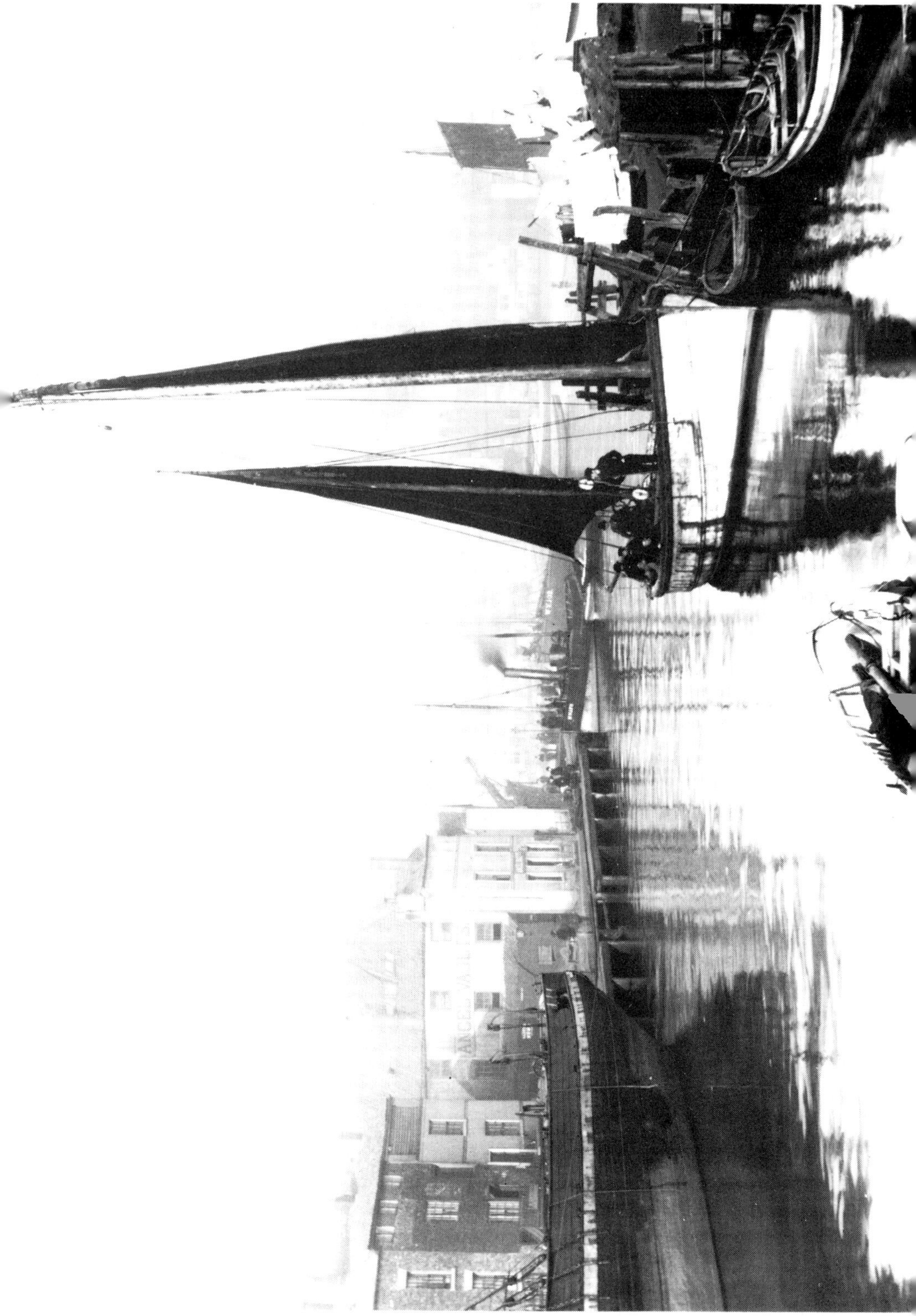

A modern view of Fishburn Park. This housing development was commenced in the late 1850s. The Freeman family were involved in supplying the bricks for the first houses. Captain Matthew Thistle lived here, at 6 Fishburn Road. *(Photograph Ray Shill)*

By a curious coincidence, Eliza Mary had lost her husband within hours of the date, November 5th, when Emma Busfield had lost Kirby Watson. Both Matthew Thistle and Kirby Watson had died outside the country and each of them had commenced a sea voyage on October 16th. Just seven years separated these two untimely deaths.

It took a year to settle Matthew Thistle's estate, which amounted to less than £200. Eliza Mary returned to live with her now widowed mother and continued to work as a milliner. The household she rejoined comprised her mother, her younger brother, Thomas, and a number of lodgers.

Eliza Mary remained a widow for the next sixteen years. When finally at the age of 49 she remarried, it was to John Ness Frankland, a 54 year old widower from Church Street Whitby, who was a Refreshment House Keeper. They were married at the Cleveland Terrace Primitive Methodist Chapel in Whitby on 20th October 1892.

The son of Richard Frankland, a white-smith, John Ness Frankland had played a leading role in the Coffee Bar movement in Whitby since its inception in 1878. The movement had been conceived by Ministers of the church, tradesmen, and other townspeople with the aim of combatting the evils of drink. By diverting the people away from the public house towards Coffee bars, it was hoped to foster the principles of thrift and sobriety in the rising generation.

AGREEMENT AND ACCOUNT OF CREW.
(FOREIGN-GOING SHIP.)

AGREEMENT No. 4439

ORIGINAL EXECUTED IN EIGHT PAGES.

Name of Ship.	Official No.	Port of Registry.	Port No. and Date of Register.	Registered Tonnage (Gross / Net)	Nominal Horse-power of Engines
Trebizond	23,320	Whitby	22 in 1862	284 / 284	—

REGISTERED MANAGING OWNER

Name	Address
Thomas Marwood	Flowergate, Whitby

No. of Seamen for whom accommodation is certified: Nil

Distance between centre of maximum load line disc and upper edge of line indicating position of the First Deck above it: 2 ft 7 in

The several Persons whose names are hereto subscribed, and whose descriptions are contained on the other side or sides, and of whom ___ are engaged as Sailors, hereby agree to serve on board the said Ship, in the several capacities expressed against their respective Names, on a Voyage from the Tyne to Cronstadt; and, if required, to any port or places in the Baltic Sea (excepting Jordan), and to the Continent of Europe for discharge of cargo if required, thence to a port of final discharge in the United Kingdom. Probable length of the voyage — six months.

Signed by **Matthew Thrills** Master, on the **14th** day of **Aug** 18**76**

Date of Commencement of Voyage	Port at which Voyage commenced
14/8/76	So. Shields

Trebizond crew agreement. *(By courtesy of the Maritime History Archive, Memorial University of Newfoundland, Canada)*

The progress of the Coffee Bar movement had been rapid and by January 1881 four coffee houses were open in the town, and proving very successful. In December 1880 Mr Frankland and his first wife, who was also called Eliza, were appointed to manage a Coffee Palace, in premises adjoining the White Horse Hotel in Church Street.

After Eliza Frankland died John Frankland married Eliza Mary Thistle. They were both committed Primitive Methodists. Eliza Mary's connections with Primitive Methodism can be traced right back to 1868 where newspaper accounts mention her name among the ladies present at the Anniversary service of the Church Street Primitive Methodist Sabbath School.

Later John Ness Frankland ran a Coffee House and Refreshment Rooms at 169 Church Street, almost opposite the Primitive Methodist Chapel in whose affairs he was involved. The building stood on the corner of Virgin Pump Ghaut and fronted Church Street. High on the wall was the name "Frankland's Coffee House" for all to see.

This was a respectable place to visit and smart dress was expected from the customers. Great efforts were made to create a comfortable surrounding. The furnishings were smart and the brasswork gleamed. John Frankland charged a penny a cup for his coffee. There were also papers on sale and various games were available.

After a long life John Ness Frankland died on the 8th January 1930. The beneficiaries of his will were his wife Eliza Mary and daughter Marina. When Eliza died has not been ascertained. However it is known that Frankland's Coffee house remained in Church Street for many years until it was finally demolished in March 1933.

Besides helping to run the coffee house, Eliza Mary Frankland was also active with her sister Emma in the Primitive Methodist Church. Mrs Eileen Leadley, one of Whitby's oldest residents, recalled that both sisters were members of the congregation at Church Street and both women were noted for their labours in raising money for the building of the new church.

Thomas Craven Busfield was the last of the Busfields to marry. He lived at home at Kilvington's Yard until his mother died. He then moved to Scarborough where he married the daughter of a blacksmith. The wedding took place on November 11th 1882 when he was 30 and his wife was Jane Elizabeth Melton, a 26 year old spinster from Scarborough. Originally a jet worker, he gave up this trade after his father's death and became a joiner. Thomas continued in this occupation until his own death in 1915, aged 62.

Emma did not re-marry until 1901, by which time she was 55 years old. Three years before, her sister Elizabeth had died, leaving Henry Freeman a widower. Now Emma and Henry were married - not in Whitby, but at the Primitive Methodist Chapel in Hartlepool. The marriage took place on the 5th February 1901.

Henry Freeman's links with the Busfield family were to span a total of more than forty years - almost the entire period he was in Whitby. The care and loyalty shown to him by the Busfields were as constant as his devotion to the Lifeboat service. Among them he found a welcome stability that had probably been lacking in his own early family life. Whatever the dangers and difficulties which befell him, no matter what trouble his fiery temperament sometimes provoked, he could always count upon the love and understanding of his wives Elizabeth and Emma. Without doubt, they were the mainstays in Henry Freeman's life, and they gave him invaluable support on several critical occasions in his career.

Henry Freeman   (Frank Meadow Sutcliffe)

CHAPTER 4

HENRY FREEMAN AND THE LIFEBOAT YEARS 1861-1866

In these days of motorised lifeboats and dinghies it is difficult to imagine a band of men actually rowing out through mountainous seas to save peoples' lives. Yet this is what the first lifeboats actually did. Over the years they were improved and special designs were built to the express requirements laid down by the Royal National Lifeboat Institution.Through trial and experience this body of people were able to perfect a design for a self-righting lifeboat which would give those manning it the greatest chance of success.

Relying on public subscription and bequests the Institution set up a ring of stations all around the coast of Britain which were controlled and organised from their base in London. At the time of Henry Freeman's involvement with the lifeboats the Whitby station was run by a private committee independent of the RNLI. After the 1861 disaster the Whitby station was incorporated into the RNLI organisation.

The rules of the Institution were then enforced and a new lifeboat called the *Lucy* built to their specific design was placed at the Whitby station. This boat had been built from funds provided by the late Mr Jaffray. His generosity had led to the placing of a new boat not only at Whitby, but also at Thurso and later St Andrews.

The *Lucy* replaced the lifeboat which had been lost in the storm. The second and surviving lifeboat, formerly owned by the Whitby Committee, which was kept on Tate Hill pier, passed to the Institution. It became known as the *Old Green Boat* and shortly afterwards was put on a carriage and stored in Pier Yard.

With the loss of the regular lifeboat crew a new team had to be formed. The choice for the Coxswain was John Pickering, a Whitby Pilot, who selected his crew from the ranks of Whitby fishermen. It was the practice to take coble fishermen because their everyday working life was spent in small craft. No one knew better than they did the hazards at sea and the limitations of a rowing lifeboat.

John Pickering's first test as coxswain was to come the Sunday before Christmas in 1862. Storms had been raging along the Yorkshire coast on the Saturday and there was an exceedingly high tide. Several buildings down by the waterfront were threatened by the rising water. Cellars, kitchens and warehouses were flooded and their contents spoilt. At the Angel Hotel and along Dock End walls were brought down, while at both the Coastguard and Volunteer Battery huge blocks of stone were knocked out of place. The Whitby Volunteers had to be mustered on the Sunday morning to drag back the guns on the Volunteer Battery to a place of safety.

Modern view of Tate Hill Pier. From 1822 until 1863 Whitby's Eastside Lifeboat was attached by davits to the side of the pier and enclosed by a wooden boathouse. Nothing remains of this early boathouse, but a plaque fixed to the pier marks the place where it stood. *(Photograph Ray Shill)*

At noon a vessel was seen to be making for the shore through the mountainous seas. She proved to be the barque *Royal Rose* under Captain J.Storm. On she came until she ran aground north of the Second Nab. All her crew had taken to the rigging for safety as a certain death awaited them if they tried to get to the land. The rescue services were alerted. John Pickering got his lifeboat crew ready with their cork jackets on and had the *Lucy* dragged out of the lifeboat house which was then a small wooden shed near to the Pier. The Coastguard assembled the rocket brigade and set off along the cliffs with the rocket apparatus. John Pickering went down to the pier to look at the state of the sea but decided it was too dangerous to launch the *Lucy*. At the scene the Rocket Brigade had no luck either. All the rockets they fired to get a line aboard the *Royal Rose* fell short of the crew.

Determined to save the helpless sailors, a group of fishermen manned the *Old Green Boat*. Because of its lighter weight, a number of men and boys were able to pull her up the Khyber Pass without difficulty then take her along the cliff tops to the wreck. Once there, the boat was taken off her carriage and carefully lowered down the cliff sides. The lifeboat set out through the storm-tossed seas on its errand of mercy.

Twelve men manned that boat: John Pickering was Coxswain, John Cass, another pilot, was Second Coxswain and ten strong fishermen pulled on the oars. On reaching the *Royal Rose* they found an exhausted crew. Time was needed to coax them into the lifeboat. This was a dangerous occupation in itself. The *Royal Rose* was tossing and rolling in the heavy sea. There was a danger that parts of the stricken barque might damage the lifeboat. The crew were taken on board but not without incident. Two fell into the water before they were dragged into the boat and another received a broken limb. A yardarm swinging in the gale hit the lifeboat with such force that a side was stove in. Carrying on regardless the lifeboat set off for the shore. They came near to disaster when a heavy wave crashed down upon them. Yet, somehow they made it back to land and all were saved, though the *Green Boat* was severely damaged.

Henry Freeman was not taken on this rescue mission, but his name became associated with another lifeboat shortly afterwards. At that time there was a third boat which remained privately owned by a small group of individuals. Originally it had been an official lifeboat for the old committee, but had been pensioned off in 1858. Called the *Fishermens Friend* this lifeboat was retained to serve the needs of fishermen themselves when their own cobles were in trouble.

After the *Royal Rose* rescue it was shown that two lifeboats were needed at Whitby. Mr Falkingbridge was authorised to repair and refit the *Green Boat* which had been damaged. On resuming duty she was christened the *Petrel.*

The *Royal Rose* rescue was to inspire those who owned the *Fishermens Friend* to obtain a lifeboat carriage for her also. For, like the *Lucy,* she could not be launched from the harbour during the storm. Mark Winn and Henry Freeman started a petition in Whitby to provide a special carriage for the *Fishermens Friend.* The task of collecting the money was left in the hands of J.Rigg, while Mr Norram, a coach builder from Whitby, was given the contract. He completed a light carriage from his own design which was tested in August 1863 and stored thereafter in Pier Yard. Another subscription was then set up for a small lifeboat house to be made for the *Fishermens Friend* on land donated by the North Eastern Railway.

In the next few years there were several incidents involving the *Fishermens Friend* which were to highlight the lack of organisation behind its operation. On some occasions the actions of its crew were more reminiscent of a Buster Keaton farce than

This view shows Dock End as it was in 1880. At this point Bagdale Brook joins the River Esk, and this marked the physical end of the harbour.
(Photograph Frank Meadow Sutcliffe)

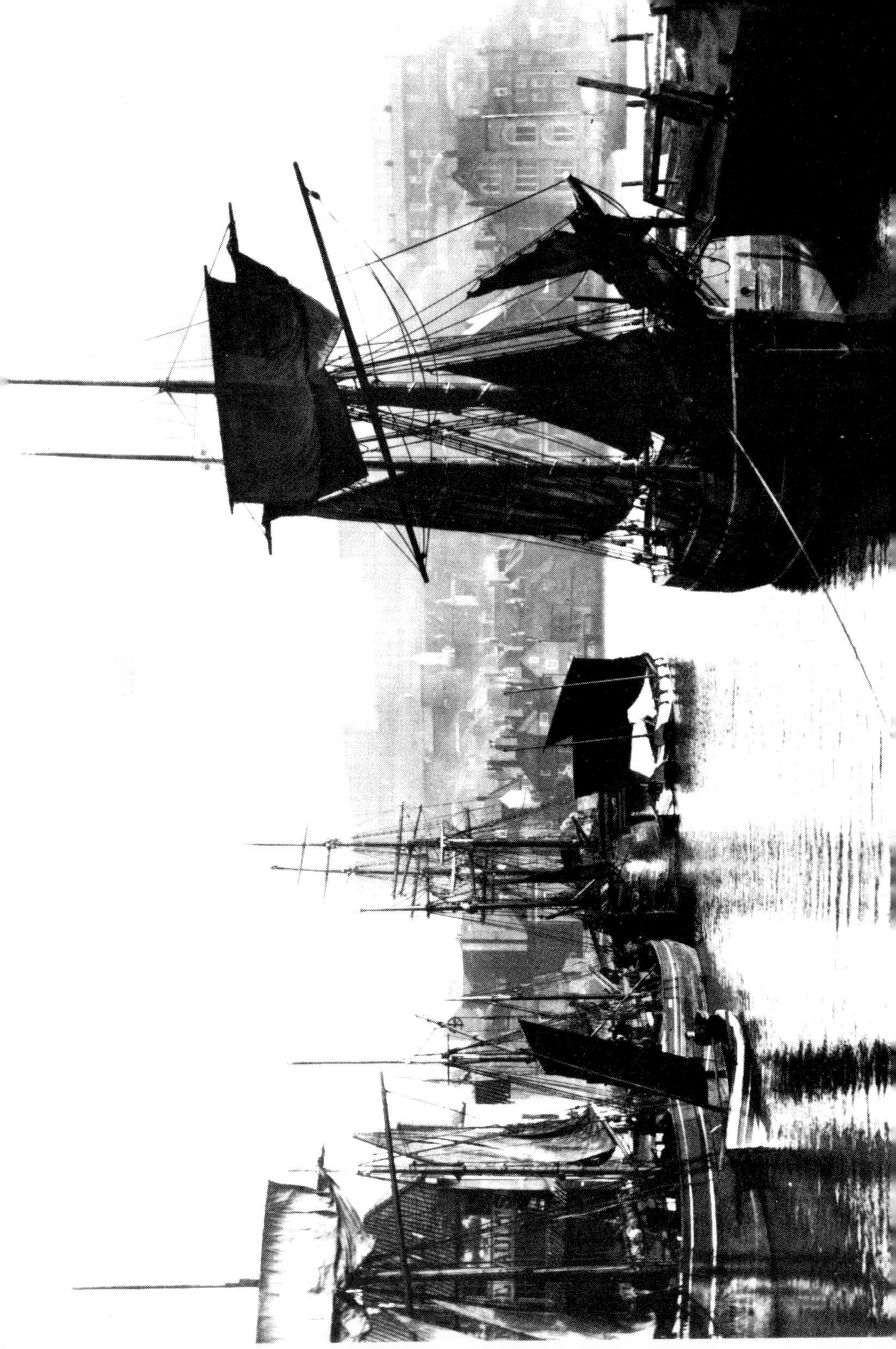

of serious attempts at life saving. Certainly, it was shown that very little can be achieved in the lifeboat service without a properly defined procedure.

On the day after the *Royal Rose* rescue, the *Fishermens Friend* was launched to follow the *Lucy* to the steamship *Alice* which had been damaged by the storm. However, she could give no help and so returned to the harbour.

One day in November the carriage and lifeboat were being moved when Mark Winn had his hand crushed between the wheel spokes of the carriage. Later the same week it was decided to put the new carriage to the test under demanding weather conditions and another exercise was arranged. The date was Friday the thirteenth, a rather surprising choice for normally superstitious fishermen. The launch met with a series of delays and nothing was really achieved.

On Tuesday the 15th March 1864, four fishing cobles were out during the day to retrieve an anchor and chain which had been dragging. The sea suddenly became stormy placing the cobles in danger. The *Fishermens Friend* was run out to the harbour side at Scotch Head, where she was lowered to the sands by a strap at each end. Despite protests from his fellows, Thomas Gains got into the lifeboat as she was being lowered. A strap broke and one end of the lifeboat fell heavily throwing Thomas Gains onto the sands. Such was the force of his fall that Mr Gains was knocked unconscious. Needless to say, the lifeboat did not venture out. Instead the steam tug *Hilda* went to help the four cobles back into the harbour. Among the rescued boats was the *Samuel and Sarah* whose master was Samuel Lacy.

Later in 1864 Henry Freeman was involved in another rescue of a rather different kind. On October 15th, he was passing down the east side of the harbour with his partners in a coble when a small boy, Matthew Snowden, was seen to fall into the harbour. Freeman's boat was close to the boy as he started to go under. Before the unfortunate lad drowned, Henry was able to reach under the surface and drag the boy into the boat to safety.

On the 19th April 1865 Pickering was able to take the *Lucy* out on her first rescue to the screw steamer *Ocean Queen* which had foundered on the rocks. The lifeboat reached the vessel and took off the 15 persons on board. The next day the ship's master employed the crew of the *Fishermens Friend* to row out to the wreck to retrieve a purse and various valuables before the salvagers got their hands on the vessel.

Shortly afterward the *Lucy's* services were again required when the barque *Maria Soames* fell foul of the rocks near the end of the pier. She was carrying a cargo of coals and coke from Sunderland to Alexandria. This time the lifeboat landed safely eighteen of the nineteen crew aboard her. The nineteenth man had been left behind by sheer bad luck. On seeing the lifeboat come alongside he had gone below to retrieve some clothing but on returning to the deck found the lifeboat already pulling away with his shipmates on board. Fortunately a brave cobleman went out and was able to rescue the laggard.

The *Maria Soames* began to break up spilling her cargo. As soon as the tide began to ebb the townsfolk were down beside the wreck like carrion. Hundreds of people laboured in the dark eager for a basket full of the precious fuel. For the poor this was a godsend.

On both rescues Pickering was coxswain and Samuel Lacy was his second in command. Henry Freeman at that time did not have a place in the crew, but that was soon to change. The RNLI had decided to erect another lifeboat station along the beach from Sandsend to Whitby to aid vessels which were stranded there. A lifeboat house was commissioned out of RNLI funds and built beside the beach at Upgang Creek. The Lifeboat Station at Upgang was completed during 1865. The running of the station came under the control of George Smales and the Whitby Coxswain.

The lifeboat was intended to be a gift from a Miss Watson but she died before her plan was realised. Her brother, Doctor Watson of Derby, chose to carry out her wishes and made funds available for the boat's construction. Called the *William Watson*, this lifeboat, which was smaller than the *Lucy,* had her harbour trials on the 22nd June.

The local society now had the problem of finding a crew to man the lifeboat and no doubt this was Henry Freeman's opportunity to gain a place as a regular lifeboat crew member. Not long afterwards he went out on several rescues with the National Lifeboat.

The Whitby lifeboat station kept duplicate returns of the services of the Whitby and Upgang lifeboats which were compiled by the secretary of the local committee. In 1865 when these records commenced George Smales was the secretary. For the next ten years John Pickering was coxswain while Samuel Lacy was usually the second coxswain.

Henry Freeman's first recorded rescue took place on the 19th October 1865. Just after noon on that day a schooner was seen to be in distress about two miles off Whitby. The *Lucy* was launched, but was scarcely afloat before the vessel foundered. Her crew were seen to take to their small boat but this sank as well, and nothing more was seen of the men. Meanwhile the lifeboatmen on the *Lucy* found it impossible to take the boat through the surf. The situation was hopeless and the *Lucy* returned to her station. If the vessel had not gone down so quickly her crew might have been saved by the Upgang lifeboat. The schooner was believed to have been the *Elizabeth* of Goole, under the command of Captain Calverson.

The next rescue undertaken did not involve any lifeboat, but Samuel Lacy's coble, the *Jane Ann*. On Monday 7th January 1866 several fishing boats were seen

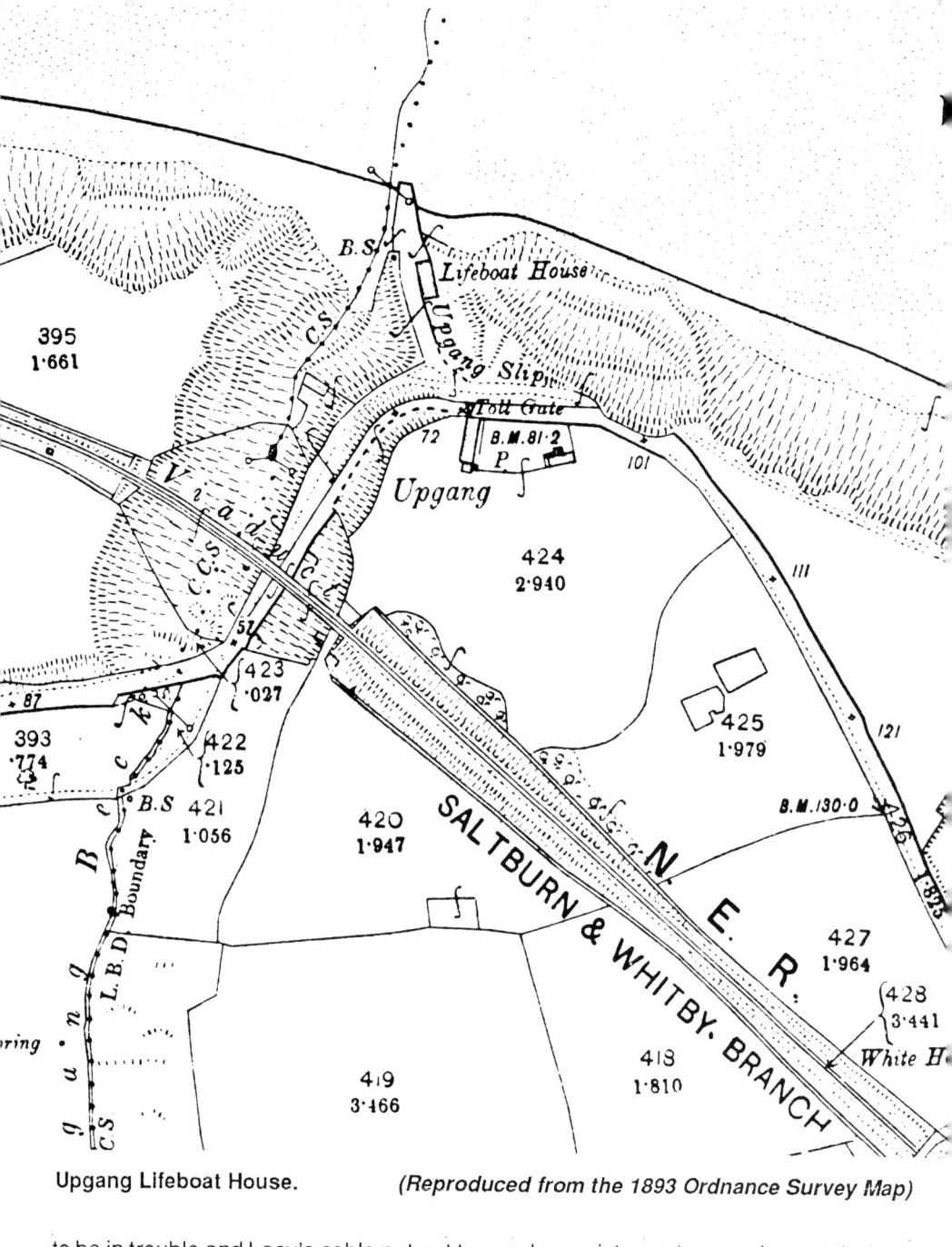

Upgang Lifeboat House.   *(Reproduced from the 1893 Ordnance Survey Map)*

to be in trouble and Lacy's coble put out to render assistance to one whose sails had been blown away. On board the *Jane Ann* were Lacy, Henry Freeman, Thomas Gains, Peter Langlands and Joseph Patten. All of them were serving members of the lifeboat team. The stricken coble proved to be the *Lena,* which was found three miles out to sea. Her crew of three were totally exhausted and as Lacy's coble drew alongside a mast and a sail were supplied. Two of Lacy's crew went aboard the *Lena* while one of her men came on board the *Jane Ann*. The pair of cobles now made for Scarborough but encountered another coble in danger called the *Maria*. This boat was also disabled with its sail blown away and its crew lay exhausted in the boat. The *Jane Ann* took the *Maria* in tow and all three cobles with the eleven men reached Scarborough in safety.

Sometimes the *Fishermens Friend* did venture out and provided a useful service for cobles in trouble. On December 30th 1866 four West Hartlepool Pilot cobles were seen to be in danger off Whitby. One made it safely to harbour and another capsized and the pilot was believed drowned. The *Fishermens Friend* was launched and rescued four men.

On December 31st, 1866, it was the *Lucy* which went into action. A heavy gale was blowing mixed with snow showers. The schooner *Lion* of Goole was being blown on shore. She was sailing from London to Sunderland and was heavily laden with a cargo of wheat. Seeking shelter from the storm Captain Flowers, her master, tried to get the vessel into Whitby harbour. Unfortunately, being low tide, there was not sufficient depth of water on the bar to allow her entry. Seeing the danger, the Harbour Master signalled the Captain to head for the beach in the hope that this was the best way of saving the crew. This was done and the *Lion* ran aground on the sands.

The RNLI lifeboat *Lucy* was launched at 10.45. On board her were thirteen men: John Pickering (coxswain), Samuel Lacy, William Harland, Henry Freeman, Thomas Gains, William Holmes, George Boyes, Francis Osborne, Samuel Hodgson, Thomas Hartley, Joseph Patten, William Fletcher and Richard Stainthorp. The wreck was soon reached and the crew of four men and a boy were safely ashore by 11.30. It was a speedy rescue but a hazardous one. Three oars were broken on the lifeboat by the heavy seas.

After this date Henry Freeman is not mentioned at all in the records for the remainder of Pickering's term as Coxswain, even though there were several further rescues made by the *Lucy* and one by the *Petrel*. It was as if Henry Freeman had fallen out of favour with Pickering. The reason for this might have been Henry Freeman's nature. He could be headstrong and quarrelsome, and he was also ambitious. It is understandable that Pickering would have resented it if Freeman had challenged his authority.

It was Henry's fate to be kept on the sidelines for the next few years. Freeman was attached to the reserve crew which manned the Upgang lifeboat. Although Pickering could have called on Henry, he chose not to use his services. The Upgang Lifeboat was not required to perform a rescue mission during this time, so Henry saw little action. His placing at Upgang, however, was by no means a handicap to his advancement in the Lifeboat service. Ironically it was to prove to his advantage at a later date. For the meantime Henry remained first and foremost a fisherman.

CHAPTER 5

HENRY FREEMAN FISHERMAN

There are many differences between the port of Whitby and Flamborough where Henry Freeman grew up, but the type of fishing Henry was to engage in for the rest of his life was common to both. He chose to be a cobleman.

The coble was to be found along the length and breadth of the Yorkshire coast. Its design was such that it could beach where other craft could not. It had a flat bottom with two keels, a high steeply rising prow and usually one mast which could be taken down. A cheap boat to make, it was well favoured by Yorkshire folk and it was used by the fishermen of Flamborough whose inhospitable shores prevented most other boats from getting close to land.

The coble is still very much in evidence today. It can be seen in common use at the small fishing communities such as Flamborough and Staithes, while Whitby still has several coblemen working out of the port. The only difference from its nineteenth century predecessors is that sail has given way to the diesel or petrol engine.

When Henry became a coble fisherman, it represented a radical change for him. Prior to this time Freeman had led a largely independent life. To be a fisherman, however, required a man to be part of a team. The numbers of men in a boat could vary according to the type of fishing undertaken with perhaps two or as many as five men in a boat. Henry Freeman would now find himself working with different partners throughout the year.

In the winter Henry went long line fishing. Usually the coble put out with three men on board each of whom provided his own fishing equipment. It was common to keep two sets of lines, one to be baited while the other was being used. Before taking up fishing, therefore, Freeman had to obtain his own gear, no doubt at considerable expense to himself.

The gathering of the bait was an arduous task, but no less important than the fishing was. Because of the time needed to find the bait and fix it to the lines, it was a role which was frequently performed by the fishermen's wives.

One of Frank Meadow Sutcliffe's best known portraits. Henry Freeman is shown here wearing the cork life jacket which saved his life in 1861.

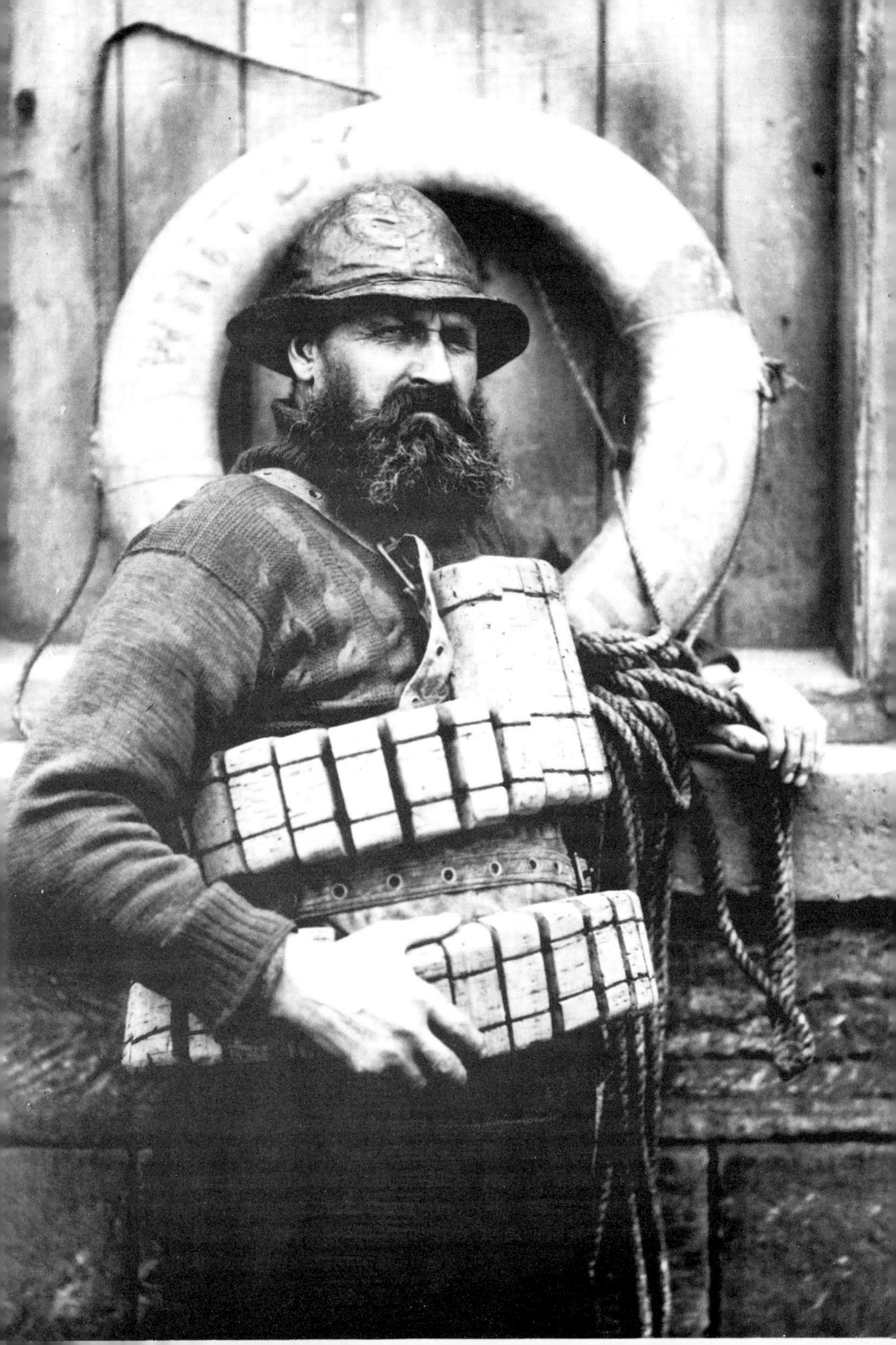

The bait came in different forms. Sometimes it was sand eels, but usually it was mussels. When mussels were not available limpets were used. Both the mussels and the limpets were gathered off rocks at the base of the East Cliff, or the scaurs, as they were known locally. The bait seekers had to scramble amongst the rocks hoping to fill their wicker baskets. All during the winter months, sometimes in the harshest of weathers, the women would be out gathering the bait.

Mussels could also be bought. They were shipped in from the Tees or Hull and some people made a living from selling them to the fishermen. This saved time and labour but reduced the profits made from the catch.

Whether the shellfish were bought or taken from the scaur, the shells still had to be removed, a process called skaning, and this was usually done at home by the fishermen's wives. The lines were baited with the fresh shellfish and as each line had hundreds of hooks many mussels or limpets were required.

As coblemen engaged in long line fishing, Freeman and his partners went out in the evening. On reaching the fishing ground the work commenced with the attaching of an anchor to the end of a baited line which was then tossed overboard, a procedure which was called "shooting the line". The coble then sailed away and the baited line was paid out until the end was reached when another was attached and perhaps another after that. Maybe a thousand yards of line was allowed to fall to the sea floor. Each section had a float or a "Dan" attached to it marked in such a way that the fishermen on returning to the spot could recognise their own lines. Most of the following morning was spent retrieving them.

Their catch was fish such as cod, skate or haddock which fed on the sea bed. Upwards of thirty stone could be caught in a night's work. As the lines came aboard the fish were taken off the hooks, sorted and deposited in a crib. On reaching the harbour the fishermen sold their fish to a local buyer on the quayside, then shared the profit. Prices varied according to the type of fish caught and the time of year. Cod could fetch a shilling each and haddock up to four shillings and sixpence a score.

Sometimes the men returned to port after shooting their lines. Coble fishermen used this time for many things including scavenging the beaches for the flotsam and jetsam lying there.

From March to August crab and lobster fishing were undertaken by a few fishermen, but Freeman appears not to have been amongst them. They worked in twos and threes laying specially constructed pots. The crabs and lobsters caught were then sold by auction along the quayside. Crabs were placed in small barrels called kits, but the lobsters were sold separately. Between 25 and 30 crabs might fill

Coble on Tate Hill Beach. The fishing coble was the most common type of fishing boat owned by Whitby fishermen. *(Photograph Frank Meadow Sutcliffe)*

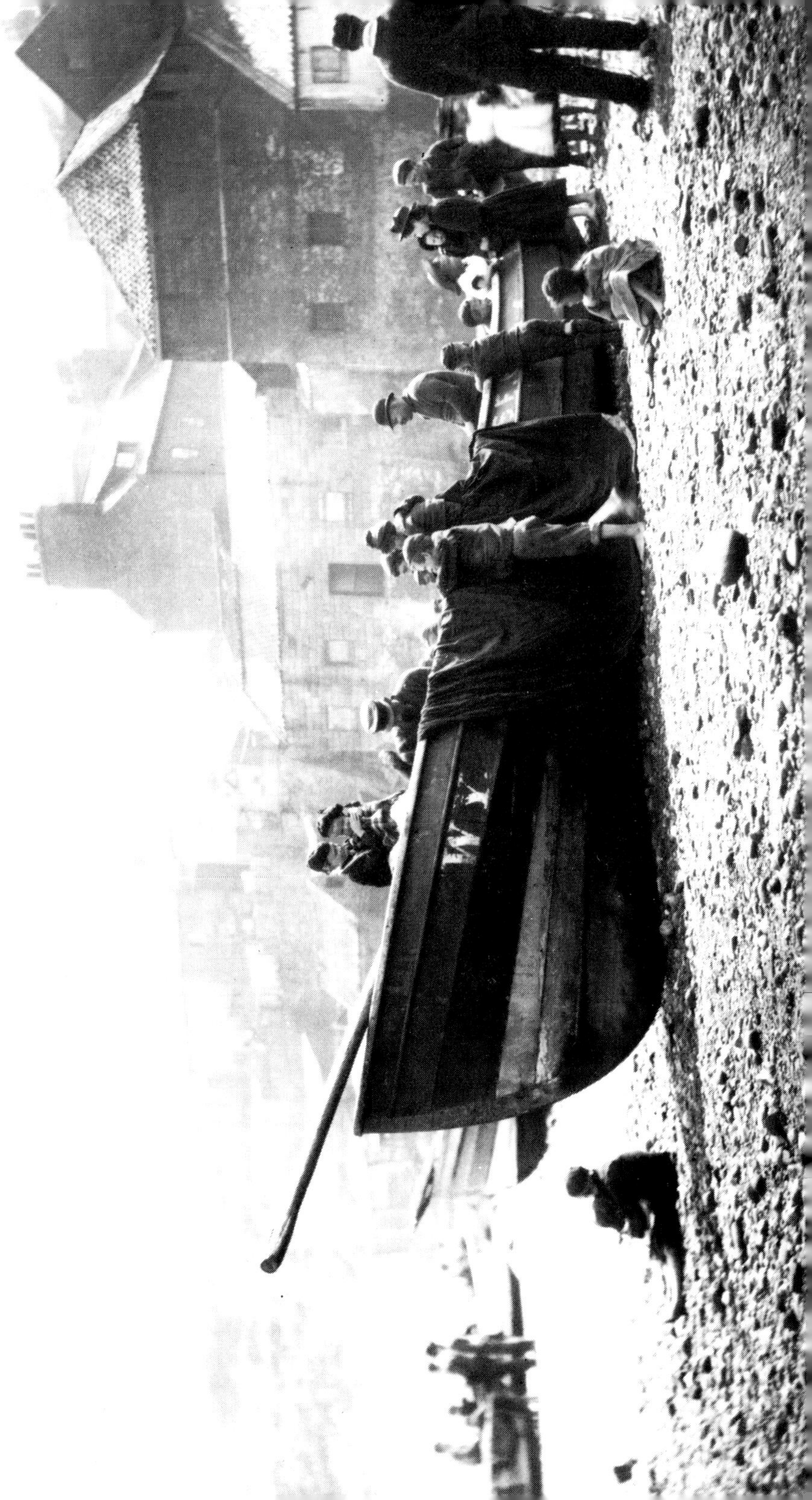

A recent view of cobles moored at Dock End. The design of the cobles has changed little since Freeman's time. *(Photograph Ray Shill)*

a kit and by mid-summer a fisherman could expect to get 4s for a kit, while lobsters ranged from 6d to 1s 6d depending on the season. Each year the number of crabs caught far exceeded the number of lobsters.

Long line fishing went on all the year round, but in summer many fishermen changed to catching herring with nets. Boats now carried four or five men who went out at night to net the surface-feeding herring. These were to be found in large numbers off the Yorkshire coast between July and October.

During these months the population of Whitby increased considerably. Besides the holiday-makers who arrived, the numbers were further swelled by additional fishermen who came there during the herring season. Regular visitors were the boats from Cornwall, Lowestoft and Scotland. Along with them came the fish buyers and the itinerant labour who descended on the port to help with curing the fish and filling the barrels so that they could be rushed to market. Some even came to help on the boats. Indeed Henry Freeman, himself, may have found this a way of earning a little money while still a brickmaker and in this fashion have become acquainted with the Whitby fisherfolk.

Two women gathering bait on the Scaur, a rocky beach off Whitby's East Cliff.
(Photograph Frank Meadow Sutcliffe)

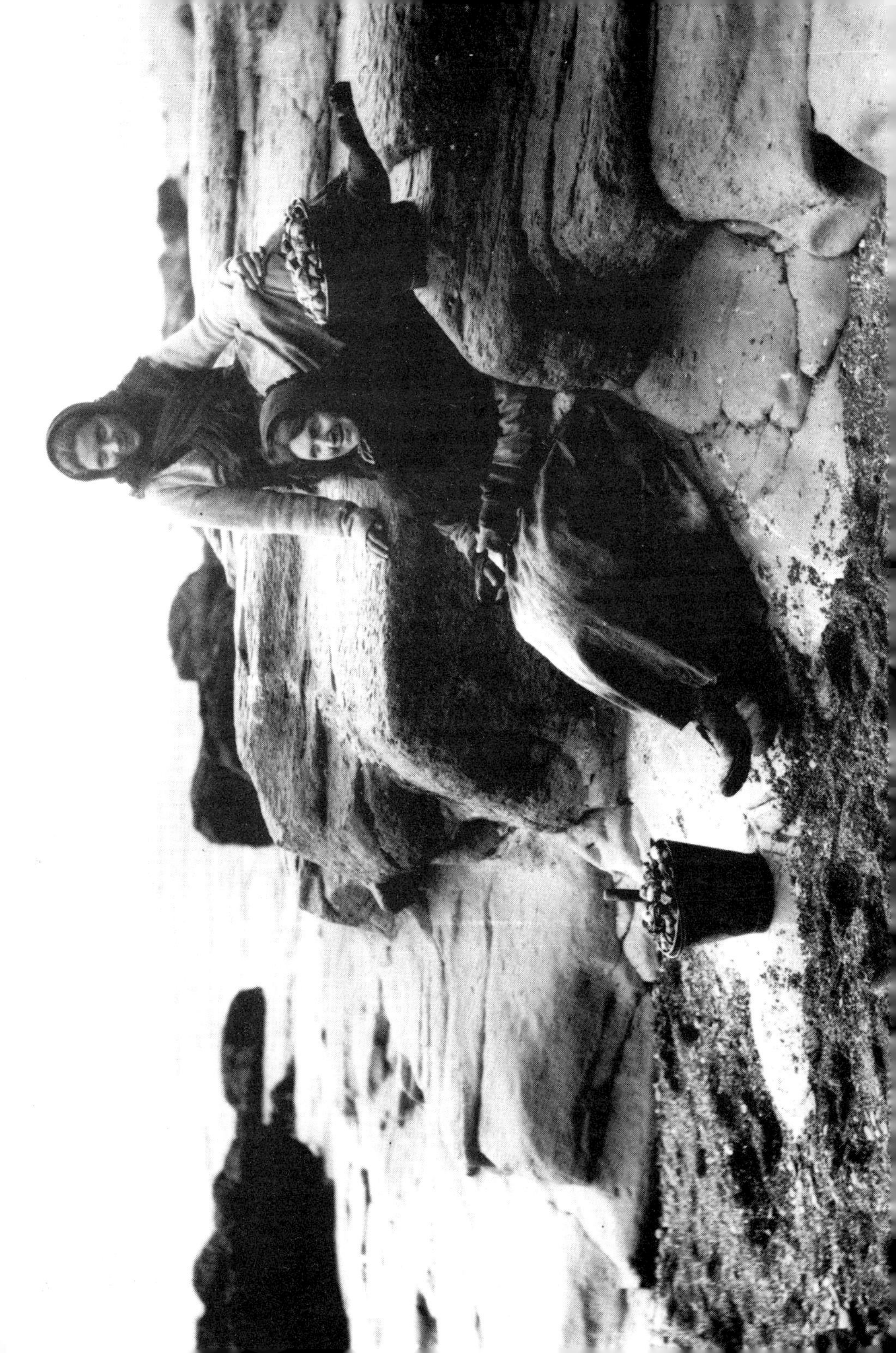

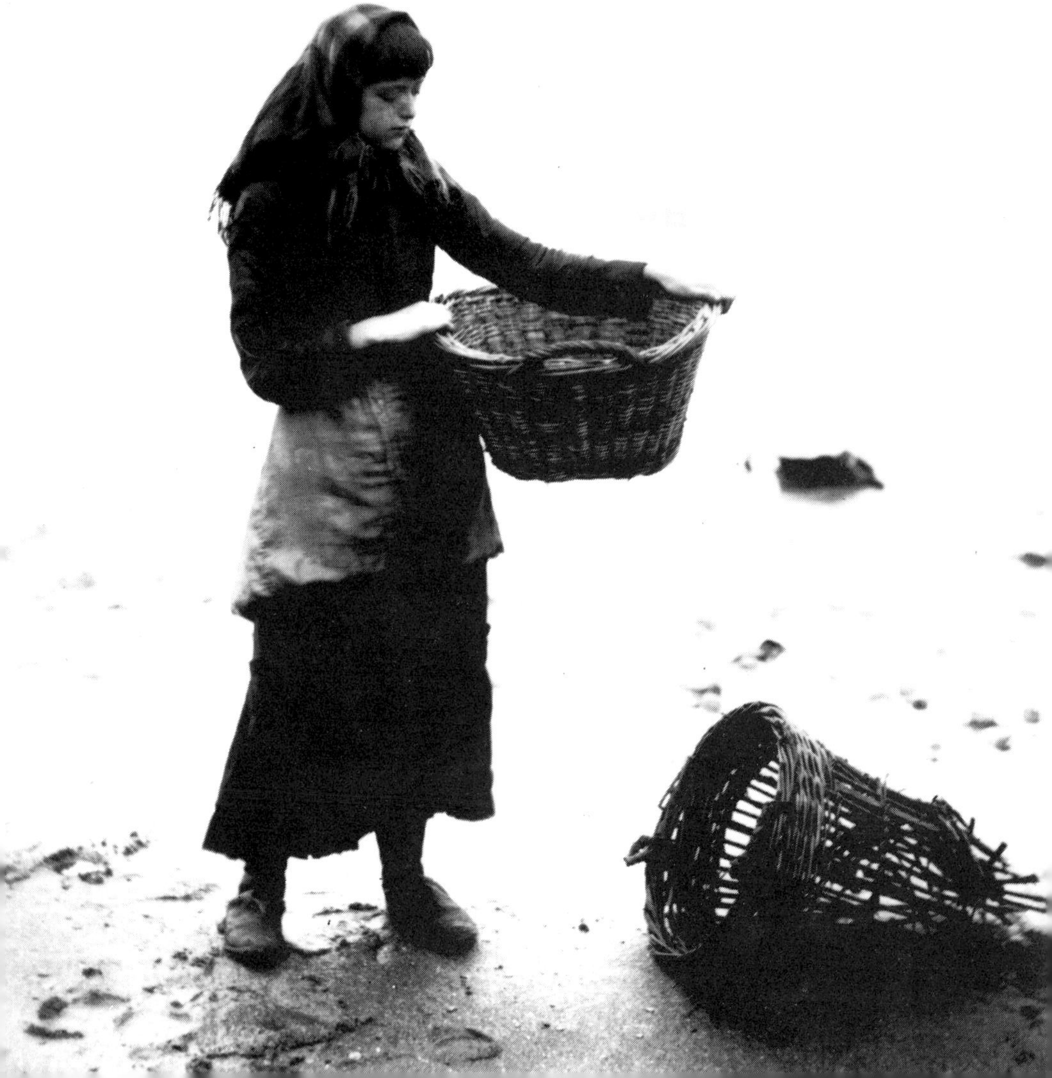

The herring were caught using nets made of cotton. Each net was about 60 yards in length. The larger boats would bring in between 6000 to 7000 fish a night while for the coblemen about 1000 would be a reasonable take. Later when steam vessels became more common in the fishing grounds amounts over 10,000 were recorded.

On reaching port the fish were sold along the quayside by an auctioneer who received a commission for the work. In 1870 this commission was 8d in the £1. The buyers were mostly the wholesale salesmen whose customers were to be found as far away as Birmingham and Manchester.

During the herring season the port of Whitby was a busy place. In Henry Freeman's time the boats would unload all over the port from Colliers Ghaut to Dock End, on the Pier, and even on the sands themselves. A lot of the quayside was then wooden planking and each buyer had his pitch marked off across it. Wooden barrels were stacked high and there was the hurry and scurry of the carters taking laden barrels of herrings along the streets to the railway station. The North Eastern Railway dispatched whole trainloads of fish from their sidings up by the Dock End. Each train had the same priority as an express passenger train to hasten their delivery to market in faraway cities.

The roads and pannier ways leading from the port were congested by the traffic as carters and carriers ferried the freshly caught fish to the inland villages of the North Riding. Amongst the carters were characters like William Frank or 'Fish Willie' as he was better known, a native of Hutton-Le-Hole who for nearly fifty years tramped along the roads with his cart from Staithes to sell his fish all over Ryedale.

The herring were bought in "hundreds" and good prices would vary from 5s to 7s per hundred. As soon as a price had been arranged the boats handed over their baskets of herrings to the buyer to be packed speedily into the barrels. The method of counting involved taking two herrings in each hand and then placing the four in the barrel. This double handful was called a warp and thirty more of these warps were packed in succession to make the "hundred" up. So in fact 124 herrings constituted a "hundred". Each barrel held between five to six "hundred" herring before it was covered by straw and sackcloth to seal it. A lot of rough salt or ice was packed in with the fish to preserve the contents for the journey. A kit was a smaller version of a barrel and held up to four "hundred" herring.

As well as collecting bait, women would gather driftwood for use as fuel. Not only fishermen's wives but their daughters also would be engaged in this physically arduous work. *(Photograph Frank Meadow Sutcliffe)*

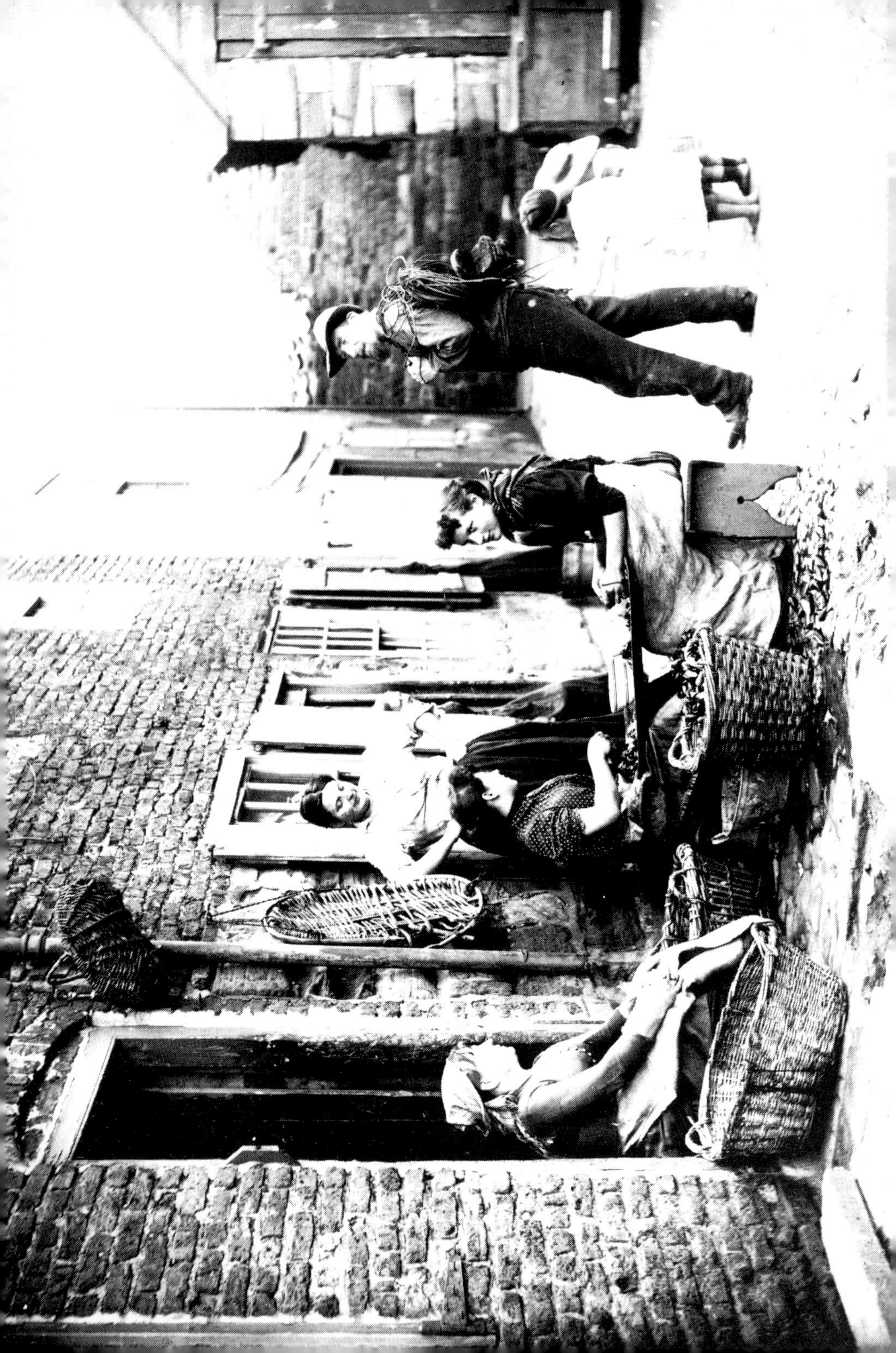

Before the bait could be used, it had to be separated from the shells, a process known as skaning. In this posed picture, women are shown skaning mussels near Tate Hill.
(Photograph Frank Meadow Sutcliffe)

Freeman seen here admiring his catch near The Fish Market, Coffee House End, Whitby. The fisherman sitting beside him is believed to be Walter Curry.
(Photograph Frank Meadow Sutcliffe)

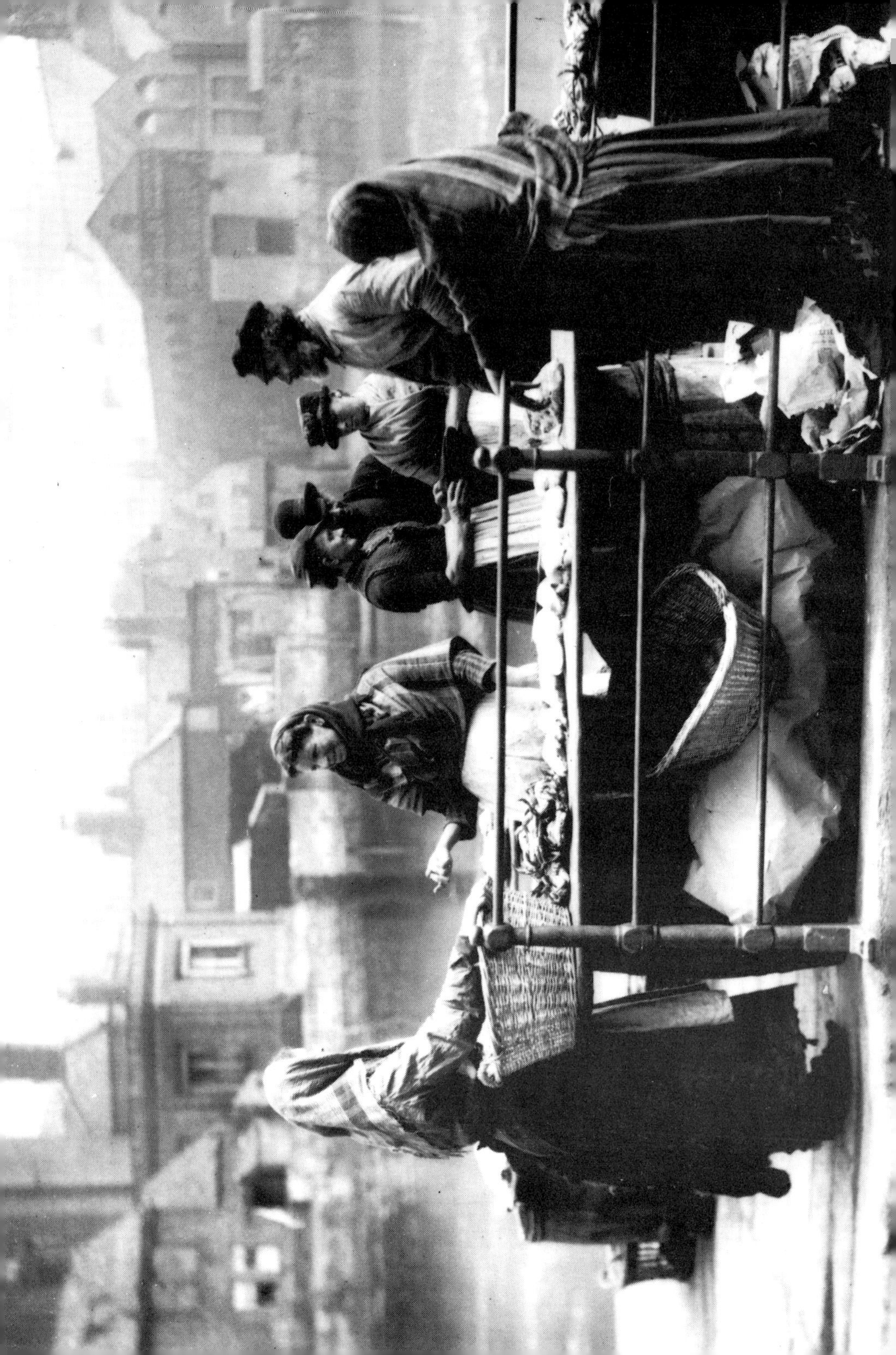

Fish stall on the New Quay, Upper Harbour.   *(Photograph Frank Meadow Sutcliffe)*

July and August were the months of the herring season in Whitby. This view shows herring cobles crowded at the Dock End. Barrels line the wooden quayside as far as the eye can see.   *(Photograph Frank Meadow Sutcliffe)*

The train journey in those early years was handicapped by the fact that the only rail link to Whitby was through Pickering and trains going that way had first to negotiate the Beckhole incline where the wagons were hauled up by a stationary engine. There were occasions when the rope broke and at least one fish train came to grief there leaving its contents to rot and offend the neighbourhood. From 1865 new railways were built which avoided this incline and the fish then had a safer passage.

Herring curing still continues behind Henrietta Street, below Whitby's East Cliff.
(Photograph Ray Shill)

Throughout the 1860s Henry Freeman was steadily becoming established as a fisherman. He went out with the Whitby boats and may have had a share in one or two. He developed a new confidence and expertise, particularly in line and herring fishing. He grew accustomed to the tides and currents, and learned to recognise swiftly the warning signs in nature which foretold a deterioration in the weather. Experience taught him also where the best catches were to be found. Prudence and wisdom made him a highly skilled fisherman and equipped him finally to become master of his own boat.

In these early years Freeman formed associations with a number of Whitby fishermen, but which of these, if any, were business partners is unknown. Newspaper reports reveal that in April 1863, Henry petitioned the local magistrate jointly with two colleagues, Mark Winn, and another man called Hunt from Staithes, for action to be taken against inshore trawling by Hull fishing vessels. Their complaint was that this indiscriminate method of fishing was reducing the coblemen's catches, and threatening their livelihood, by scooping the sea bed and taking all the bottom feeding fish, regardless of their size. For Henry the matter was to become something of a personal crusade. However, his efforts on this occasion achieved little; it was not until much later, when the North Eastern Sea Fisheries Committee was set up that any serious action was taken to remedy the situation.

Among Freeman's known associates at this time, Mark Winn seems the man most likely to have worked alongside Freeman. A man some twenty-five years older than Henry, Mark could well have been Freeman's mentor and guide. A resident of the Cragg, he was well acquainted with Whitby fishing and no doubt shared his knowledge with Freeman. Little is known of the boats Mark Winn owned, but one coble was called the *Major Worsley.* It was perhaps on this boat that the two men worked together. From time to time Henry's name appears with fellow lifeboatman Thomas Gains and it is possible they manned a fishing coble together. A third man, Samuel Lacy, seems to have been associated briefly with Freeman. But in later years there was considerable animosity between Lacy and Freeman as lifeboatmen and so it seems unlikely that their initial experience of working together as fishermen was a success.

Henry specialised in two types of fishing: line and herring fishing. Line fishing provided a small but steady income for Whitby fishermen throughout the year. Cod, haddock and ling were caught in substantial numbers and there was also a smaller catch of halibut and turbot. But chances of extra money came when the herring season arrived. In spite of competition from many visiting boats Whitby fishermen were still able to do well out of the herring.

The registration of Whitby Fishing boats commenced in 1869 in accordance with the Sea Fisheries Act passed the previous year. Freeman's name appears late in the list, after the registration of all the existing boats had been completed. It would seem, therefore, that he neither owned nor mastered a coble until later. The first recorded mention of his name appears against the date 14th June 1870. This suggests strongly that it took Freeman at least ten years to attain his goal of taking on a boat as master.

The coble listed beside Freeman's name in the register in 1870 was called the *Alexandra*. Freeman was master and the owner was Thomas Mennell. The vessel was fitted with a lug sail, carried four men and was a herring boat. Henry took her out on the first night and christened her in fine style. For on the morning of the 15th of June 'Harry Freeman', as the *Whitby Gazette* described him, brought in the first catch of the season by a Whitby boat. His catch of 1000 must have been of a poor quality because they sold for only 1s 6d per hundred. On the following morning his catch numbered 1100 and fetched a better price at 2s 6d per hundred.

Freeman purchased his first line fishing coble in November 1870. Of this he was both master and owner. The vessel was called the *William and Margaret* and she was a three man boat. He used her that winter and in the following spring before the herring season got under way.

In 1871 the herring season was heralded again by another early catch by Henry Freeman. Newspaper reports confirm that on the morning of Wednesday 28th June he brought to market a promising catch of 1000 aboard the *Alexandra*.

At the end of August he tried his luck with a larger boat called the *Quartelle*. Thomas Turner was the chief owner and Henry Freeman became the master. She was a mule and was 33ft long. Her normal complement was four men and a boy. Henry used her for the remainder of the season but gave her up at the start of the next. Apparently the boat was not favoured by him. He continued to use the *Alexandra* again.

Later that year he entered the *William and Margaret* in the race for cobles and mules which took place every year during the Whitby Regatta. The coble put up a fine show and came second. The following year (1872) Henry Freeman again entered the *William and Margaret*. This time, however, he failed to win a place, the race being won by the *Anne* from Hartlepool. It was said that Freeman was quite dissatisfied with the result and that he challenged the owner Robert Horley to another contest the next day over the same course with a wager of £5 being given to the victor.

Registration documents for the Alexandra.
(Courtesy of North Yorkshire County Record Office)

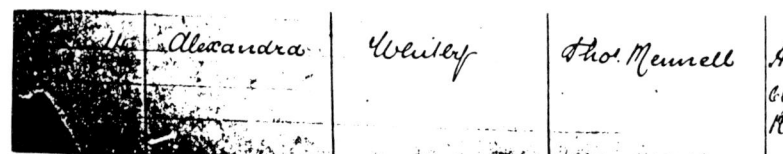

The race began in earnest and was hotly contested. Each coble had a crew of three men, but Henry Freeman himself was not in his boat. Instead it was manned by William Harland, Richard Sheppey and another unnamed man. Tragedy struck when the *William and Margaret* was opposite the Coast Guard station. Her crew were putting the vessel about when she capsized and sank in a sudden squall. The men on board her were pitched into the sea. Several craft came to their rescue but before anyone could reach him William Harland slipped below the waves and drowned. The others were rescued by a Penzance fishing boat. Sheppey was in a bad way and when brought ashore he was taken to the Marine Hotel where fortunately he was revived. The other member of the crew appeared to be none the worse for his ordeal.

After this sad occurrence Henry issued a statement in the Whitby press that the unfortunate coble race had been none of his doing. Perhaps he sought by this denial of responsibility to escape unpopularity or simply to salve his own troubled conscience. Whichever was the case the feeling must have been abroad in the town that the death of William Harland was down to him.

This whole episode reflected badly on Freeman's character. His desire to win at all costs had lost a man his life. Now his egotism prevented him from even acknowledging his part in the affair. It is hard to believe that the denial convinced anybody or increased his popularity one iota among local people. The insertion in the newspaper so soon after the accident was strangely insensitive but not inconsistent with Freeman's appetite for publicity. Always eager to draw attention to his prowess as a fisherman he saw no reason to miss this opportunity to defend his reputation in the press against adverse criticism.

There is of course a possibility that the race went ahead without Freeman's knowledge or approval although the newspaper reports would suggest otherwise. If, however, the contest was indeed promoted by him then by denying his responsibility Henry was clearly being dishonest. This trait of lying his way out of a corner was in fact to emerge on more than one occasion during his life. It would seem, therefore, that he knew all about the race but could not face up to the consequences of his actions. Perhaps this was an act of self-preservation, but it indicates a serious flaw in his character that at critical moments his judgment could be impaired.

To replace the coble he lost, Henry purchased another line fishing coble during December 1872. He named it the *Elizabeth* after his wife. In many ways this coble was identical to the *William and Margaret*: it was 19.5 feet long, weighed 2.5 tons and carried three men. Of all Henry's boats it was to be with him the longest.

By now Henry was an established member of the fishing community yet part of his time was still reserved for the lifeboat cause. Henry was attached to the Upgang team and no doubt went out on exercises with the *William Watson* lifeboat.

Meanwhile John Pickering remained coxswain of the Whitby boats. He had been out to most of the rescues and had given stalwart service to the cause. His last call to duty was at the start of August 1875 when the *Robert Whitworth* was taken out to the brig *Globe*. Pickering retired at the end of the month leaving the local committee to decide on a successor.

After Pickering's retirement it was decided by the committee to split the responsibility for the Upgang Lifeboat station from the Whitby Coxswain. They felt that a separate coxswain should be in charge at Upgang. Samuel Lacy, an experienced fisherman and second coxswain under Pickering, was given the post of Whitby Coxswain and Henry Freeman was appointed as Upgang's first coxswain.

It is curious to see why Henry won this appointment as other Whitby Lifeboatmen must have had a stronger claim. It is possible perhaps that the position was not wanted by the others. But a more probable reason was that Freeman had been associated with Upgang from the beginning. At a meeting of the Lifeboat Committee which took place on 24th October 1864, it had been "recommended that a second coxswain be appointed to Upgang". No further reference is made in the minutes to this post and it may not have been created. Yet it is likely Henry Freeman held a position of responsibility there and this would have favoured his selection as coxswain. The new job proved to be an advantage to Henry as it was to establish him in the chain of command.

A group of fishermen line the harbour rail. Henry Freeman is standing third from the left. He is clearly the tallest among them. *(Photograph Frank Meadow Sutcliffe)*

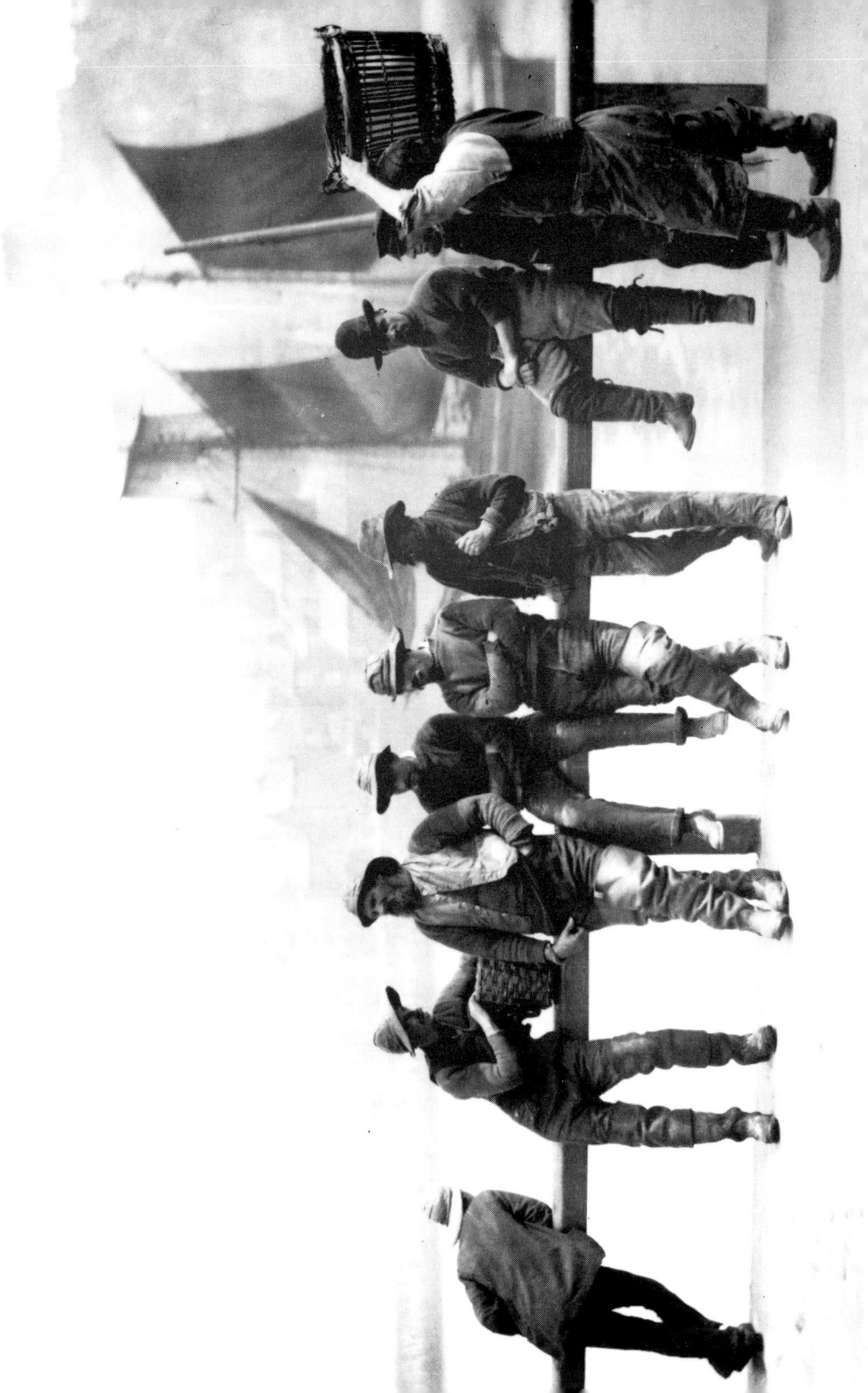

A modern view of Whitby coble fishermen. Many now supplement their income by organising fishing parties. *(Photograph Ray Shill)*

CHAPTER 6

COXSWAIN OF THE LIFEBOAT

As coxswain at Upgang, it was Henry Freeman's duty to pick the crews of the lifeboat when she was called out and have command of the lifeboat when at sea. Thomas Langlands, who had already spent some time in the Whitby boats, became his second in command. On land Henry also had to ensure the lifeboat house was kept in good order and the cork jackets were in good repair. Woe betide any coxswain found lacking in this respect when the Lifeboat Inspector came to call!

For these responsibilities the coxswain received a quarterly salary which was a welcome and regular income for Henry Freeman in addition to what he earned as a fisherman. The nationally agreed salary laid down by the RNLI was a fixed sum of £8 per annum for a Coxswain-Superintendent and £2 annually for an assistant coxswain.

George Smales had been the lifeboat secretary since 1863 and it was to him that the Whitby lifeboat coxswains were directly responsible. As secretary, Smales held the real power at Whitby. It was he who decided when a lifeboat should go out and who was in charge of the day-to-day running of the service. In effect he was the manager of the lifeboat operations at Whitby and therefore was keenly aware of the cost of launching the boat. Normally, each lifeboatman on a rescue received some payment, usually 10 shillings, but this was increased to £1 at night. Men were also needed to get the carriage out and there were standard payments for this, as well. Men on the carriage usually were paid 2s each and at least 25 and sometimes 50 were needed to launch the boat. Further expense was incurred if horses were hired.

Special tokens were issued to those who helped launch the lifeboat. When redeemed each man received payment for his service. *(Photograph Ray Shill)*

In turn the Lifeboat secretary was responsible to the Lifeboat committee who made any important local decisions. These gentlemen were appointed to the position usually because of their practical experience in seafaring matters, but in later years several of the moneyed ship-owners also gained seats on the committee perhaps guided by their belief in social duty. All major decisions such as the provision of new lifeboats were made in London.

Samuel Lacy succeeded Pickering as coxswain of the Whitby boats and Thomas Hartley was his second coxswain. Both Lacy and Hartley were involved in several rescues, but none so controversial as the salvage of the barque *Svadsfare* in 1875. The repercussions of this were to involve Henry Freeman and highlight the bad feeling which must have existed between Freeman, Lacy and Smales.

Lacy and Hartley had gone out with the No 1 Lifeboat, *Robert Whitworth* to the barque *Godstadt Minde* but afterwards they had taken refuge at Runswick Bay. Henry Bell had gone along on this trip as one of the lifeboat crew. A native of Runswick Bay his knowledge would have been useful on the rescue attempt.

The men were returning by sea on Friday, 22nd October 1875 when they answered the call for aid by the barque *Svadsfare*. Going aboard, the lifeboat crew helped to take the barque into Hartlepool and returned the following day with the *Robert Whitworth*. Unfortunately this act of salvage was done in such a way that it incensed other Whitby fisherfolk including Henry Freeman.

During the Friday afternoon the *Svadsfare's* signals were seen at Whitby. Henry Freeman, branch pilot John Douglas and other fishermen went out in a coble to see if they might be of assistance. Evidently the situation did not warrant the launching of the *Harriott Forteath*, but they believed that they could get the vessel to another port and claim salvage rights.

On reaching the Swedish barque they found Samuel Lacy and his lifeboatmen already aboard. Lacy was trying to run the vessel ashore. Those in the coble shouted to Lacy not to attempt to beach her, but to head for another port. They also shouted up to Lacy that they were willing to help with the task.

Lacy must have then realised the prospect of a salvage reward and perhaps wishing to share it with as few people as possible had the barque turn about and head for Hartlepool leaving the coble in the boat's wake. Whether or not this was intended as a direct snub to Freeman will probably never be known, but certainly it was insensitive of him as the coble had to get back into harbour.

At that time the sea on the bar was rough and as the coble approached the Whitby Piers there were calls made to George Smales to launch the *Harriott Forteath*. This he declined to do but instructed the Coastguard to throw a line across the harbour which the coblemen could catch hold of in case the coble overturned or was swamped with water. In the event the line was not needed and the men reached a safe berth.

A special meeting was held by the local committee on the Monday to sanction payments made to Lacy and his crew for both rescues including the expenses for leaving the *Whitworth* at Runswick. The meeting also commended his actions over the salvage of the *Svadsfare*. Henry Freeman's claim for salvage rights was also discussed during the committee meeting but it was turned down. Samuel Lacy was backed all the way by the committee. The minutes even include the suggestion that Lacy should return to Hartlepool as soon as possible to meet with the Inspector of Wrecks and collect the salvage money.

The same day a letter was written to the Royal National Lifeboat Institution in London which crystallised the grievances Henry and his colleagues had. It bore his name, that of John Douglas, Whitby pilot and coxswain of the *Fishermens Friend*, Samuel Hutchins, fisherman and a fellow lifeboatman and three other fishermen. All the signatories appeared to have manned the coble which went out to the *Svadsfare*. A copy of this letter was published later in the *Whitby Times*. Clearly the authors intended to cause trouble for the local lifeboat committee. Their letter ended with the threat of using the *Fishermens Friend* against the National lifeboat whenever the opportunity arose.

It caused a volcano to erupt amongst the Lifeboat Committee in much the same fashion as Oliver Twist's asking for more in the Workhouse. The fact that Henry Freeman, coxswain of the Upgang boat, had the temerity to question the local committee's decision was sorely felt particularly by George Smales.

Meanwhile the local committee were also in conflict with the parent institution in London over the payment of 40s per man over the *Godstadt Minde* rescue. London believed the sum to be excessive and recommended a maximum payment of 30s. The Whitby Lifeboat Committee met again on the 28th October and reaffirmed their decision to pay Lacy and his crew 40s per man. London grudgingly agreed the payment.

The matter of the letter to London was set aside for another meeting on the 1st of November. Present on this occasion was Captain Ward, the Chief Lifeboat Inspector from London who had come to resolve the difficulties highlighted in the dispute.

The meeting took the form of an inquiry. First Samuel Lacy gave evidence; then Henry Freeman, John Douglas and Samuel Hutchins were all called to have their say. Lacy was completely exonerated and in fact it was concluded that Lacy would not have done his duty if he had refused to go to the barque's aid.

The Whitby Times

And North Yorkshire Advertiser.

THE WHITBY COBLEMEN AND THE NATIONAL LIFE-BOATS.—We have been requested to publish the following letter, which has been transmitted to its destination this week:—

Whitby, 25th October, 1875.

To the Secretary of the National Life-Boat Institution, London.

Sir,—On the 22nd inst. the barque *Svadsfare*, of Porsgrund, came off Whitby, making signals of distress, about 3 P.M. A pilot coble with five men and a branch pilot in company put off in a heavy sea at the risk of their lives to render assistance, and succeeded in reaching the vessel. At the same time the National life-boat, No. 1, *Robert Whitworth*, came alongside, and took possession of the ship. The coxwain left his boat and acted as a branch pilot, and turned the coble and her crew adrift, not caring whether they reached the harbour or not. As soon as the coxwain of the life-boat was on board, the ship's head was turned to the shore, with the apparent intention of running her on to the beach. The coble again came alongside, and asked what they were going to do with the ship, and were told that they were going to run her ashore. They (the coblemen) replied, "Don't do that, as we are willing to come on board and help you to get her to a northern port;" whereupon, they put her about, and proceeded to Hartlepool, taking the life-boat with them, and leaving the coble and six men in extreme peril to get back as well as they could. Meanwhile, the National life-boat No. 2, *Harriet Forteath*, was got out, and the pilots and fishermen put on their cork jackets, intending to launch her for the benefit of the coble and her crew, but the secretary told them that the boat was not got out for that purpose, but merely to let the public see that there was another life-boat, and saying that the coble was in no danger, although he went immediately to the chief of the Coast Guard, and got him to take the rocket apparatus to the harbour mouth and throw a line across, so that if the coble was swamped the men might get hold of it and so save themselves. Now, the boat would have been launched and put back again clear of expense to the Institution. The coble succeeded in entering the harbour in safety, but if such is to be the practice when men incur risk to render assistance in cases of distress, we shall on all occasions have to launch the *Fishermen's Friend*, a private life-boat, and work against the National life-boats whenever opportunity serves us, as the using the National boats in opposition to private enterprise is contrary to the Institution's regulations, and is in effect taking away the bread from our families.

JOHN DOUGLAS, Pilot.
SAMUEL HUTCHINS, Fisherman.
HENRY FREEMAN, Fisherman and Coxwain of the Upgang Life-Boat.
WILLIAM COOPER, Fisherman.
RALPH STORR, Fisherman.
WILLIAM AUSTIN, Fisherman.

Freeman was cautioned by Captain Ward because his name had appeared on the letter. Henry denied ever having seen it. Unlikely as this was, there may have been some truth in his denial. Like most of his fellow fishermen, Henry Freeman could not read or write and always signed by his mark. Henry quite literally may not have seen the letter, but whether he knew and approved of it is another matter. Without doubt he must have shared most of the sentiments expressed in it. Freeman came very close to losing his job. It was perhaps because of the difficulty in establishing whether Henry did or did not give his mark to that letter that he continued as coxswain at Upgang.

To set matters right in the eyes of the public George Smales had a reply published the next week in the *Whitby Times* laying out Captain Ward's exoneration of Lacy and justifying his own actions in not launching the *Harriott Forteath* to the rescue of Freeman and his fellow fishermen in the coble.

George Smales's letter was well written and no doubt it had the desired effect. But it does not satisfactorily explain why the lifeboat could not be launched as a crew were willing to give their services voluntarily. There was never any danger of a precedent being set, because the lifeboat had been launched before to cobles in trouble and the crew manning it had given their services free of charge.

Smales's written account of the *Svadsfare* rescue in the surviving lifeboat records is rather brief and mentions none of the friction which seems to have existed between him and Freeman. But later events make clear that friction did exist between the two men.

The antagonism between Smales and Freeman may well have been of a long standing nature. George Wakefield Smales belonged to a successful and wealthy Whitby family whose interests included mast making, timber importing and ship owning. He and his brothers were influential Whitby businessmen.

George Smales was only two years older than Henry Freeman. Henry might well have resented the fact that someone his age had risen to such a position of authority, especially if Smales had gained that position through family connections, rather than on his own merit. Clearly the *Svadsfare* incident did little to enhance Freeman's confidence in George Smales's capabilities.

The animosity may not, however, have been confined solely to the Lifeboat Secretary but may also have involved the Whitby Coxswain, John Pickering and his second-in-command Samuel Lacy. These two men had the authority to exclude Freeman from rescue missions. Freeman's name was certainly absent from the lifeboat crew lists for almost nine years prior to his appointment as Coxswain at Upgang. This may not have been purely because of his desire to concentrate on his fishing; the actions of others may have played a part here. It is interesting that in barely

Whitby Times 5th November 1875

LETTERS TO THE EDITOR

THE NATIONAL LIFEBOATS AND THE COBLEMEN.

Sir,—As the Committee of the Whitby and Upgang Branch of the Royal National Lifeboat Institution consider the letter published in your last week's issue is calculated to give the public a wrong impression of the services rendered by their boat *Robert Whitworth*, on the 22nd October, in saving the barque *Scaldifare* and her crew of 16 hands, I beg to hand you copy of the resolutions passed by this committee at their meeting held on the 1st inst., at which Capt. Ward, R.N., Chief Inspector of Lifeboats to the Institution, was present—viz., that the Committee and Capt. Ward not only exonerate Samuel Lacy, the coxswain, from all blame, but consider he would have neglected his duty had he not proceeded to the assistance of the barque on perceiving she had shown a signal for aid; and they are further of opinion that his doing so did not infringe the rule of the Institution which requires its boats not to be used so as to interfere with private enterprise. The subsequent rejection of the services of the coble and her crew rested entirely with the captain of the barque, who naturally preferred the assistance of the safer boat and the larger body of men to accompany him to Hartlepool.

The Committee consider their hon. secretary, with the assistance of Mr. Richard Smith, the Chief Officer of Coast Guard, took every precaution for the safety of the crew of the coble, and that the launching of the No. 2 Lifeboat was uncalled for. Such, Mr. Editor, being the opinion of Capt. Ward and a committee of 13 practical and most of them nautical men, I shall be obliged by your giving it publicity in your paper, that the public who support our boats may divest their minds of any wrong impression which they may have formed from the letter you inserted last week.

I remain yours truly,
GEORGE W. SMALES,

Whitby, 2nd November, 1875.   Hon. Sec.

---

two months after his promotion to Coxswain conflict flared between Freeman and Lacy.

At the start of May 1876, in preparation for the summer fishing, Henry bought a mule called *Wings of the Morning* from William Griers and his partners. This vessel was registered for herring fishing and was able to carry four men. Henry barely had time to take it out before he was called upon to give his first service as a lifeboat Coxswain.

It happened on Wednesday 24th May 1876. Eight fishing cobles had gone out between 3 and 4 in the morning to fish and Samuel Lacy was among them. There had been no sign of bad weather, but this soon altered. The wind increased and a storm blew up. The cobles turned about and made for home. Entering the harbour in such a wind, however, could easily capsize a small vessel. Richard Smith, the chief coastguard officer was soon down at the pier with the rocket apparatus and had a line put across the harbour mouth. Suspended from it were a lifebelt and buoys so as to help those returning in the boats. Three cobles got back safely into the harbour, but there were fears for the others. Another three were seen in the distance approaching the port. Thomas Hartley assumed the role of Coxswain and took out the smaller No.2 boat, the *Harriott Forteath,* with crowds of onlookers lining the piers and the West Cliff. They rowed out and took all the men from the cobles. Six men were taken off including Lacy himself.

Hartley had returned to the shore and beached the lifeboat when another coble came into sight. The time needed to replace the *Harriott Forteath* on her carriage ready for relaunching was considered to be too long and the *Robert Whitworth* with Henry Freeman as coxswain was taken out for the rescue. Several of the crew who had been out with Hartley manned the lifeboat with Freeman including John Storr, son of the coxswain who perished in the 1861 disaster. John Thompson and John Palmer were there as well.

The launching was very rapid but not without incident. Henry launched the boat far too quickly, while two of his crew were still on the carriage trying to get into the lifeboat. One man was dragged aboard by his fellows but the other, William (Bendy) Patterson, a jet worker by trade, grabbed onto the stern of the lifeboat and came close to being crushed as he was dragged through the surf between the lifeboat and the wheel of the carriage. Fortunately Patterson retained his hold and was taken into the boat after the launch, dripping wet but none the worse for his ordeal. It was a hard row against wind and tide to the solitary coble which belonged to James Midwood. He and the other two fishermen in the coble were transferred to the *Robert Whitworth* which then returned to the shore.

This was the only time Henry took out a lifeboat in the course of a rescue whilst he was the Upgang Coxswain. The Upgang lifeboat was never called out and further rescues were carried out by the Whitby boats under the command of Lacy or Hartley.

At the start of November 1876 William Tose died. He had been harbour master at Whitby for 26 years and had been a regular sight along the pier giving instructions where needed to the fishermen and lifeboat crews. He was replaced by Captain Robert Gibson, a Whitby born merchant seaman. Robert had served for many years on the shipping which plied the North Eastern coast and had a share in different vessels. He was a very able man and well suited to the task before him.

One of his first problems was to be the schooner *Agenoria* which had arrived from Hartlepool with coals for Whitby on the 9th January 1877. She had dropped anchor in Whitby Roads. A storm then arose. About midnight the vessel made for the harbour, which was a dangerous thing to do in such a gale. Both Robert Gibson and

Richard Smith saw the *Agenoria* approaching and tried to warn it off, first by signals and later by a lighted tar barrel.

The master at first complied but returned about 1.30 am. The vessel was close to the outer side of the West Pier-end when Gibson noticed her again. With one of the pilots he hailed the vessel and ordered the captain "to put his helm down and get his ship off to sea again", which was done. Just at that time a very heavy wave struck the *Agenoria*. The master lost control of her and she drifted on shore, a quarter of a mile to the north of the West Pier.

Gibson and Smith made their way to the stricken vessel with the rocket apparatus and tried to get a line aboard. Their progress was hampered by repair work which was being done to the main sewer which had collapsed, but they managed to get the apparatus to the spot and set it up.

Meanwhile, the lifeboat crew had been called out. Lacy and his men had been roused from their beds about midnight, when the *Agenoria* was seen to be in danger. Because of the damaged sewer the *Robert Whitworth* had to be left in her boathouse and instead they took the *Harriott Forteath*. When the lifeboat was launched, at 1.30am, the seas were rough and they could not see the ship in the pitch darkness. The stormy seas came close to filling the boat as they rowed through the waves. On board was the Upgang second coxswain Thomas Langlands who acted as bowman on this rescue. John Storr and Thomas Gains were there, as well, to pull on the oars.

A lifeboat battles through rough seas with survivors from a wreck.

(Collection Mrs. Pat Pickles)

They rowed to the north in the hope that they might then see the ship. With the prevailing wind the vessel could not make the harbour and must strike the beach in the direction they were going. Using a sea anchor or drogue held by Thomas Hartley to keep the boat steady in the water Lacy then tried to get the lifeboat back to where they thought the vessel lay.

A huge wave suddenly crashed down on the *Harriott Forteath*. Sam Lacy saw it coming and called out "Boys, stand fast". It turned the boat over onto her port side. A second wave finished the job, turning her completely over and casting the crew into the inky water. Only Luke Walker remained with the boat the whole time as he became entangled in her ropes. The rest of the crew grabbed for the boat's lanyards or whatever they could take hold of. But some were not so lucky. Three men drowned, Samuel Lacy, John Thompson and Richard Gatenby. It was a tragic loss.

As the lifeboat righted itself the survivors climbed back into it. John Dryden, oarsman, was fortunate. The strings of his lifejacket broke in the water, yet he still managed to get back into the lifeboat. John Storr actually swam ashore and made it to the beach.

The first Gibson knew about the tragedy was when John Storr struggled out of the water near where he was standing. The loss of the *Harriott Forteath* might have sealed the fate of those aboard the *Agenoria,* but Robert Gibson and the Coastguard were successful in their rescue bid. A line was thrown aboard the *Agenoria* and her crew of three were safely taken ashore.

At the inquest the Coroner found that the men had accidently drowned when the lifeboat capsized. Both the inquest and the RNLI inquiry held at Whitby noted the fact that the lifebelt strings had broken in some cases. Thomas Hartley was questioned about the strings breaking and on oath he stated that he and Lacy had inspected the lifejackets two weeks earlier. When it was suggested, also, that he may have let go of the sea anchor, he denied this. Afterwards the inspector reported back to the RNLI in London and no blame was attached to any of the lifeboatmen.

After this inquiry three things happened. Firstly, a circular was sent round all lifeboat stations urging the need to examine regularly lifeboat equipment such as the straps and strings on the lifebelts. Secondly, the *Harriott Forteath* was replaced by another boat bearing the same name. And thirdly, Henry Freeman was elected coxswain of the Whitby boats.

The decision of the Whitby Committee to promote Henry Freeman was hotly contested. Captain Wharton had proposed his appointment at the close of the committee meeting called on 12th January. About two weeks later, at the next meeting, the actual appointment was discussed. Hartley was brought before the committee and was offered the Upgang Coxswain's job. This he declined and he refused to work with Freeman as Second Coxswain under any circumstances.

Hartley was a strong candidate to succeed Lacy. He had more experience in the lifeboats, and had acted as coxswain on several occasions during 1876 when Lacy was not available. He was well liked by his crew.

Nevertheless, Freeman's appointment was confirmed a week later. The committee were split over which man they preferred for the post but the majority voted in favour of Freeman. Smales resigned in protest but his resignation was not accepted by the committee. He remained in his post temporarily until a successor could be found.

The Whitby committee now voted to promote Thomas Langlands to Upgang Coxswain. After this Thomas Hartley played a lesser role in lifeboat matters. No doubt he felt slighted at being passed over and may even have wondered if in some people's minds blame was attached to him for the lifeboat disaster the previous month. Hartley carried on fishing until his death in 1882, at the comparatively young age of forty-eight.

Henry now had the task of reforming the lifeboat crew and he gathered about him some able men. His crew frequently included James Pounder as second coxswain, and John Storr, who gave his services in a variety of ways either as an oarsman or as bowman and sometimes as second coxswain. Thomas Langlands went out with him as well, usually as bowman.

At Whitby he had charge of the two lifeboats. The No.1 boat was the *Robert Whitworth* a 32 feet long self-righting boat with ten oars. The other was the smaller *Harriott Forteath* which had been placed at the No.2 station in 1872 to replace the *Petrel*.

After the drowning incident the *Harriott Forteath* was little used. Records show she went out only once in September 1878 to render assistance to some cobles. The old Wexford No 2 boat was sent to replace her in 1879. However, the *Robert Whitworth* was to accompany Freeman on many rescues, some of which verged on the spectacular. She was the first lifeboat he took out as coxswain in 1876 and she would be there when he needed her right up to 1886.

The names Henry Freeman and Robert Whitworth were seemingly fated to be together. How this came about was quite remarkable. The first lifeboat to bear that name was stationed at Henry's home town of Bridlington. She had been completed at Forrest's yard in London in 1864 through funds provided by the South Manchester branch of the RNLI whose secretary was Robert Whitworth, a Manchester Cotton Merchant. After being christened in Manchester the *Robert Whitworth* was paraded through the streets. The boat was then sent on loan to Tynemouth whose own lifeboat had been damaged in a rescue.

The *Whitworth* did not arrive at Bridlington until January 1865. Another parade was organised and the lifeboat was taken through the streets. She was then launched into the sea as cannons blasted a salute. Unfortunately the Bridlington men did not approve of her and the boat was sent away to Whitehaven in 1866.

A 32 ft replacement boat was given the same name, but fared little better. She proved a difficult boat to row in the conditions which existed in Bridlington. Her test came at the start of February 1871 when a number of vessels in the bay were threatened with being blown on shore in a storm of near hurricane proportions. The *Whitworth* went out and rescued the crews of two vessels, but her own crew was totally exhausted and could not go out again. Present at the time was another private lifeboat called the *Harbinger* built by a local man David Purdon. The *Harbinger's* men went out time and time again to save the crews of the ships as they came on shore. It was a perilous mission. On her sixth trip out she was capsized with the loss of three lives including that of her builder David Purdon. There was a terrible loss of life that day as vessels sank and men drowned. The coastguard tried in vain to use rockets but they were useless in such a wind.

After this the second *Whitworth* was taken off station and replaced by a boat designed to meet the special needs of the port. This presented the RNLI in London with a problem. Robert Whitworth and his team at Manchester had been extremely active on their behalf and by that date had succeeded in placing over fifteen boats along the coastline of Britain. To ensure proper recognition of their efforts it was decided to rename an existing lifeboat the *Robert Whitworth.* The boat chosen was already stationed at Whitby. Then called the *Lucy,* this vessel was relatively new. Placed on station at Whitby the previous year she had already seen service in a number of rescues. Successfully tried and tested she was a worthy boat to bear the name of *Robert Whitworth.*

Henry Freeman's first opportunity to take out this lifeboat as Whitby coxswain was lost, however. Henry was out fishing. On the 23rd February 1877, three fishing cobles were observed at noon making for the harbour under sail. A fresh breeze blew from the NNE and though the sea was calm, the River Esk was swollen creating a lot of rough water at the bar. Amongst those watching on the pier were Richard Smith and George Smales. Both were concerned about the cobles entering the harbour. A member of the coastguard, George Wilson, took the rocket apparatus, line and lifebuoy out to the West Pier, where he stood ready. The first coble got in safely but the second, the *Ann and Elizabeth,* manned by David and Thomas Dobson and Edward Musgrave, was caught in the rough water and upset. The Dobson brothers were both unable to swim and to save themselves clung to mast and oars in the water. Edward Musgrave was carried to the East Pier and was saved by a line thrown to him. The third coble tried to pick the others up but was carrying too much sail and ran past them. Lowering the sail the coble rowed to where the men were and got them into the boat. Thomas Dobson was saved but David had already drowned.

Thomas Langlands took out the *Robert Whitworth* to the third coble and brought the four men and the Dobson body back on shore. Thereafter the lifeboat was kept afloat to help other cobles should it be needed. At 5 o'clock Henry Freeman and the crew of his coble were assisted into harbour by the *Whitworth*. It seems to have been an occupational hazard with Whitby Coxswains, but Pickering, Lacy and now Freeman had been rescued by their own lifeboat! In the official report to the RNLI Smales praised Langlands for "acting with great promptitude".

A few days later Freeman had the chance to take out the *Whitworth* himself. On Sunday 28th February the Norwegian brig *Christopher Hansteen* loaded with a cargo of pit props was off Whitby signalling for a pilot and a steam tug. The vessel had sprung a leak and her crew were exhausted from the pumping. Unfortunately her signals were not seen and it was decided to abandon the ship. The crew of eight along with the ship's dog got into the small boat and headed for the shore. Their plight was not noticed until the next morning. A group of quarry workers on the East Cliff saw the small boat in danger of running onto the rocks. Fortunately, the workmen were able to warn the mariners in time and they pulled away. One of the workers was sent to inform the Coastguard of what had happened. The alarm gun was fired. The Coastguard officer quickly assembled the lifeboat crew and within an hour Henry Freeman had the *Robert Whitworth* manned and ready to put to sea. In a short time the *Whitworth* had been rowed out to the small boat, rescued all the crew and landed them safely. Afterwards George Smales and several fishermen went out with the steam tug *Emu* in order to beach the brig on the sands.

At the start of May 1877 Captain James, a National Lifeboat Inspector arrived at Whitby to examine the boats and equipment. In the aftermath of the recent lifeboat tragedy this was not a surprising event. He found everything in order and returned to London.

The first Monday morning in September found Henry out with the *Garland* after a night netting herring in appalling weather. For the herring season Henry used the *Garland* which he had bought together with John Mitchell in 1876, but had taken sole ownership of her from the 7th June 1877. She was a Keel Boat and certainly the largest vessel Freeman ever mastered. Her weight was fourteen tons, her length was thirty-seven feet, there was a lug sail aboard her and she normally carried a complement of five men.

On returning to Whitby he found himself in a dangerous situation. Several vessels were making for the port after a hard night out on the fishing grounds. The rain had been continuous. There was a strong breeze from the North East and a heavy sea while the River Esk was swollen. Crossing the bar suddenly became a precarious business. The first coble to come to grief was the *Thomas and James* which struck the East Pier and began to sink. Her crew of four leapt to catch hold of ropes thrown from the East Pier and were saved. Shortly afterwards Freeman was coming into the harbour with the *Garland* when the Hartlepool coble, the *Water Lily* was driven into her by the force of the sea. The *Garland* was badly damaged, but the *Water Lily* sank and her crew had to transfer smartly to the *Garland* which then limped home to a

Damaged Brig being assisted into harbour by steam tug.
(Courtesy of National Maritime Museum)

safe berth. Thomas Langlands took out the *Robert Whitworth* and patrolled the harbour ready to give assistance to any other vessels which might get into trouble, though fortunately all other boats entered the harbour safely.

Henry Freeman's second call to duty as coxswain came on the 5th January 1878. On this occasion his lifeboat saved no less than twenty-two lives. The steam ship *Oscar* of Leith had stranded on the rocks at Whitby. The *Robert Whitworth* was launched at 10.40pm with Henry Freeman in command, and Thomas Gains as second coxswain. The *Oscar* was reached in twenty minutes and the crew were taken off. In the morning the lifeboat went back with the captain to inspect the waterlogged ship and to retrieve some of his clothes.

George Smales relinquished his post as secretary to the local committee in 1878. The post then passed to Robert Gibson, the Harbour Master. He proved to be an invaluable choice and his enthusiasm was soon to manifest itself.

Robert Gibson's first duty came on Monday 8th May 1878. Two Scarborough fishing boats were attempting to enter the harbour, but heavy seas were making the task virtually impossible. It was a risky situation for the four fishermen on the *Eliza* and the *James and Sarah*. Robert Gibson ordered the *Robert Whitworth* to be launched. Amongst Henry Freeman's crew were John Storr and Thomas Langlands. The lifeboat proceeded to take the men off the boats and landed them on the beach. One of the fishing boats, the *Eliza,* sank shortly afterwards near Upgang.

During the next couple of years there were a number of fishing boat rescues. Sometimes Langlands went out, sometimes it was Freeman and both RNLI lifeboats saw action. On one occasion, 15th April 1880, Henry took out the *Harriott Forteath (II)* to assist two of his regular lifeboat crew, John Storr, master of the *Star of Peace,* and John Hodgson on the *Lady Morris*. There was a danger that their boats might be swamped when they crossed the bar.

That winter the fishermen of Whitby had a hard time. Bad weather kept them off the fishing grounds. There was destitution in the Port. During January Sir George Elliot MP distributed coals to the poor. Twenty tons of coal were given to the fishermen.

Shipping also suffered. There were several reports of ships stranding and getting free again. On Wednesday 12th March 1879 there was what the papers described as a "violent equinoctal gale" which had swept across the Atlantic to Britain causing a great deal of damage. Two vessels had difficulty in entering Whitby harbour. The brig *Otterburn* ran aground at Colliers Hope while the steamship *J.H.Lorentzen* struck the rocks near the harbour entrance as it tried to come into the port. In ballast from Rochester to Sunderland, the steamship had run short of coal at sea and had made for Whitby. Its plight was soon seen. The lifeboat *Robert Whitworth* was launched within 15 minutes. Henry Freeman with his by now regular combination of men which included John Dryden, Thomas Langlands, James Pounder and John

Rescues were often conducted in perilous conditions.   *(Courtesy Mrs. Pat Pickles)*

Storr manoevred the lifeboat towards the wreck. With great difficulty and at considerable risk to themselves, they took all seventeen men off that ship and had them back on shore within an hour. It was quite a feat of seamanship. The *J.H.Lorentzen* became a total wreck and a few days later was cut up and disposed of as scrap.

Each year since 1870 the autumn and winter gales had become progressively worse causing havoc amongst the shipping on the Yorkshire coast. The steep forbidding cliffs between Hull and Hartlepool left few safe havens where ships could take shelter when in trouble. Whitby with its long stretch of beach to Sandsend was one of the few places where ships' masters believed they had a chance of survival. So in severe storms the lifeboat services at Whitby frequently came under pressure.

Henry Freeman and his lifeboat crew were to face their gravest task in the winter of 1880/1881 when the gales and storms were to reach a crescendo. In what was a replay of the severe weather conditions of 1861, a hurricane swept across Britain. The gale was blowing ENE and many vessels were soon in danger keeping the rescue services busy along the whole coast.

Shortly before noon on the 28th October 1880, a vessel was in trouble near Whitby Rocks. She proved to be the schooner *Reaper,* in ballast from Ostend to Sunderland. Robert Gibson ordered the *Robert Whitworth* out of its house in readiness. Henry Freeman assembled his crew about him all wearing their cork lifejackets. There were James Pounder, William Winspear, John Waters, Edward Gash, Henry Hodgson, John Clarkson, F.Foster, John Davidson, Walter Curry, R.Pounder, William Richardson and John Batchelor.

The *Reaper's* master, Thomas Shimings, skilfully avoided the rocks, but was unable to prevent the vessel from being driven past the harbour to run aground on the sands. The lifeboat was immediately launched. Sixty men were on the carriage to drag her to the sea. The lifeboat surged ahead and within fifteen minutes was beside the besieged schooner. Four of her crew were safely taken off and landed, but unfortunately her master Thomas Shimings was drowned.

The *Whitworth* was brought ashore at 12.05, replaced on her carriage, and dragged back to her station by a team of horses. The lifeboat was not there for long, however. At 1.30pm a large fishing yawl was running towards Whitby sands. She was obviously in distress. Gibson had the *Whitworth* launched again. This time Henry had a different crew: John Storr, John Hodgson, John Dryden, Thomas Langlands, Matthew Gales, William Brown and G. Hodgson were in the boat. Only James Pounder, Walter Curry, John Waters, H.Hodgson and John Clarkson remained of the first crew. As before sixty eager helpers launched the boat without delay. The yawl was the *Good Intent* of Staithes and she had barely run aground before the lifeboat was beside her. For the lifeboatmen it had been a gruelling pull through the mountainous seas, but they were spurred on by the thought that the men on the deck of the yawl would have little protection from the sea once she hit the sands. It took twenty minutes hard rowing but the lifeboat reached her goal and the crew of eight were taken off. Within ten minutes the *Whitworth* had pulled to the beach and landed the exhausted men.

Little more than an hour later, at 3.15pm, another schooner was observed making for Whitby. She was the *Elizabeth Austen* of Rye, in ballast from Rye to Sunderland. The *Robert Whitworth* having beached some distance from the port, Mr Gibson decided that it would be more expedient to launch the *Harriott Forteath,* instead of waiting for the *Whitworth* to get back to her station.

Henry Freeman took out the *Harriott Forteath* with a smaller crew. John Dryden, John Clarkson and John Waters stayed out of the boat while a newcomer,

William Cummings, took their place. Again the whole crew of the vessel were saved and safely landed. Henry Freeman and his men were not happy with the performance of the *Harriott Forteath*. Gibson wrote in his RNLI report: " The Harriot Forteith is not approved of by her coxswain and crew she is too deep and narrow to me she seems to pull very heavy I must admit I do not like her preformance."(sic)

At 4.15pm yet another schooner was making for the beach. She was the *John Snell* bound for Newcastle with wheat from Great Yarmouth. Many people had gathered on the pier to watch the ship struggling through the sea. Mountainous waves continually swept over the vessel and there were times when she was completely lost from sight. It was feared that she might sink, yet she managed to stay afloat and finally struck the beach.

By now the *Robert Whitworth* had been dragged back to her station by the team of horses. She was launched at 4.30pm, again with a slightly altered crew, for the rough seas were taking their toll amongst the rowers. Only Freeman, Curry and James Pounder remained from the original team. New members were Thomas Gains and William Waters, while back in the boat were John Dryden, John Clarkson and William Winspear. Henry Hodgson was absent on this occasion. After rowing hard for forty minutes through the waves the lifeboat finally reached the *John Snell*. Fortunately the return to shore was easier and her crew of five were landed after twenty minutes.

The speed at which the rescues had been carried out was a credit to the organisation of the lifeboat services at Whitby. Only after regular practices could they have honed their response down to such a fine margin. But speed was not the only factor. The grit and determination of the lifeboatmen had triumphed over the extraordinary weather conditions against considerable odds. The rescues had been a total success apart from a single fatality.

Henry Freeman's own personal contribution was outstanding. His was the driving force behind the men and the stamina which kept them going. In gratitude for his services that day the RNLI presented Henry Freeman with his second silver medal. It was an honour which he justly deserved.

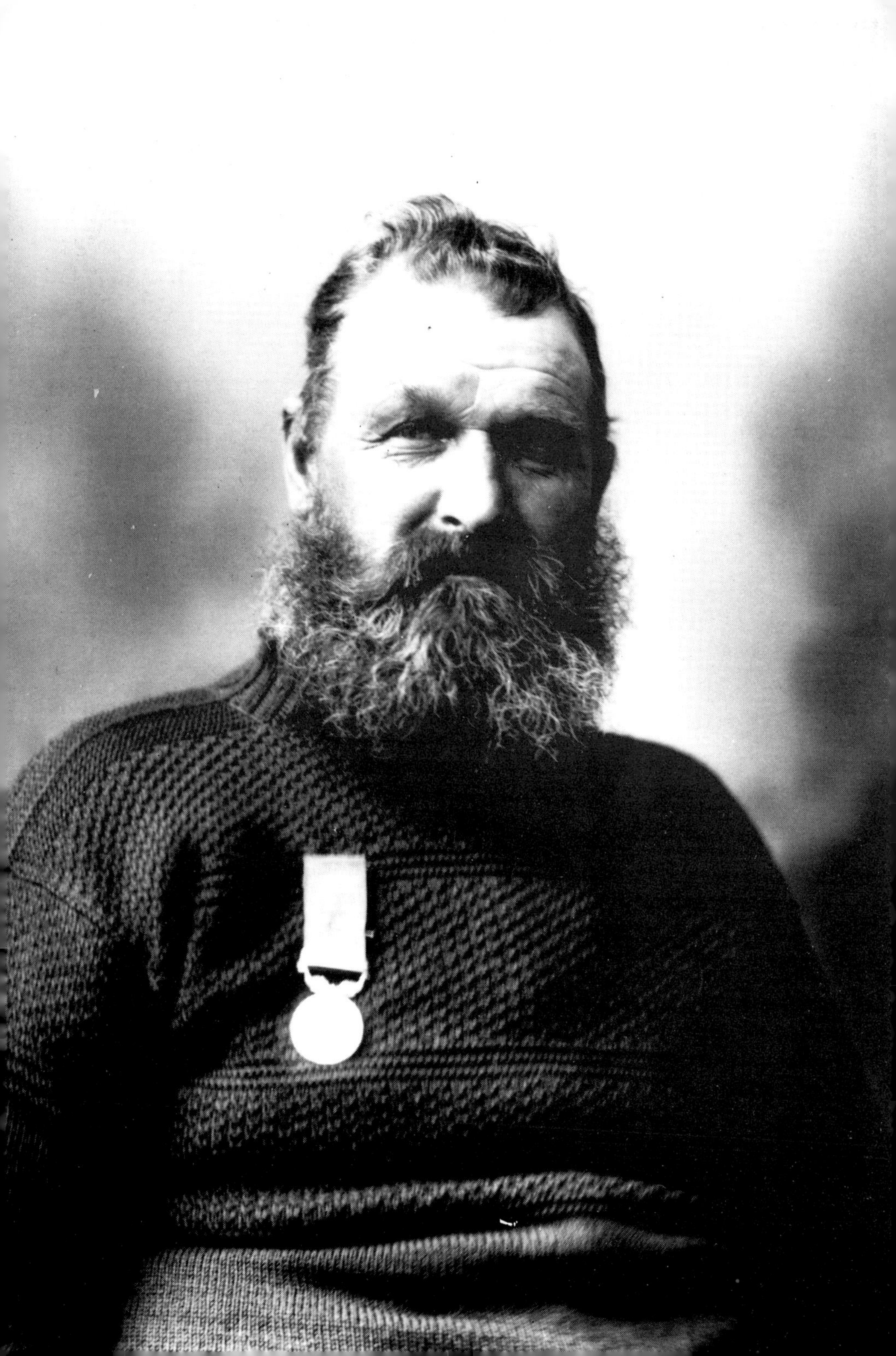

The RNLI Silver Medal as presented to Freeman in 1861. It bears Freeman's name on the rim: Henry Freeman dated 4 April 1861. His second medal took the form of the silver clasp with the words Second Service inscribed across it.

Henry Freeman seen here wearing the RNLI's silver medal for his services during the rescues of February 1861 and the silver clasp for the 1880 award.

(Photograph Frank Meadow Sutcliffe)

CHAPTER 7

THE WRECK OF THE VISITER 1881

It was a hard winter. The October gales of 1880 were a prelude to some of the harshest weather that century. For Henry and his fellow fishermen it was to be a portent of lean times to come.

One cold January morning in 1881 found many men working around Northumberland Dock in Newcastle. The date was Saturday the 15th. The frost lay thick on the ground colouring the wood of the railway sleepers a snowy white. An old North Eastern Railway locomotive was pushing some coal wagons onto a staithe. The sound of metal on metal carried across the dock. Wagon couplings clanked, wheels spun round as they slipped on the icy rails and dark clouds of smoke flecked with steam belched into the January sky.

The name Cowpen and North Seaton Coal Company was written in large letters on the side of all the wagons being propelled along the wooden staithe. As each reached the end, their contents were disgorged into the hold of the sailing vessel below. Only a few hours before, the coal had been hacked out of the ground far below the Northumberland countryside. Now it was lying in the sailing vessel *Lumley* destined for Carthagena in Spain.

The *Lumley* was a Snow, and was large by the standards of the ships which were usually employed in the coal trade at that time. Built at Seaham in 1856, her length was 101 feet. She was registered in South Shields and her master was John Woodhouse, a South Shields man.

With her crew aboard, preparations were made to set sail. At three in the afternoon, the *Lumley* slipped her moorings and made for the centre of the River Tyne. Here she was taken in tow by a steam tug. On board the tug was James Woodhouse son of the *Lumley's* master.

Half an hour later the Snow was safely over the bar and the tow rope was let go. John Woodhouse exchanged farewells with his son, then set his course for the Mediterranean.

By 9.30 pm the *Lumley* was sailing close to the North Yorkshire coast and was a mile or so from Whitby. It was pitch black owing to the dense cloud overhead and intermittent snow showers lashed the faces of the captain and his crew on deck. Waves rose high around the ship pounding her sides with increased ferocity.

These were dangerous waters for John Woodhouse to be in, for he was sailing virtually blind in an area of the coast where submerged rocks abounded. Had the tide been full the experienced sea captain might have weathered the storm, but it was low water and it was the *Lumley's* misfortune to strike Upgang Rock, a mile off-shore.

When he realised that his ship had been holed, Captain Woodhouse had a signal flashed in the direction of the Coastguard station on Whitby Pier.

At first the Coastguard lookout could not believe his eyes, for the weather was not particularly bad and he could not see why a vessel should be in trouble. However, when the signals were repeated the reality of the situation became clear. Signals were exchanged and the mortar was fired to alert the rescue services.

The Royal Naval Life Saving Brigade proceeded to the shore with the lifeboat apparatus. At the same time both the Upgang and the Whitby No.1 lifeboats were brought out of their boathouses.

Robert Gibson went to Upgang to organise the operations from there. He had Thomas Langlands take the *Joseph Sykes* out to be launched. Thomas Hartley went out in the boat as his second coxswain. The launch from Upgang was a difficult one. A gigantic wave fell on the lifeboat and it looked as though the crew would be overwhelmed, but Thomas Langlands remained calm and rallied his men. With renewed vigour they set off into the raging sea.

Once the men were on their way they found the sea extremely rough. For Langlands and his men it was a battle to make the slightest headway. Huge waves descended on them from the total blackness, and snow whipped them remorselessly as they struggled on. Ahead of them they could just see the *Lumley,* partly illuminated by a burning tar barrel on her deck. It was this burning barrel which became a beacon for Langlands to aim for. From time to time wraith-like figures could be seen moving in front of the smoky flames, proving the crew were still alive and spurring the lifeboatmen on to greater effort.

The *Joseph Sykes* was buffeted, tossed and turned by the sea. Waves washed over the lifeboat, sometimes with such force that some of the oarsmen were stunned by their strength. After almost two hours of sustained physical effort the lifeboat crew was exhausted. Thomas Langlands realised the cause was hopeless and returned to the beach. His crew was drained of all their strength. Two were almost insensible and had to be taken off the boat. The *Joseph Sykes* was in no better condition. Her bottom had been stove in and three of the oars had been broken.

Richard Smith and his brigade of volunteers tried to fire rockets towards the ship but all fell short. Realising that this was a wasted effort, Smith, the Chief of the Coastguard, deployed his men along the beach at intervals so that they could give aid to any of the mariners who might swim successfully ashore. Each man held a white light in his hand to act as a guide.

Meanwhile the *Robert Whitworth* was launched down the slipway beside the coastguard station. Henry Freeman was at the tiller and James Pounder stood beside him as second coxswain. Ahead of them was their quarry, the Snow *Lumley*, indicated by the burning tar barrel. The decision to launch had been taken by Freeman, but was later approved by Robert Gibson.

Henry Freeman and his crew beat their way through the heavy seas and came close to reaching the vessel. But the lights onshore misled him. He took the white lights to be blue or green which signified that the crew of the *Lumley* had been rescued. Henry turned for home. The row back was just as difficult as the outward journey. A violent snow storm overtook the *Robert Whitworth* and came close to wrecking her. Finally the lifeboat reached the shore and was beached near the base of the West Cliff Saloon.

Her weary crew then dispersed. Many made for their homes, but others walked back along the beach towards Upgang. Henry was left with some of the launchers to put the lifeboat back into her house.

Robert Gibson was unaware of these events. He sent Thomas Cass back to Whitby with a message to have the *Whitworth* held in readiness as the *Joseph Sykes* had failed. After seeing to the needs of the Upgang men, Robert Gibson went back to Whitby with one of the coastguardmen. Henry Freeman was found beside the lifeboat and the great mistake was soon apparent.

It took time to assemble a second crew to man the *Robert Whitworth* for a further rescue attempt. In the meantime the tide had turned, making it impossible to relaunch the *Whitworth* from where it was. Instead it was decided to take the lifeboat by road to Upgang. The *Robert Whitworth* was placed on her carriage and taken by a team of horses up the Khyber Pass, along Skinner Street, St Hilda's Terrace and then Upgang Lane. Ultimately the lifeboat reached Upgang.

At the scene of the wreck, all had gone quiet. The burning tar barrel on the deck of the *Lumley* had gone out plunging the ship once more into darkness. As the *Whitworth* arrived, the moon started to show herself and the ship became visible again, for one brief, awful moment. As all those on the beach watched in horror, the *Lumley* slowly sank beneath the waves. The time was five minutes past two in the morning. The combined efforts of Whitby's life saving organisation had been to no avail. Nine mariners had lost their lives.

The next morning the bodies of the *Lumley's* Captain and a Swedish sailor, A. Jansen, were washed ashore. The rest of the crew were never found, nor were the circumstances surrounding the vessel's sinking ever fully determined.

An inquiry was held by the RNLI at the Seamans Hospital, Church Street. Captain Gibson pressed for the fullest investigation as grave reflections had been cast upon him. The proceedings were dominated by the issue of the lights allegedly misinterpreted by Henry Freeman. The reputations of both Robert Gibson and Freeman were at stake. Gibson was vindicated when it was proved that no green light had been shown. Freeman was then called to defend his decision to turn back when he had almost reached the wreck. Commander Napean for the RNLI argued that when a man was nearly blinded with snow and salt water he might easily be mistaken about the colour of a light. It was not a green light that Freeman had seen, but he was not to be blamed for putting back to the shore. At the close of the inquiry the committee passed a vote of confidence in both Captain Gibson and Henry Freeman and expressed the opinion that everything possible had been done to save life.

THE CREW OF THE LUMLEY

Name		Age	Abode
John Woodhouse	Master	61	South Shields
William Martin	Mate	50	South Shields
William Temple	Boatswain	45	South Shields
James Hunter	Cook/Steward	35	South Shields
Richard Bellman	Able Seaman	20	South Shields
A. Jansen	Seaman	21	Stockholm
Johnson Taylor	Ord. Seaman	18	Percy Main
George Yeog	Ord. Seaman	19	Dundee
William Hogan	Apprentice	15	Willington Quay

Two days prior to the inquiry a letter had appeared in the *Northern Echo* from a correspondent at Sandsend who called himself "an eyewitness". The letter contradicted a number of major points contained in the official reports. The writer criticised the delay in launching the Upgang lifeboat and the subsequent failure to reach the wreck. He placed the time of the launch of the *Joseph Sykes* at 11.30 pm, while Gibson recorded 10.30pm. He described the sea as calm while Gibson wrote in his report "seas mountainous". Furthermore, according to him the wind was not as strong as believed. His attack was clearly directed at Langlands and his men, but careful examination of Langlands during the inquiry revealed no evidence to support this "eyewitness's" claims.

Freeman was fortunate, for had the inquiry found blame in his actions, then he would have lost his job at Whitby. However, other events may well have influenced Commander Napean's decision. Between the fateful day of the *Lumley* sinking and the holding of the inquiry Henry Freeman was to be involved in a highly successful and most memorable rescue.

CORRESPONDENCE.

LIFEBOAT SERVICES AT WHITBY.

TO THE EDITORS OF THE "NORTHERN ECHO."

GENTLEMEN,—I venture to invite the attention of your readers to some facts in connection with the wreck of the brig *Lumley* at Whitby, reported in the *Northern Echo* of the 17th inst. Shortly before ten o'clock on the evening of Saturday, the 15th inst., signals of distress were observed at Sandsend from a vessel in the direction of Upgang. The readiness with which the Coastguard at Sandsend, with the volunteers of the rocket apparatus, proceeded to the scene of the wreck is most commendable. The impossibility of reaching with the rocket a vessel nearly 700 yards beyond low-water mark soon became evident, and so the Upgang lifeboat, close at hand, was launched after a considerable delay. Subsequent events, however, have shown that it would have been well for the crew of the ill-fated vessel if this delay had been indefinitely protracted. It was half-past eleven o'clock before the lifeboat, manned with what has been described by one paper as rather a mixed crew, put out into what has been caused to appear as a terrific sea. The night, however, as the hundreds assembled on shore can testify, was bright and calm from ten o'clock to nearly an hour past midnight. There was, as usual, a little broken water along the shore, but as the lifeboat is said to have approached within 150 yards of the vessel, this, the faintest approach to "seething waves," must have been passed over in safety. If the observation of old and experienced mariners is of no account, the fact that a tar barrel, around which some of the crew were seen moving, was blazing for two and a half hours does not reconcile itself with what has been dramatically described as a merciless surging sea. If, as was the fact, there was no wind, how is it that a strong wind is said to have detained the Whitby lifeboat for two hours in a space of little more than a mile? About half-past twelve o'clock a green light, signifying a successful rescue, was shown by one or other of the two lifeboats, and the public, for whose dispersion homewards it was also a signal, did not receive—and then with sorrow not unmingled with indignation—the almost incredible news of the loss of the *Lumley's* crew until the morning was far advanced. Messengers were despatched again for the Whitby lifeboat—a fact which is suggestive of the opinion of the public concerning the gallantry of a portion at least of the Upgang crew; but the vessel had broken up by three o'clock on Sunday morning, and not one of her men has been left to tell the tale of the skilful and fearless efforts made to rescue them.—Yours sincerely,

AN EYE-WITNESS.

Sandsend, January 20th, 1881.

Extract from the Northern Echo

Some particularly dramatic rescues have been made along the North East coast by lifeboats. One particularly outstanding rescue, which was launched off the coast of Robin Hood's Bay in January 1881 has been recounted by several authors. Nor has it ever been forgotten by the local inhabitants. This was the rescue of the crew of the brig *Visiter,* on Wednesday 19th January 1881.

It was a rare operation where many worked together as a team to bring an imperilled crew of six men to safety, regardless of the appalling weather conditions.

Yet without the combined efforts of two quite separate communities and the outstanding bravery of the lifeboatmen, all hands on board the brig would have lost their lives on that bitterly cold January day.

Visiter was an old vessel, built in Sunderland in 1823 for the coal trade. She had had several owners and masters during her long life plying the waters of Eastern Britain. A group of Whitby businessmen had bought her in 1840 and from then on she had remained a Whitby registered vessel. The *Visiter* usually sailed laden with coal from the ports of Hartlepool and Middlesbrough to London, Chatham and Rochester. Her master for many years was Robert Simpson Adamson, but when he acquired a share in the brig *Medora* he gave up his mastership to Trueman Robinson, who took a quarter share in the *Visiter* at the same time.

For nearly a quarter of a century Trueman Robinson, a Robin Hood's Bay man, was her managing owner. He took her regularly on voyages to London and his son George was apprenticed on the brig. George sailed with his father many times thereafter as seaman and mate. In time Trueman Robinson took a less active role, leaving the command of the ship to other men.

On the fateful last voyage William Todd Anderson, another Bay man, was on his second trip as master of the *Visiter*. On the fifteenth of January 1881 the ship was moored at Tyne Dock, Newcastle, when his crew came aboard. After filling with coal from the staithes during the next day the *Visiter* was towed across Tyne bar and set her sails for London.

By 4 o'clock on the afternoon of Tuesday 18th January, the brig had reached Flamborough when the wind changed and rose to gale force. Driving snow began to lash the faces of her crew as the heavy seas increased in violence.

THE CREW OF THE VISITER

Name		Age	Abode
William Todd Anderson	Master	48	Robin Hood's Bay
William Bell	Mate	47	Robin Hood's Bay
James Sherry Storm	Able Seaman	20	Robin Hood's Bay
Edward Hughes	Ord. Seaman	19	London
Algernon C. Dodd	Apprentice	19	London
Charles Burrell	Apprentice	18	London

All with the exception of Edward Hughes had been aboard the *Visiter* on her last voyage. Seaman Hughes joined the ship at Shields, his last ship was the *Violet*.

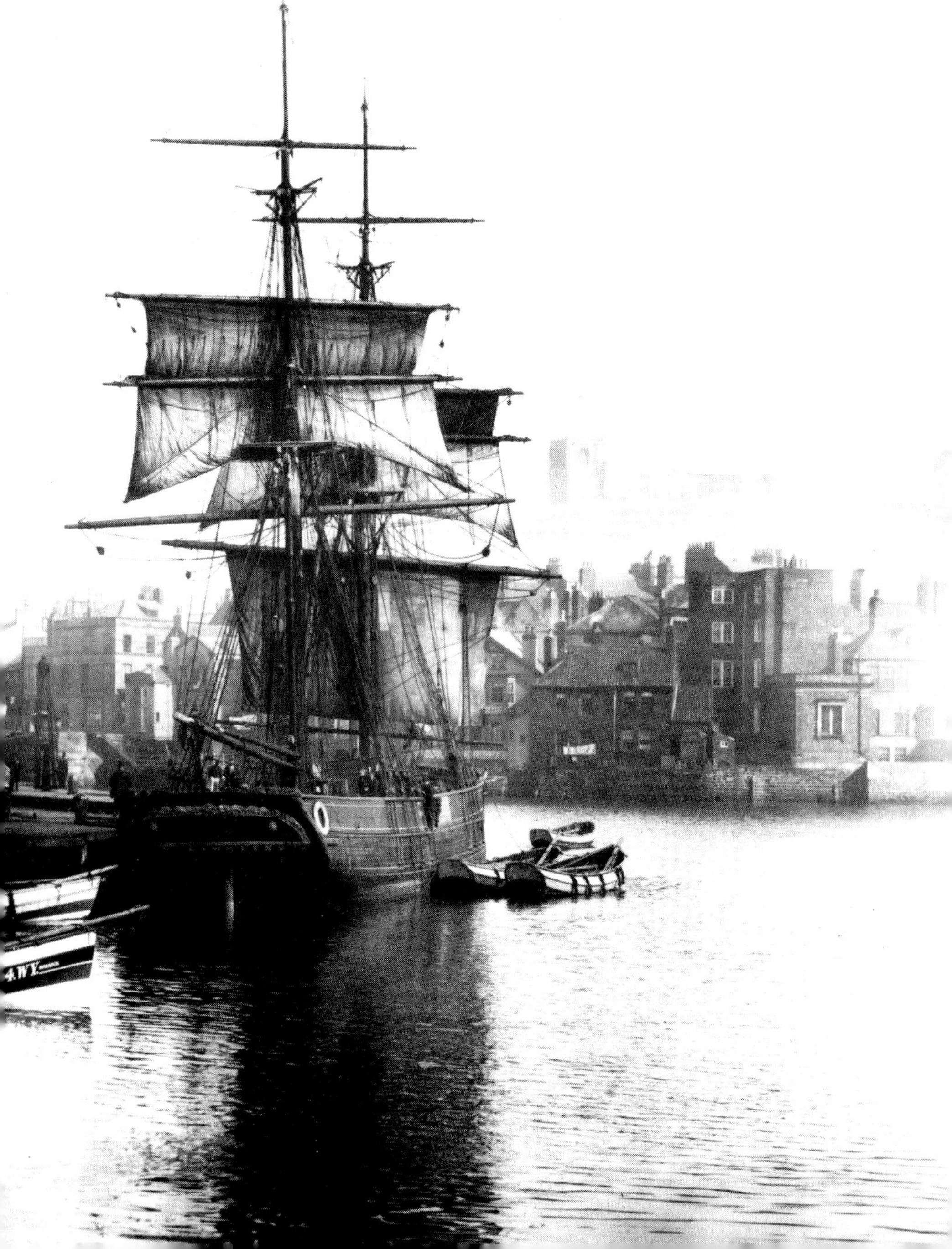

Inland, the whole of the country was in the grip of a raging blizzard which had caused widespread havoc. Trains were left stranded, roads were blocked, buildings were blown down and whole towns and villages were suddenly cut off, in what proved to be the worst storm for many years. What chance did the fragile brig *Visiter* stand now that this fury was unleashed off shore?

The brig was driven north by the storm with most of her sails blown away. By 2.00 a.m. on the 19th she was four miles off Robin Hood's Bay when Captain Anderson decided to drop anchor in order to save the vessel from being blown ashore. The wind was approaching hurricane strength and water was rising in the hold. The atmosphere amongst the crew was tense. The captain and the mate, Willie Bell, conferred closely together, at ever more frequent intervals, throughout the long night.

By 8.00 a.m. the water was five feet deep in the hold. There was now only one course of action left: the captain ordered the ship to be abandoned. The crew climbed into the longboat to ride out the storm in the lee of the stricken brig. Last to leave was one of the apprentices, Algernon Dodd, who swam to the longboat as the *Visiter* finally began to sink. Now all six men were together in an open boat, tossed and buffeted by the mountainous waves.

At first light, their plight was observed by the folk in Robin Hood's Bay. A hasty conference was called in Mr White's store near the Way Foot. It was soon decided that it would be pointless to call out the coastguard. Joseph Cooper's rocket brigade had saved many lives in the previous October when storms had driven four vessels into the Bay, but on this occasion the coastguard could do nothing. The *Visiter's* crew were too far out to sea for rockets to reach them.

The Bay had its own lifeboat, but it was old and considered unseaworthy. To have her launched in such a savage sea would have been suicide. Help, if it was to come, had to be called in from outside. Captain Richard Robinson suggested that they should send immediately for the Whitby Lifeboat. The Bay's resourceful and widely-respected vicar, Robert Jermyn Cooper, wasted no time taking up the suggestion, and telegraphed Robert Gibson requesting assistance. A similar message was also relayed to Scarborough.

Commander Grant received the message at Scarborough but was unable to offer immediate assistance because his tugs were aground in the harbour. In his reply he undertook to dispatch a tug with their lifeboat as soon as conditions improved. Everything now depended on what Gibson would say.

The *Opal* is a typical example of a brig, but when she was built in Scotland this vessel started service as a two-masted schooner. *(Photograph Frank Meadow Sutcliffe)*

The first page of the *Visiter's* Crew agreement as completed by William Anderson 6th January 1881 prior to sailing for London. The spelling of the ship's name *Visiter* is to be noted. It is often mis-spelled as *Visitor*.

(By courtesy of the Maritime History Archive, Memorial University of Newfoundland, Canada)

Name of Ship	Official Number	Port of Registry	Port No and Date of Register	Registered Tonnage	Managing Owner Name	Address
Visiter	671	Whitby	1823	18	Freeman Robinson	Robin Hood's Bay

Left Whitby 16 Jan 81. Vessel found...

		Names of the MASTER and the Crew	Age	Town and County where born	No. of Fund Ticket	No of Royal Naval Volunteer's Certificate	Ship in which he last served, and Port she belonged to, or place of Employment	Date and Place
		W. T. Anderson	40	R. H. Bay	—		Same, Whitby	24/12/80
		William Bell	47	R. H. Bay			do do	do
		James Perry Storm	21	R. H. Bay			do	do
		Edward Hughes	19	London			Violet	1/8
		Clamon C Dodds	19	London			Same	
		Charles Burrel	18	London			Same	

Articles lost with vessel

The crew members of the *Visiter* at the time of the last voyage.

105

The Reverend Robert Jermyn Cooper, Vicar of Fylingdales. He played a leading role in organising rescue efforts at Robin Hood's Bay.

(Photograph Fylingdales Local History Group)

The Post Office and General Store, Robin Hood's Bay. From here, the telegraph message was sent to Whitby to alert the Whitby rescue services of the *Visiter's* peril. The shop has changed little since Freeman's day. *(Courtesy of Daisy Hardy)* (old view)

(Photograph by Ray Shill) (Modern view)

Robert Gibson did not disappoint the Reverend Cooper. After consulting with his lifeboat crews, it was decided to take one of the Whitby lifeboats overland to Robin Hood's Bay, so that they might save the *Visiter's* men. He telegraphed back to Cooper that he was leaving at once and needed men and horses to be got ready to meet him on the way. Only a short time later, the lifeboat *Robert Whitworth* was on its carriage and being hauled through the streets of Whitby by the lifeboat crew and their helpers.

The lifeboat had to be taken by hand from the boat house, along Haggersgate and over the Bridge. At the top of Church Street horses were attached at Gibson's request. Fresh horses were provided as the need arose by local farmers whose lands lay along the route.

The *Robert Whitworth* was brought along St Ann's Staith and taken across the drawbridge. This view portrays the scene as it appeared in 1881.
(Collection: Mrs. Pat Pickles)

News of the emergency did not only bring help from the local farmers, however. Word soon spread among the ordinary people of Whitby and their response was instantaneous. As the dramatic lifeboat procession passed through the streets of the town, it drew with it a steadily growing number of people, all of them willing to help. Houses and shops were suddenly deserted as tenants and traders rushed to join the men who were clearing a way through the deep snowdrifts, or pulling the ropes attached to the carriage. At last some two hundred people were toiling in the snow with spades and axes. Men, women and children alike did their utmost to speed the carriage's slow progress.

When they had gone about a mile a couple of travellers met the party. They told the rescuers that the way ahead was impassable. The roads were one mass of ice and snow and they had been forced to abandon their horses and traps in the drifts. Undeterred by their warnings the men with the boat pressed on.

Meanwhile from Robin Hood's Bay, a team of men had also set out to clear the way, under the charge of Robert Cooper, son of the Vicar, who directed the work on horseback. It was at Stainsacre that this party made its rendezvous with the team from Whitby.

ON THE COAST — THE WHITBY LIFEBOAT ON ITS WAY TO ROBIN HOOD'S BAY

Outside Stainsacre Matthew Wellburn took charge. A farmer at Bay Ness, his skill with horses helped the progress of the lifeboat considerably. On his initiative, walls and gates were broken down and the boat was taken across the fields because the route was easier. In those days the road system had not been developed in the way that exists today and following the old road through Stainsacre village would have involved unnecessary delay. (The lifeboat's course followed closely the route of the present A171). After great efforts the procession emerged at Bay Bank Top where a large crowd was waiting.

Built in a fissure between two steep cliffs, Robin Hood's Bay was an old fishing village. One road wound through the centre of the village and then climbed steeply to Bay Bank Top. Even today, its gradient remains a test for the fittest amongst us, and this was the route by which the lifeboat would have to descend to the Bay!

Towering above the crowds who had come out to see the spectacle or lend a hand, the lifeboat carriage was unyolked from the horses and lowered down the last mile by ropes. Matthew Wellburn had ten men go in between the shafts of the carriage to ease its descent. The difficulties of this part of the operation were tremendous. What foothold could the men have found on a slope which was too icy even for horses to negotiate? Yet, somehow, by slithering and sliding through the snow, they started down the hill.

The greatest test was at the Laurel Inn. Here the road is not only steeply graded but turns a tight corner. Imagine the difficulty of getting a thirty-two foot long lifeboat and carriage past this obstacle. Yet, again, this was done though with barely an inch to spare.

Now the gradient levelled out as the road approached the narrow bridge over Kings Beck. The lifeboat was dragged across the bridge and down the Way Foot onto the shore. The six mile treck was over. It had taken just three and a half hours to reach the Bay from when Captain Gibson had received the telegram in Whitby.

Thereafter it was Henry Freeman who took charge. He took his place at the rudder and with a cry of "now pull away lads" the thirteen men set off on their mission. Though weary after their exertions on land, they rowed strongly to reach the men of the *Visiter*. They knew that the brig's crew must be in a bad way and would not survive for much longer.

For an hour the ten rowers pulled at full strength. Then suddenly a massive wave crashed down on the lifeboat, breaking six of the oars as if they were matchwood. With most of the oars useless, two of his crew semi-conscious and the rest exhausted, Henry Freeman decided to put back to the Bay. The lives of the *Visiter's* crew still hung in the balance.

John Storr, who was second coxswain on this rescue, suggested that the old Bay lifeboat's oars be used to replace the broken ones. While they were being fetched, fresh men replaced those who were injured after the first attempt. Once more the boat went out, this time with eighteen men, some double-manning the oars.

The new band of rescuers comprised men from different lifeboats. Members of the *Robert Whitworth* regular team sat shoulder to shoulder beside men from the Upgang Lifeboat. Leading the way was the only Bay man present in the crew, John Skelton. A mariner himself, who had at one time served on the *Visiter,* he was able to guide the lifeboat through the hazardous rocky scar to the wreck.

Roused by John Storr and Henry Freeman they rowed through the raging seas for three quarters of an hour, until at last they reached the longboat. The frozen crew had to be lifted into the lifeboat. After seven hours adrift, all were suffering from exposure, and two were delirious.

On their return to shore, a deafening cheer went up from the crowds which had gathered there. Warm clothing and medical attention were provided at once for the rescued men and the rescuers. Those who were half dead from exposure were quickly taken to the warmth of nearby houses to thaw out. Mrs Cooper, the Vicar's wife was amongst those lending assistance to the men.

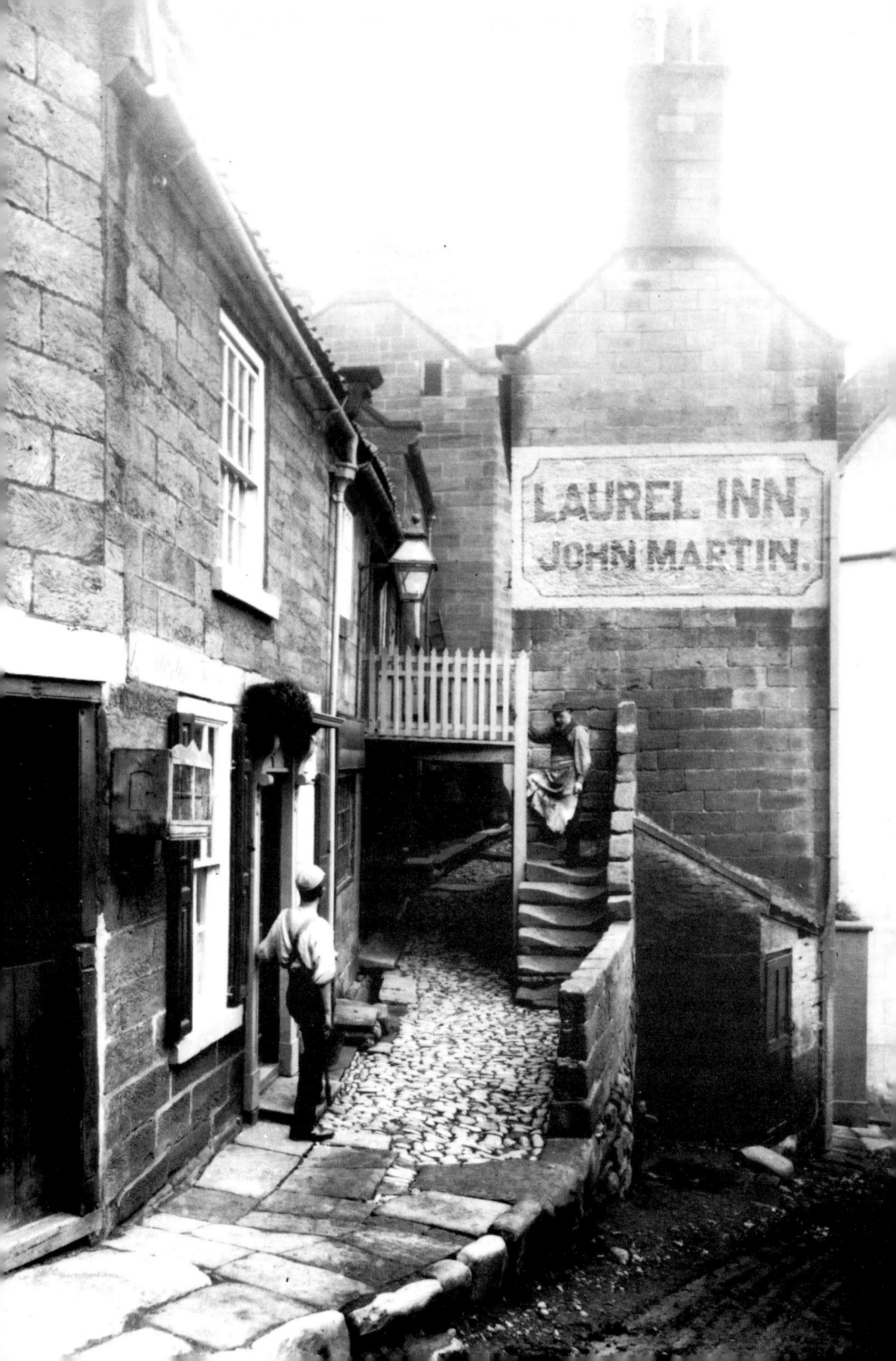
LAUREL INN,
JOHN MARTIN.

A local Robin Hood's Bay man, John Skelton, accompanied the crew of the *Whitworth* on their second attempt to reach the *Visiter,* guiding them through a safe channel between the hazardous rocks. *(Courtesy of Mr. R.P. Pennock)*

Rough sea at Robin Hood's Bay. *(Courtesy Fred Lane)*

The Laurel Inn, Robin Hood's Bay, provided a serious obstacle to the lifeboat's progress when it was let down Bay Bank to the Way Foot.
(Photograph Frank Meadow Sutcliffe)

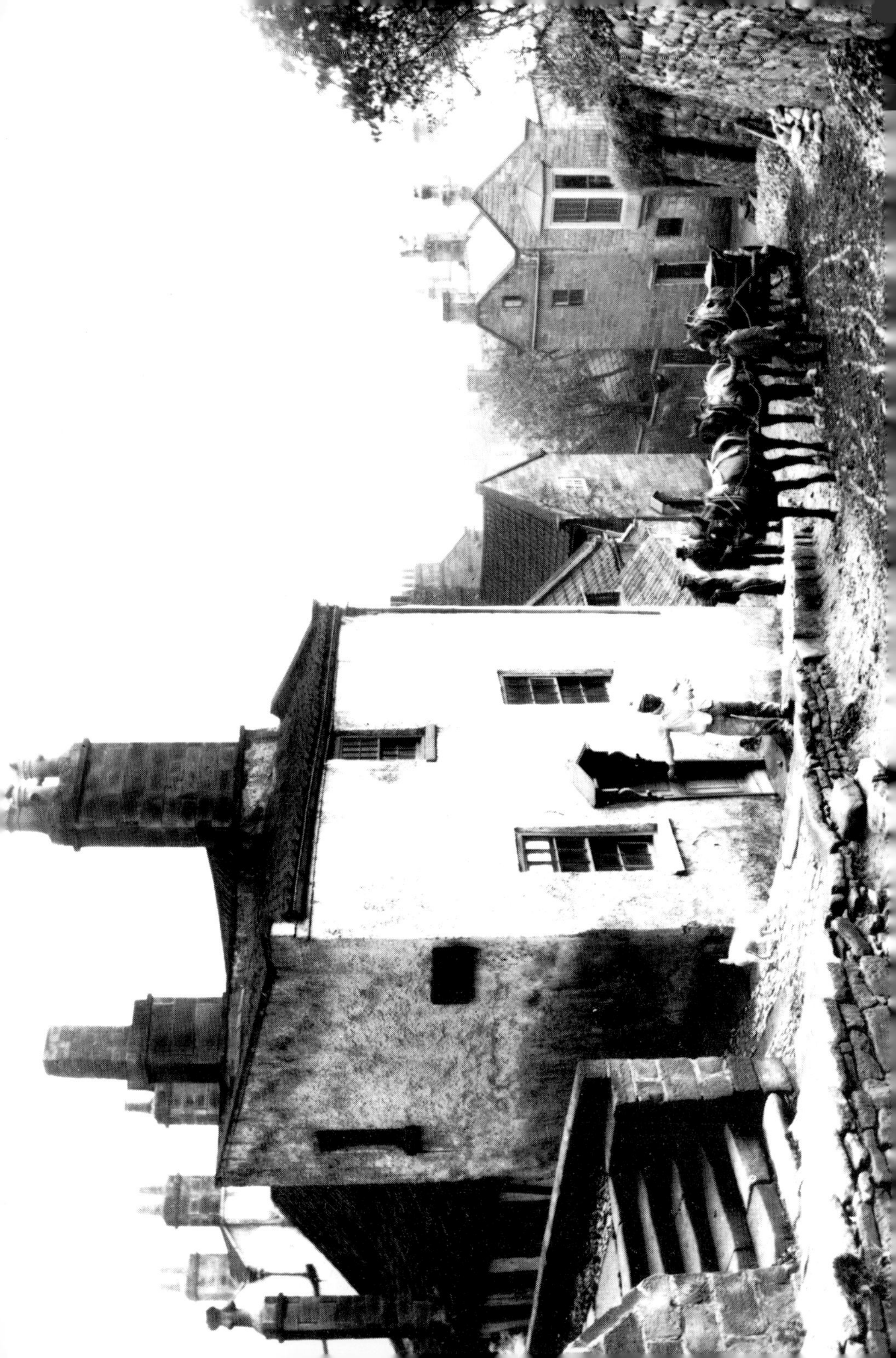

A personal recollection of these events has been supplied by Mrs Dorothy Burnett whose mother Isabella Harding in 1881 lived in her father John Newton's, house, above the butcher's shop in King Street. "The morning of the rescue, mother was washing up in the kitchen. She went out at the back to look across the Bay at the *Visiter* with the dish cloth in her hand. When she went back into the kitchen, it was frozen stiff. They had to warm it very slowly and carefully to get it off without taking the skin off her hand. Then she went across the road to help Mrs Anderson, wife of the *Visiter's* captain to get ready to receive the rescued men."

Captain Anderson and his crew had been lucky. Several ships foundered that night and many lives were lost. Some gallant lifeboatmen forfeited their lives too. But for Whitby and Robin Hood's Bay it was a day of celebration. John Barry, local landowner and gentleman was so moved by the rescue that he gave the lifeboat crews two gold sovereigns to share between themselves. Later a collection was raised in the Bay where a further £19 16s 6d was given in gratitude for the lifeboatmen. At their next London meeting the Royal National Lifeboat Institution allowed double the usual amount paid to the Whitby crews in recognition of their bravery.

This was a truly historic rescue. Literally hundreds of individuals had been involved: Captain Robinson, whose idea it was to summon the Whitby lifeboat; Reverend Cooper and Captain Gibson whose quick thinking had despatched the lifeboat so swiftly; the farmers who lent their horses; Matthew Wellburn whose skill with horses ensured the safe arrival of the lifeboat at the Bay; the townspeople of Robin Hood's Bay and Whitby who cut a path through the deep snow; the lifeboatmen from Upgang and Whitby who toiled together as one crew under the capable charge of Henry Freeman and John Storr; John Skelton who steered a safe course for the lifeboat; and finally the ordinary families of Robin Hood's Bay who had thrown open their homes to care for the wet and frozen men.

Bay Bank, Robin Hood's Bay. The muddy slope of Bay Bank provided a severe test for the transport of the period. The *Robert Whitworth* was lowered down the steep hill to the Bay in January 1881. *(Photograph Frank Meadow Sutcliffe)*

A modern view of Bay Bank shows that little has changed in the last century.
(Photograph Ray Shill)

Freeman and his crew photographed after the 1881 *Visiter* rescue.
(Courtesy of Whitby Literary & Philosophical Society)

Royal National Life Boat Institution

Return of Service on the 19th day of January 1881

DATES AND CIRCUMSTANCES OF THE CASE

(If this space is insufficient, please continue the account on the next page, the blank left for the Hon. Secretary's remarks.)

On the date at 10 a.m. I received telegram from the Rev. R.Cooper Vicar of Robin Hds Bay six miles south from Whitby stating vessel sunk Crew in open boat riding by wreck, send Whitby lifeboat if practicble, replied coming with lifeboat at once, send men and horses to meet us, I at once dispatched a group of men with shovels to cut the snow in front which was in some places seven or eight feet deep, with the assistance of some twelve or fourteen horses and some two hundred men we started from Whitby happy to say with the assistance of the men and horses from Robin Hds bay the boat was safeley gott to the scene of the disaster and about 1.30 p.m. were launched and proceeded on her errand of mercy after pulling in the terrific seas for about one hour a tremendous sea struck the boat breaking six oars steer oar included it was then quite patent to her coxswain and crew they must return for more oars and men, on a call made for volunteers eight responded which was deemed by her Coxswain Mr H.Freeman to be sufficient, the boat with her brave crew amidst the cheers of the hundred of spectators was again launched and right nobly pulled through the mass of broken and terrific seas to the frail craft containing the crew six in number of the ill fated vessel, Visitor, the whole of which had to be lifted out of their boat into the lifeboat, this accomplished the lifeboat was headed for the shore and about 4pm succeeded in landing the poor fellows nearly froze to death after being exposed in an open boat for nearly ten hours fortunately medical aid was at hand with the kindness and assistance of the Robin Hds Bay people they soon showed signs of recovery, I beg particularly to bring to your notice the great kindness and assistance rendered by the Revd R.Cooper, Mr Mathew Wellburn, Mr Ralph Smith and others.

1. Name of Vessel, and where belonging to?
2. Name of master, and of Owners?
3. Rig, Tonnage, Number of Crew and persons on board the vessel
4. Where from?, Where bound to?
5. What Cargo? or in Ballast?
6. Probable value of Ship and Cargo?
7. Wind, Weather and State of Sea
8. Time of day? State of Tide?
9. Exact spot where wrecked
10. Number of lives saved by lifeboat?
11. Number of lives lost
12. Supposed cause of wreck
13. Was it a total wreck, or stranded or sunk?
14. Time of launching lifeboat?
15. Time of reaching wreck?
16. Time of returning ashore

1. Visitor - Whitby
2. Willm Anderson.
3. Brig, six
4. Sheilds. London.
5. Coals
6. £800.
7. ESE Gale.Sea very mountainous
8. 1.30pm. Low Water
9. Robin Hds Bay
10. Six.
11. None.
12. State of weather
13. Sunk
14. 1.30 pm - 2nd time 2.45pm.
15. 3.30 pm.
16. 2.30 pm - 2nd time with crew 4.00pm.

17. How did boat behave? 17. Well
18. By whose authority was she ordered out? 18. Your Hon Sec.
19. Was any damage done to the boat? Extent of repairs required? 19. None

20. State names of the Crew of the lifeboat on this occasion and number of times these men have been off in the lifeboat to a wreck noting(in third column) any special case of individual exertion.

NAME OF CREW	Number of times afloat in the Lifeboat	NAME OF CREW	Number of Times afloat in the Lifeboat
H. Freeman Coxn	Twice	James Hodgson	Twice
Jno Storr 2nd Cox	Twice	Thos Palmer	Twice
H. Hodgson	Twice	Walter Curry	Twice
Willm Winspear	Twice	Walter Cummings	Twice
Jno Dryden	Twice	Shotten Gill	Once
Thos Walker	Once	James Thompson	Once
Willm Richardson	Once	G. Townsend	Once
Jno Richardson	Once	Jno Esdale	Once
Richard Wright	Once	William Dryden	Once
Jno Skelton	Once	William Moat	Once
One man unknown	Once	Jno Millburn	Once

In the third column R Gibson had written : number of times afloat this wreck.
Certified 22 January 1881, Robert Gibson (his signature)
                                                                Honorary Secretary

CASE OF THE WRECK OF THE Brig Visiter
A return of expenses incurred by the Robert Whitworth lifeboat on the 19th January 1881, in rendering assistance to the crew of the as per annexed Wreck return:

NATURE OF EXPENSES	£ s d
1. Lifeboats crew of 22 men for service 19th Jany by saving in ESE wind, the lives of six persons from the VISITOR wrecked at Robin Hds Bay at 10 shillings per man.	13 -0 -0
For crew afloat and bringing boat back to Whitby by sea Nine men afloat. (margin note)	4-10 -0
2. 60 persons for assisting to launch and haul up lifeboat at 5 shillings each person.	15 -0 -0
20 men employed in cutting snow at 4/- each. (margin note for both- These men went from Whitby to R.Hd's Bay and returned in wet frozen clothes distance 14 miles.)	4 -0 -0
3. The hire of 14 horses or other means for transport of lifeboat to site of wreck at distance of 7 miles at 15 shillings each horse.	10-10 -0
TOTAL	47 -0 -0

Total with extra awards to crew and helpers £70-10s
Margin notes: Several panniers and others brought their horses as we proceeded along and hooked on, no claim from them up to the present time been made.
Signed Robert Gibson, Richard Smith, and Henry Freeman(his mark) 22 January 1881.

CHAPTER 8

CALM BEFORE THE STORM

A week later on the following Wednesday, a special thanksgiving ceremony was held in St Michaels Church, Whitby. In the afternoon, at the invitation of the Reverend Cooper, a dinner was held at the Belle Hotel, to honour those men who helped in the rescue. Coxswain Freeman proposed a toast to Matthew Wellburn and paid tribute to the assistance which he had given. John Barry proposed the health of Henry Freeman and praised his skill and bravery. The rest of the evening was devoted to singing and recitation.

The RNLI recognized Captain Gibson's part in the rescue. At a meeting held at their offices in London on 3rd February 1881 the following minute was recorded in the books of the Society:

Resolved that the thanks of the Royal National Lifeboat Institution accompanied by a binocular glass be presented to Captain Robert Gibson in acknowledgement of his general, valuable and skilful services in the preservation of life from shipwreck and especially for his valuable co-operation the occasion of the rescue by the Whitby Lifeboat of the crew of the brig Visitor of Whitby at Robin Hood's Bay on 20 Jan 1881.

This minute formed part of the special thanks written on vellum which the RNLI presented to Gibson together with the binoculars.

Freeman was now, suddenly, a popular figure in the port. His standing was high and it was not uncommon at lifeboat functions for his health to be toasted. Yet this achievement was not his alone. Two men, in particular, had made significant contributions to his success. Fate now conspired to take both of them from him.

The *Visiter* rescue did a lot to enhance the reputation of John Storr. The country-wide publicity it attracted led to a new lifeboat, the *Ephraim and Hannah Fox* being placed at Robin Hood's Bay in September. John Storr was to become her first Coxswain.

Henry became angry at this decision fearing the loss of one of his most capable crew members. He even talked of resignation to Gibson, but did not carry out his threat. No doubt he realised that John Storr could still go out with him if the occasion arose, in the same way Langlands did. In fact John Storr did accompany Henry on other rescues and soon tired of being Coxswain at the Bay.

The sudden death of James Pounder, however, did rob Freeman of a key man. James had been a lifeboatman for many years and was a regular member of

Freeman's team. Apart from the ill-fated launch to the *Lumley*, he had been second coxswain on several successful rescues including all those which took place on the 28th October 1880.

James Pounder died during a lifeboat exercise aboard the *Harriott Forteath* on the 8th August 1881. The lifeboat had been launched just after two in the afternoon. Apart from the regular crew, Richard Lewis, secretary to the RNLI and Captain Napean, the Lifeboat Inspector, were aboard. The boat had only just cleared the harbour pier when James, who was standing beside the steer oar, collapsed and fell forward. Henry Freeman picked him up, his neck cloth was loosened and his face bathed with water. But nothing could be done. He was dead.

During the inquest, Henry Freeman stated that he had known James Pounder for eight years. His Second Coxswain had usually been in good health, but had fallen on the Scaur during the last winter injuring his shoulder. James was off work because of this accident for at least a month and afterwards complained that his shoulder still hurt.

James Pounder was 45 when he died leaving a widow and six children. A public appeal was lauched on their behalf and raised a reasonable sum of money. Richard Lewis contributed a guinea to the fund.

The exercise was probably organised to examine the *Harriott Forteath II* which had behaved poorly during the October rescues. Captain Napean and Richard Lewis no doubt decided the boat had to be replaced, for a new lifeboat was sanctioned for the Whitby station using funds provided by Mrs M.Ellis.

Mary Ellis, the widow of the Reverend Robert Ellis, a Yorkshire vicar, had decided to give £800 to the Institution. The money was to be used to place a lifeboat on the Whitby coast. A new boat was soon completed, but owing to the poor health of Mrs Ellis, the RNLI decided that it would be inappropriate to expect her to travel to Whitby for the naming ceremony. Instead they brought the new boat to York, where she lived, and performed the launch there.

The ceremony took place on Friday 2nd December. The lifeboat had been brought up by train to York railway station. It was carefully placed on its carriage then drawn through the streets of York by a team of six horses. Aboard her were members of the Whitby lifeboat crew. Upon reaching the River Ouse at a place near the Blue Bridge, the launch was prepared. Several speeches were made including one from Captain Napean who praised the Whitby station's past achievements. Mrs Ellis who had remained in a bath chair beside the lifeboat then christened her the *Robert and Mary Ellis*. In the time-honoured tradition, she broke a bottle of wine over the boat.

The Dean of York stepped into the boat which was then placed into the river. Freeman gave his usual command "Now pull away lads" and the lifeboat was rowed away. The Artillery Band played "God Save the Queen" as they were taken down the river by a strong current. The Whitby crew then brought the lifeboat back up stream again before turning into the River Foss where the Dean left the vessel. The York launching ceremony was quite a spectacle and proved good publicity for the lifeboat cause. In later years the RNLI were to make use of such events to raise money, but this time the demonstration was just to mark a new lifeboat on the Northern Coast.

The *Robert and Mary Ellis* arrived in Whitby the next night where she was installed as the new No.1 lifeboat. The *Robert Whitworth* remained in Whitby as the No.2 boat. The local committee had decided in October to retain her and send the existing *Harriott Forteath* away. Thus the *Robert Whitworth* became the third *Harriott Forteath*, while the *Harriott Forteath II* was sent back to London.

After the *Visiter* rescue until the autumn of 1882 there was a brief respite from bad weather. It was a welcome breathing space for sailors and fishermen. But for the lifeboatmen this led to a drop in earnings.

The *Robert and Mary Ellis* first saw action on Wednesday 20th September 1882. That day there was a heavy sea and a strong ENE breeze. A Danish schooner, the *William* was approaching Whitby with a cargo of deals for Charles Smales (a Whitby timber merchant, and brother to George Wakefield Smales, the former Lifeboat Secretary). Her master, Neilson, brought the ship in at the wrong angle and missed the harbour entrance. The vessel was obliged to come to anchor just outside the harbour mouth. Here the schooner rolled about and appeared to be in some danger.

At about 11.00 a.m she showed a signal of distress by raising her ensign. Gibson responded by having the No.1 Lifeboat launched. Henry Freeman and his crew were down the slipway to the schooner's aid in fifteen minutes. Thomas Cass, branch pilot, and two extra men were on board in case their services were required.

When the lifeboat reached the water the *William* lowered her ensign, but the *Robert and Mary Ellis* continued on to the schooner and came alongside her. Despite requests from the lifeboatmen the crew of *William* insisted on remaining aboard. After two hours Henry Freeman came away with a message to get a tugboat. Only the steam tug *Emu* was in harbour at that time and she was undergoing repairs. Eventually the tugboat *Admiral* was summoned to the *William* and succeeded in towing the vessel away to sea.

Two lifeboats were in action that day. Thomas Langlands launched the *Joseph Sykes* from Upgang and reached the *William* only five minutes after Freeman. On seeing that his services were not required, Langlands returned to Upgang.

Both Freeman and Gibson were impressed with the behaviour of the *Robert and Mary Ellis*. Gibson wrote in his return to the RNLI "her coxswain and her crew speak very highly of her capabilities and expressed themselves highly pleased with the performance on this occasion."

The lifeboat practice held on the 17th October produced a large gathering of spectators. Mrs Ellis was invited to see her boat perform but continued ill-health prevented her attending. The *Robert and Mary Ellis* did well in rough sea and heavy rolling waves. Afterwards the lifeboat crew were treated to a substantial dinner at the Angel Inn. It was a warm-hearted affair. A toast was drunk to Mrs Ellis and another to Henry Freeman.

On December 6th the brig *Star of Hope* in ballast from Dieppe to Newcastle was seen struggling northwards in tremendous seas. When the vessel was half-way to Upgang, she turned for the shore. Robert Gibson told Freeman to get his boat ready and to launch if the brig missed the harbour. Gibson then went to the end of the pier with a red flag in the hope that he could guide the vessel into port should she come his way. Disappointed in his efforts he returned to the lifeboat house to find that Freeman had already launched the lifeboat with John Storr as his second coxswain.

It was another speedy rescue. The vessel, which lay 250 yards north of the West Pier was soon reached. Six men were taken off the brig and landed ashore. The whole operation lasted only twenty minutes, but was not without difficulty. Two oars were broken and a boathook smashed.

Gibson criticised Freeman for placing an extra man in the lifeboat (there were 14 on this occasion), but justified the use of 70 men to handle the carriage because of the difficulty of the launch.

After James Pounder's death, Henry found it difficult to find an able assistant. William Cummings took on the role of second coxswain, although he does not appear to have taken part in any rescues with Freeman during this period. In January 1883, Robert Robinson replaced Cummings as the official second coxswain.

For Henry Freeman the start of the decade had brought him honour and recognition. It had taken him to the pinnacle of success. Now things were to go badly wrong. In the years that followed, his reputation, his business and his family life were all to suffer.

The Robert and Mary Ellis stands at Scotch Head with Henry Freeman in the boat surrounded by his fellow lifeboatmen. The carriage used to launch the lifeboat can be clearly seen. *(Photograph Doran Bros. Courtesy Mrs.Pat Pickles)*

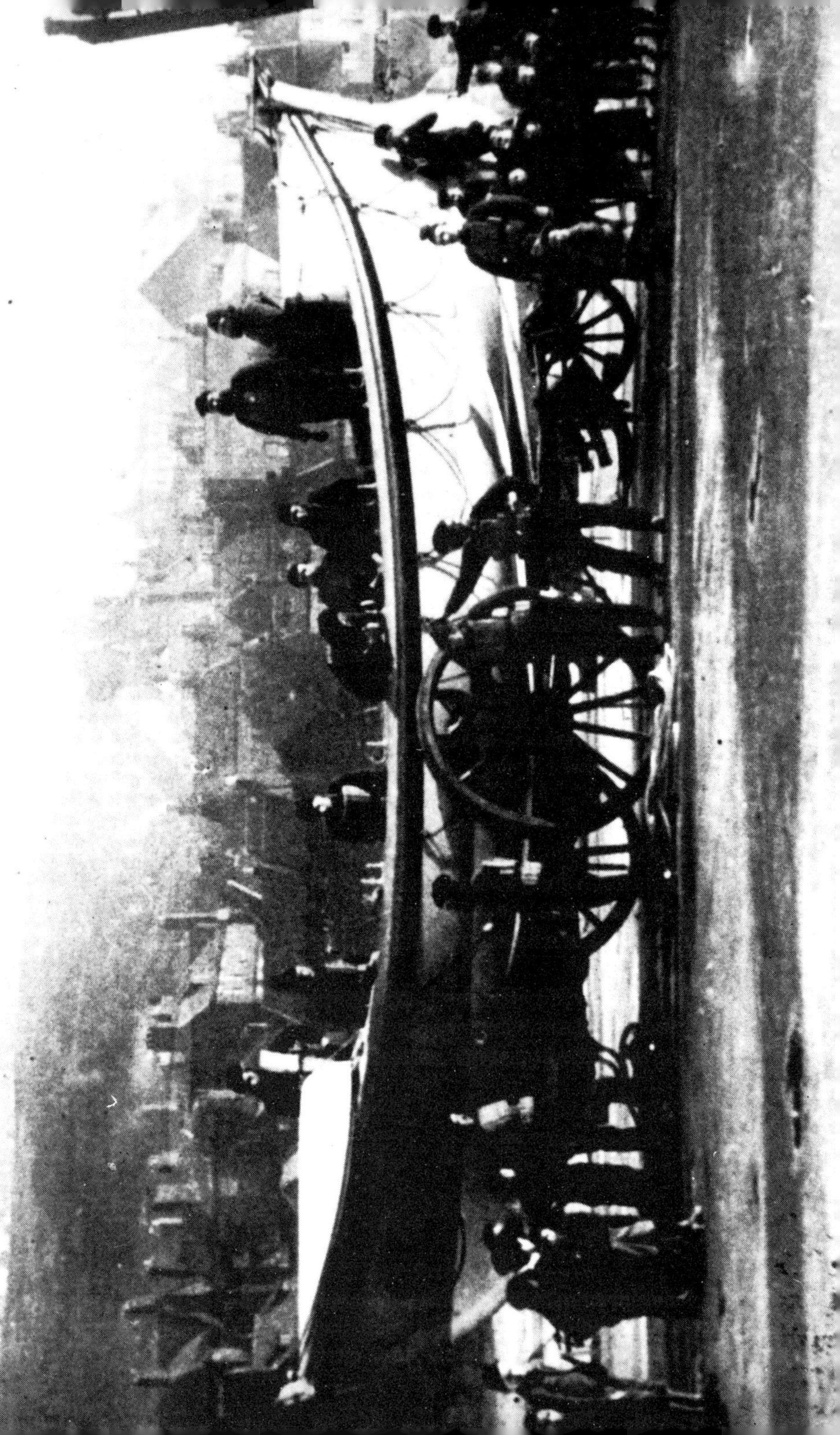

CHAPTER 9
BEFORE THE MAGISTRATES

The year 1883 was a memorable one for Whitby in general and for Henry Freeman in particular. The town as a whole experienced a fairly successful year, while Freeman personally suffered disgrace and humiliation.

Developments in the transport business brought improved communications to the town, both by land and sea, and gave a boost to the local economy. New rail links were forged between Whitby and neighbouring towns. New steamships launched from the Whitehall shipyard enhanced the prosperity of the port. With these changes came jobs and a measure of added security for many local families.

These developments did not guarantee everybody an easier life, however. The year 1883 was a particularly tragic one for those men who were employed aboard the steamers. In the first four months of the year, Whitby lost three of her steamships at sea, the *James Gray,* the *King Arthur,* and the *Wykeham,* with all hands aboard. In December of that year, a further steamship the *Beatrice,* belonging to Thomas Turnbull and Sons, also went down. Tragedy and loss of life was still, then, very much part of the sea-going experience, in spite of the added speed and comfort of the steamships. The melancholy poem "Loss of the Wykeham" which appeared in the *Whitby Times* of April 27th, 1883, describes the loss of all the ship's twenty-one young crew members. It highlights in a most poignant way the vulnerability to the elements of this new generation of vessels.

Of course, for the Whitby fishing community, life was never easy, and the dangers at sea were nothing new. But now there was a challenge of a different kind. In the previous year, concern had grown about the plundering of the fishing grounds off the North East coast by Belgian trawlers. The herring fishery had suffered: catches were down on preceding years and prices had fluctuated. No doubt the indifferent season of 1882 sharpened feelings of insecurity among the fishermen of Whitby at the start of the following season. Possibly, the unpredictability of their situation lent a keener edge to the competition between individuals for the best catches.

It was against this background that Henry Freeman's own personal fortunes took a sudden turn for the worse. In April 1883 he found himself before the Whitby Petty Sessions on a charge of theft. A complaint had been laid against Freeman by some of his fellow fishermen that he and his three partners had stolen some fishing lines which the plaintiffs had left at sea.

It would be difficult to exaggerate the seriousness of the charge. The laws protecting property provided strong penalties against transgressors, and in Freeman's day the courts were not slow to mete them out. Those who were convicted of such a felony were frequently imprisoned. Stiff fines were sometimes imposed, but not without very clear mitigating circumstances.

There was more at stake, however, than the severity of the law. Freeman's whole credibility in the local community would be undermined even if he were acquitted. His predicament was not only a grave personal humiliation, but also a serious embarrassment to the lifeboat service upon which, until now, he had brought the greatest honour.

Only months before the court case, the *Whitby Times*, in its Local Gossip column had proudly contrasted the men of the Whitby lifeboat services with those elsewhere, and had boasted: "We are fortunate in Whitby in never having any lifeboat scandals." Now one of the most respected members of the lifeboat team, the Coxswain himself, stood accused of being a common thief. Whitby's lifeboat management must have agonised over the dilemma Freeman had placed them in.

Freeman's credibility in the eyes of his superiors was arguably of less importance than his standing among his brother fishermen. If suspicion and mistrust of him were generated by the court case, not only would his life as a fisherman be a more difficult and uncomfortable one, but his position as a Coxswain of the lifeboat would be untenable. The management committee would find it impossible to keep a man who had lost the confidence of his subordinates.

For Freeman, therefore, things could hardly have looked more bleak. At best, he stood both to lose his job as Coxswain and the respect of the Whitby community; at worst, he could lose everything, including his very livelihood, and be sent to prison.

A heavy responsibility, therefore, rested on the shoulders of Freeman's legal counsel, Mr W.R.Fawcett from Stockton. Everything depended upon whether or not he could turn two key factors in the case to the advantage of his clients. Firstly, the evidence against them was far from clear-cut. No one had actually observed his clients taking the lines. Without eye-witnesses to support the prosecution, it ought at least to be possible to present a strong defence. Secondly, Freeman's standing in the community as Coxswain of the lifeboat constituted an excellent character reference. The prosecution's indictment was that Freeman had originally intended to commit theft. It was Fawcett's task to demonstrate that it was not in Freeman's nature to be dishonest.

The case was heard before the Staffordshire and Yorkshire Ironmaster, Charles Bagnall, Chairman of the Bench, and two other presiding magistrates, Thomas Turnbull, and Mr.C.Richardson on Saturday April 21st. Before the court were Henry Freeman, James Philpot, William Barrett and Robert Coulson, all fishermen from Whitby. They stood charged on the information of Henry Bell and others with stealing fishing lines at sea between 21st March and the 2nd April.

The charge against these fishermen was the most serious being dealt with by the magistrates at the Police Court that day. It occupied most of the session, although a string of less important cases involving vagrancy, excise evasion, non-attendance

This recently discovered portrait is believed to be that of Charles Bagnall, J.P.
(Courtesy of Whitby Literary and Philosophical Society)

at school, and drunk and disorderly behaviour, had to be heard first. There was great public interest in Freeman's case, and so the court was crowded when at last Superintendent Ryder stood to read the details of the alleged offence.

The first witness to be called was Henry Bell, a fisherman from the Cragg. He described what had happened on the night of the 20th. March. Bell had put out to sea that night in his boat, the *Lily*. With him were Frank Unthank, Thomas Bell and Thomas Gaines, his usual fishing partners. When they reached a spot some ten miles offshore they began to shoot their lines. In all, twenty-three lines, or "overs" were shot early in the morning, amounting to some 320 fathoms of line. Attached to the lines were about a hundred hooks. The lines were held down on the sea bed by six or seven anchors and marked on the surface by buoys.

At about 9 o'clock on the morning of the 21st they began to pull in their lines. By three in the afternoon all but a quarter of their overs had been hauled in when bad weather intervened and they were forced to stop work. They made for home arriving at Whitby early on the 22nd.

When they left off they had seventeen overs in the boat, and had left behind just six, with two anchors and two buoys attached. One of the two buoys was produced as evidence, bearing Thomas Gaines' initials, and the abbreviation for Whitby, "Wy". Bell explained that he could identify his own "overs" by the "snoods", or short lines, which connected the hooks to the main line, or "over". Two of the six lines left in the sea belonged to him, and there were two snoods with peculiar nozzles on them, which he described. A fellow fisherman, Robert Crosby, who was later to give evidence, produced a snood of the kind Bell was describing for the court to see.

The Police Court in Spring Hill where Henry Freeman and his fellow fishermen were tried in 1883. The building was demolished in 1977.

(Courtesy of Scarborough Borough Council)

Continuing his evidence, Bell stated that they went out to sea again on Saturday 24th March to reclaim their overs. When they reached the spot they were unable to see either their buoys, or the land, because of the misty conditions. All they managed to see were the defendants, Freeman and his partners, in their boat somewhere in the vicinity, but they did not speak to them. Unable to locate their buoys, they gave up the search and returned to Whitby.

The next attempt to get their overs had to be postponed until the 2nd April, owing to bad weather. They found their buoys at the place where they had left them, but when they hauled in the lines, they found only three overs. Three overs and a part of another were missing. Both anchors were intact, but one of the buoys was gone. The missing over had not been cut off, but had been carefully untied.

Bell and his colleagues returned to Whitby that night and lost no time in accusing the defendants of taking the overs. Bell himself told the Court he had not discussed the matter with Freeman at all but had challenged Robert Coulson at home, where he was in bed. Coulson had denied Bell's accusations, and an argument had ensued over the number of overs Coulson claimed to have hauled. When it became clear that Bell had found out from another source already how many overs he had hauled, Coulson had become evasive. He could not say exactly how many he had hauled.

Bell concluded his evidence by stating he had been a fisherman for 45 years. It was a long-established practice to leave lines at sea, and if he had come across any while fishing he would have known they were not his property and would have left them. The value of his missing lines was about £4. No doubt Henry Bell was hoping to impress the court with his long experience and with his position as a senior member of the Whitby fishing community. In reality he was not much more than five years older than Freeman and like Freeman was not Whitby born but a native of Runswick Bay.

Under cross-examination by Mr Fawcett, Henry Bell showed shrewdness and caution. He yielded little to the defending counsel and anticipated Fawcett's line of questioning in a way that obviously caused amusement to those present in court.

Bell had to concede that when they went out after their lines, the defendants' boat, which was seen lying beside their own buoy, was not the only one they noticed; there were one or two others besides. But Freeman's boat, he insisted, was near to the place where Bell expected to find his own buoy.

The question of distance was of crucial importance here, both to Bell and to Fawcett. Bell's intention was to make clear that Freeman and his partners had the best opportunity to steal the lines. Fawcett was seeking to demonstrate that the proximity of Freeman's buoys to Bell's could equally have led to the men's lines becoming accidently entangled.

When Fawcett asked Bell exactly how near Freeman's boat was, the canny fisherman refused to be drawn. When a distance of half-a-mile was suggested to him, he made light of it: "Half-a-mile is not far at sea," he declared, amid appreciative laughter from the back of the court. Fawcett admitted that he was not a nautical man. A confident Bell at once took advantage of the admission. In a manner which bordered on condescension he invited his examiner to "come over for a week and go with us." The retort again drew laughter, at Fawcett's expense. Bell was unashamedly playing to the audience. Beneath his wily humour he was making it very clear that it would take more than an out-of-town lawyer without even a rudimentary knowledge of fishing to get the better of him.

Undeterred, Fawcett asked Bell if lines did not get entangled when they were left at sea as his had been. At first, Bell would not accept the suggestion, but later he reluctantly conceded this might occur, just occasionally.

The tone of Fawcett's cross-questioning became sterner at this point. He demanded to know whether or not Bell had offered to give Coulson a sovereign if he would say that Freeman had got his lines. Bell refuted the suggestion. He had told Coulson he would give him a sovereign if he would tell the truth. Coulson was adamant that they had got only thirteen lines. Bell denied that he had ever attempted to bribe Coulson to incriminate Freeman. What he had said was that the matter would get settled up if he were to tell the truth. Coulson refused to co-operate and rejected the money.

Fawcett pursued the matter further, and asked Bell if he had ever offered anybody else a sovereign to assist in his inquiries. Bell said that he hadn't but some sovereigns had been offered to him. Fawcett adroitly side-stepped this reply by saying dismissively. "Yes, just so; and you did not take them, I suppose." Bell at once replied no. His intimation that he had been offered money to drop his accusations was not explored further in the court. From the press reports, it appears that no attempt was made to discover the truth of this claim.

The next witness to give evidence was Francis Unthank, one of Bell's men. He confirmed Bell's evidence that when they went to recover the overs some of them had been untied. The three remaining had been tied onto the second anchor. One over belonged to Bell, one was his own, and the third belonged to Thomas Gaines. He had gone to see Freeman, and asked if he had any of their gear. Freeman replied "No" and denied ever having seen the buoy belonging to Thomas Gaines which had been produced earlier in the court. Unthank had challenged Freeman to swear that he had never seen the buoy. Freeman repeatedly said no he hadn't. He then went down into Freeman's boat, the *Alexandra,* to see for himself. William Barrett, one of Freeman's associates was present when Freeman showed him eleven overs which he said were all that he had. He could tell by the splices and the buoys that none of the eleven overs belonged to him or any of Bell's fishing party.

Coulson's original total of thirteen overs, stated to Henry Bell, conflicted with the eleven which Freeman had shown Unthank in the boat. Had Coulson, in an unguarded moment, come close to disclosing the true figure, perhaps having awoken suddenly from sleep, and being caught unprepared? If so, then Freeman had not shown to Unthank all the overs he had, but had concealed or disposed of some.

The next witness to testify, Ann Oxley, soon made clear that this was the case. Ann Oxley worked in Mennell's sail loft, near Spital Bridge. She was employed there mending herring nets. On Tuesday 3rd April, only hours after Bell and his associates had confronted the defendants about missing overs, two people had come up to the first floor sail-loft, where she was working. They had arrived between nine and ten in the morning. One man had a large bag on his back. He carried the bag upstairs to the floor above where she heard him walk across the floor and stop just overhead. It was not long before he returned downstairs. He spoke to her briefly, before following the other man back downstairs to the street. The man who spoke to her she identified as Robert Coulson.

Half an hour after the visit by these men, she again heard someone in the loft, and heard him go down. When she looked out through the window she could see Freeman. Afterwards, she went upstairs onto the second floor which was used for repairing the herring nets, and in a spot near where the men had been she found a large canvas bag, full of very damp, sandy fishing gear. The following Friday, she took her brother to see the bag and its contents. It was hidden behind some herring nets, which were hanging up in a dark corner. Her brother went and cut some pieces out.

On the Tuesday after, she saw Coulson and Freeman, who both came to the sail-loft when she was working. Someone went upstairs and came down, but she was not sure who it was. She had asked Coulson, "Are those Harry Bell's lines you are taking away?" and he had replied, "We have not had any of Harry Bell's lines." The next day she saw Harry Freeman in the loft, and told him about Bell's lines. She said she thought he was going to get into a row about them. His reply was: "I have not got them. I only wish I had."

According to Ann Oxley's testimony, it wasn't until the following day that Freeman at last admitted to stealing the lines. Freeman had come down again, and began to talk about the lines. She said it was a pity about them, and he replied: "I wish I had never taken them. I should not have taken them, but for the other men. I cut them to get my own lines clear." After that, Freeman went down every day, and said something about the lines. On one of these occasions, he said: "If you don't put upon me, it will be alright." She replied: "If the men come to me, they won't get anything out of me."

Ann Oxley could not say when the bag was removed from the loft. But on Tuesday 10th April, Freeman's boat was moored immediately below the loft where she was working. Somewhere between three and four in the afternoon she remembered noticing an unusual amount of smoke coming out from the boat. She spoke to Robert Coulson about it. When she said she could smell something burning, he replied that he had just lit his pipe. Evidently unconvinced, she retorted that it was not tobacco smoke she could smell.

Two days later, Thomas Gaines came to see her to make some inquiries about his nets. Afterwards, she told Freeman that Gaines had questioned her, but Henry did not say much. On the following Saturday, when Freeman was at the loft, she had said to him: "There's Harry Bell coming." He said he would go and get hid, and hurried upstairs into the other loft.

The next witness to give evidence was Ann Oxley's brother, William Clark Oxley, who was a sail maker by trade. He had visited the loft above the one where his sister worked on the 6th April. She showed him a canvas bag containing fishing lines which were dirty and damp. He had examined them and cut off pieces of line, which he later gave to Robert Crosby. He had seen snoods before like the one he took, but never on a fishing line.

The evidence given by the Oxleys was highly damaging, but it was the testimony of Robert Crosby, a sailor and fisherman, which sealed the fate of the accused. Crosby said he visited the loft on the 9th, and saw the bag there. He was there again on the following day, the 10th., when Freeman came. Henry said: "This is a bad job; how long have you known these lines have been here?" to which Crosby had replied: "I've known they've been here long enough, Harry." Freeman then went upstairs to the loft where the lines were and Crosby followed him. Henry went straight to the bag which was in a dark corner. Pulling aside some nets, he had lifted it out and said: "I wish the ***** things had been at the bottom of the sea, yet, before I had anything to do with them."

They both went down into the street. There, Freeman had told Crosby that Mennell had ordered him to get the things off the premises. He then asked Crosby what he thought was the best thing to do with the lines. Crosby's advice was " Give them back to the men they belong to. What else can you do with them?" Freeman's response was:" No, that ***** old Harry Bell will send us off." Crosby had retorted: "No, you will be far more likely to be sent off if you don't give them up." Freeman had replied: "Look at the disgrace there would be. I should lose my life-boat job. I know Mennell is alright. You'll say nothing about it. I'll destroy them. I'll bring the boat up here as soon as there's water and have a good fire on and burn them. If they're once burnt and out of sight, I durst stand before all the judges in England and swear I never saw them."

Later that day Crosby saw Freeman with Coulson. Henry said to Coulson, "The key is there, get down when you like and make a good fire on again, there is water

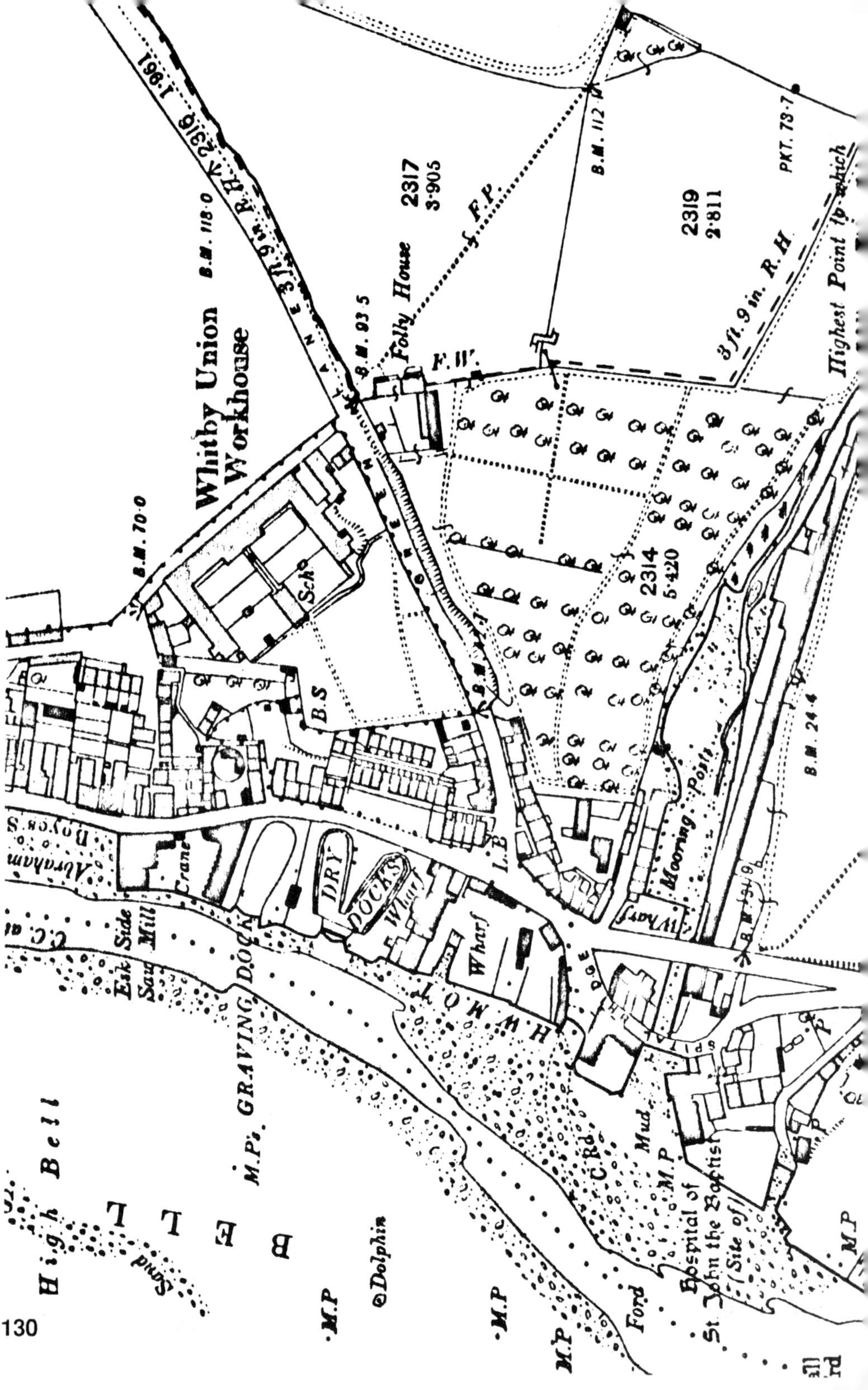
Whitby Union Workhouse
Folly House
F.P.
F.W.
2317
3·905
2319
2·811
2314
5·420
B.M. 118·0
B.M. 93·5
B.M. 70·0
B.M. 112
B.M. 24·4
PKT. 73·7
Sch.
B.S
L.B
3 ft. 9 in. R.H
Highest Point to which
Mooring Posts
Wharf
Wharf
Wharf
DRY DOCKS
Crane
Esk Side Saw Mill
M.P's GRAVING DOCK
Abraham Boyes S
H.W.M.O.T
Mud
C. Rd
Ford
M.P
Hospital of St John the Baptist (Site of)
BELL
High Bell
Dolphin

to get up to the loft." In the afternoon Crosby was at Spital-bridge ghaut-way, and he saw the *Alexandra* come up between three and four o'clock. All the defendants were on board. They took the boat up towards the Lock then steered right under the loft and moored her there. After a while, he saw smoke coming from the funnel of their boat - more like a steamer than that of a fishing boat. Crosby went into the loft, then went onto the pier. There Coulson said to him: "I've left the keys at Mennell's." Crosby said "That's alright. Have you got the overs all burnt?" Coulson at once denied the suggestion: "No, we didn't burn them." Crosby retorted: "What's the use of saying that to me when I know you have?" Coulson replied: "Well, is it likely we should say we did it?"

The same night, Crosby testified that he saw Barrett and Philpot at the top of Bridge-steps. Barrett had said to Crosby: "There's Jim Philpot standing there, and if he likes to speak the truth, if they had done as I wanted them, they would never have touched the lines." Philpot had remained silent. Barrett then asked Crosby if he knew who had taken the lines up into the loft. Crosby said, "Yes, I believe Coulson did." Barrett said: "Well, he didn't take them up. I took them up myself, while Coulson kept the young woman in talk."

Mr Fawcett put the question to Robert Crosby: "Did Barrett tell you that the lines had got entangled with theirs?" Crosby replied: "Yes, he did." That concluded the case for the prosecution.

The magistrates granted a request by Mr Fawcett that his clients' cases be taken separately. Their consent was of some importance. Had the Bench refused the request, and taken the cases together, the value of the property taken by all four defendants would have exceeded forty shillings and the cases could not then have been settled in that court.

Mr Fawcett proceeded to address the Bench on behalf of his clients. In this case, he argued, the Magistrates were not dealing with notorious thieves. One of the defendants occupied a prominent position; he was a man well known to the Magistrates. As Coxswain of the lifeboat, he had many times risked his own life to save the lives of others. He would ask the magistrates to consider that Freeman's former good character might stand him in good stead in this instance. He recognised that, in the light of the statements made by several witnesses, it would be futile for him to deny that the overs which were missed had been taken by Freeman into his boat, and later destroyed. He had no wish to waste the time of the court.

The Spital Bridge area of Whitby. There were several sail lofts in this part of the town. Mennell's loft is believed to have been part of the 'L' shaped building situated between Spital Bridge and the spot marked "Hospital of St John the Baptist".

(Reproduced from the 1893 Ordnance Survey Map)

The building, centre left, at 32 Church Street, now converted into holiday flats used to be a public house called the Ship Inn, and was owned by Thomas Mennell at the time of the fishing lines incident. Coulson would have left the keys for the *Alexandra* here on his way to the pier where he met Crosby. *(Photograph Ray Shill)*

Andrews Sail Loft still stands at Spital Bridge. This is believed to be the building where Thomas Mennell rented a floor as his sail loft. *(Photograph Ray Shill)*

Another view of Spital Bridge and the Sail Loft. Henry Freeman was said by Robert Crosby to have brought the Alexandra *up to the lock and moored under the loft here.*
(Photograph Ray Shill)

The question was whether the lines were taken with a felonious intent. There was no doubt that they were taken wrongly. But they were taken because the lines were entangled together. That was the original cause of the theft. The defendants had lost several lines themselves and when these lines became entangled with their own, they were prompted to take them. If later the idea occurred to Freeman to destroy them, that did not alter the fact that the original taking was not a felonious one.

Of course, what took place afterwards was most blamable, for Freeman did not speak the truth. He hid himself away, knowing that he had done wrong, and remarking that old Harry Bell would get him sent away, instead of acting upon the honest advice which Robert Crosby had given him, which would have ended the matter.

It was the case of a man taking a false step, and telling untruths to shield his conduct. For four or five years he had been Coxswain of the lifeboat and for sixteen years or more had been connected with the crew. He had a morbid fear of losing that situation, and he trusted the Bench would consider his general good conduct. A man who suddenly yielded to temptation, and admitted the wrong, was not to be placed on a par with an ordinary felon.

Fawcett also added that at the time Freeman's wife was ill in bed, and by implication indicated the harm which might befall her should he be sent to gaol.

As to the other men, Fawcett concluded that no evidence existed to show any felonious intention on their part. The Chairman, Charles Bagnall, intervened here to point out that the other men were present when the nets were taken, and when they were burnt. Mr Fawcett agreed, but argued that they were acting under the orders of Freeman, their master.

After some deliberation among the magistrates, the Chairman gave the verdict of the Bench. The charge against the defendants had been most clearly proved. They had been very ably defended by Mr Fawcett, who had made a powerful appeal for leniency. Freeman's position and the gallant services which he had rendered were circumstances which they should take into consideration on this occasion. But they must remember also that fishermen were very much at the mercy of their fellow fishermen when their property was left unprotected at sea. It would be very unfair indeed to allow a case of this sort to pass without severe punishment.

In consequence of Freeman's good character, and there being nothing serious against the others (they had been before the Bench charged with drunkenness), the Magistrates would not commit them to prison, but would inflict severe fines. Freeman was ordered to pay £15, or two months' imprisonment, and the others were fined £5 each, in default one month's imprisonment.

The Police Court was in session for more than six hours that day. The major part of that sitting was spent on the investigation involving Freeman and his associates. His case had been preceded by some half a dozen others, all minor offences, but it is sobering to reflect that the very first case of the day, which had been a charge brought against a tramp, of sleeping out in a haystack at Fylingdales at night had attracted a penalty of fourteen days' imprisonment with hard labour. This is perhaps a measure of just how serious Freeman's predicament had been. From the magistrates' summing up, it is clear that only Freeman's previous good character had saved him from a prison sentence.

In view of the heavy penalties for theft, it is hard to understand why Freeman would ever have taken such a risk. His motives were not explained during the court case. Only one sentence in Mr Fawcett's summing up speech provides any kind of clue: "The defendants had lost several lines themselves, and these lines becoming entangled, they were prompted to take them." If they had indeed lost some lines, Freeman may not have had the ready money to replace them. With the recent difficulties in the herring fishery, he may well have been short of money. Perhaps Freeman's motive was not an entirely selfish one: one witness reported him as saying

" I should not have taken them but for the other men." Another possible explanation was that competition among fishermen for catches might have prompted the deed. The possibilities are many, but one thing is certain: the consequences were the near ruin of him.

Equally difficult to explain is how, when the penalties were so severe, Henry Bell could even have countenanced the idea of reporting Freeman and his men to the authorities. Freeman's behaviour was certainly provocative but Henry was not a notorious thief. His previous good character, and his lifeboat service record might surely have given Bell pause for thought before pursuing the matter. To bring these charges against him, Bell and his friends knew full well that they risked destroying Freeman completely. Could this, indeed, have been precisely their intention? Were they motivated purely by malice? Or had they been driven to these extreme lengths only as a last resort by severe financial pressures and Freeman's refusals to make amends?

From the available evidence, it is possible to draw either conclusion. Arguably, some pointers are provided by the evidence given by Henry Bell during the trial. Could it be significant that when Bell gave his account of the first effort to recover the overs, he stated that when they failed to locate their buoys, they saw the defendants in their boat, but did not speak to them? Might this suggest, perhaps, that there was some enmity between Bell and Freeman even at this stage, long before it was even realised the lines were missing?

Why was it indeed, that when the lines were lost, Bell by his own admission, did not discuss the matter with Freeman at all, but chose to confront Robert Coulson? Were the two men simply not on talking terms? Did Freeman, in fact, have good grounds for his fear that " ***** old Harry Bell will send us off?" If he and Bell were on terms of mutual hatred, he could well have had substantial grounds for supposing that Bell wished him ill.

It certainly appears that Bell was driven by an extraordinary zeal to pin the blame for the missing nets on Freeman and his men. Only after cross-examination by Mr Fawcett did Bell acknowledge that other boats besides Freeman's were in the vicinity when he made his first attempt to reclaim his overs on Saturday 24th March. Earlier, he had volunteered no mention at all of any other boats being nearby. To neglect even to mention that other boats were present; to attempt to dispel any suggestion that Freeman's boat was near enough for the lines to become entangled; to have questioned Freeman's men before anybody else, when others might have had the same opportunity to take the lines; to wake Coulson in his bed in the middle of the night to interrogate him; and to have offered him a sovereign as an inducement to incriminate his own master - all these are suggestive of something more than a simple desire to recover lost property. Taken together, they indicate a profound determination either to secure justice, or, equally to exact vengeance.

Henry Bell was fortunate in being able to identify so successfully the overs which belonged to himself and his colleagues. This would have been a much more difficult task but for the salvaging of a unique type of snood by William Clark Oxley. It was a type of snood with a special nozzle used only on lines owned by members of Bell's fishing boat team and were instantly recognisable. According to Mr Oxley such snoods were not usually used on fishing lines. Could it be that these snoods had been introduced by Bell and his fellow fishermen for the purpose of setting a trap?

Henry Bell was also fortunate in having the testimony of Robert Crosby who had been master of the *Alexandra* since May 1877. Having disposed of the *Garland*, Freeman was in need of a large fishing boat. The *Alexandra* was a vessel he was acquainted with, having been her master, himself, a few years earlier. Crosby's consent to Freeman's use of it begins to look suspicious when Crosby's testimony was so damning. Might there have been collusion between Bell and Crosby to seal Henry Freeman's fate?

What is not known is whether Crosby's testimony was obtained under pressure of interrogation or whether he made his statement voluntarily. If he was a friend of Freeman, then any statement he made would have been carefully worded to cast Freeman in the best light. Yet in court it was Crosby who produced the snood which positively linked the stolen lines to Bell and when his turn came to give evidence he clearly identified Henry Freeman as the culprit. With a "friend" like Crosby Henry Freeman would hardly need an enemy like Bell!

But if malice was Bell's motive what could be the cause of it? One can only speculate. In the past he had been out in the lifeboat under Samuel Lacy. When the barque *Svadsfare* was salvaged Henry Bell was present amongst the crew. Was he offended by Freeman's subsequent outburst? Bell may have seen himself as a potential coxswain and may have been hostile to Freeman's appointment. Was he annoyed because of his continued exclusion from the crew when Freeman took charge? Or was his dislike of Freeman already so well established that he would not serve with the man?

Of course, malice may not have been the prime motive behind Bell's actions. Perhaps it was a burning sense of injustice, and not a warped desire for vengeance, that drove him to seek redress from the courts. If so he must have been sorely provoked. Is it possible that this incident was not an isolated one, but actually a culmination of a whole series of similar incidents? This might, at least, provide a clue as to why Bell was so sure about who had taken his property, and why he pursued them so vigorously.

Having been tried and found guilty, Freeman was faced by a most damaging financial burden. His own fine was a very large sum, fifteen pounds (nearly two years of his salary as Coxswain). In addition, he still had his solicitor's fees to pay. It is significant that by 1885 Freeman was no longer living in Church Street but was in a much poorer area of the town, the Cragg.

Freeman found little sympathy in the local press when the case was over. In its editorial column almost a week later, the *Whitby Times* reflected: "The case presented several very bad features, and but for the previous good character of the chief offender, and the gallant services that had been rendered by him in the life-boat in times of great peril, the punishment meted out to the accused would have been in all probability, of a much more severe character. Property left at sea by fishermen, in the way fishing lines were left, and which by the way, is not an unusual thing with them, is at the mercy of all comers; but any person who may be prone to dishonesty will do well to remember that the strong arm of the law will be sure to overtake them, and mete out the punishment for their misdeeds. After the revelations of Saturday, it is to be hoped we shall hear no more of this kind of pilfering."

Most Whitby folk believed that Henry was guilty. But, the damage done to his reputation was less severe than might have been expected. Somehow he managed to retain the loyalty of those around him in spite of everything. Perhaps they were of the opinion that the version of events presented by Henry Bell was not as accurate as it should be. Henry Freeman retained his post as Coxswain of the lifeboat and in time was able to regain the respect and esteem which the court case had tarnished. That the affair was largely forgotten is some measure of his quality as a man and of his resilience of character.

Henry Freeman had moved to the Cragg by 1885. Accommodation at the Cragg was cramped and of a generally poor standard. Harkers Buildings, now demolished, exemplifies the sort of living quarters Freeman may have occupied at this time.
(Courtesy of Whitby Literary & Philosophical Society)

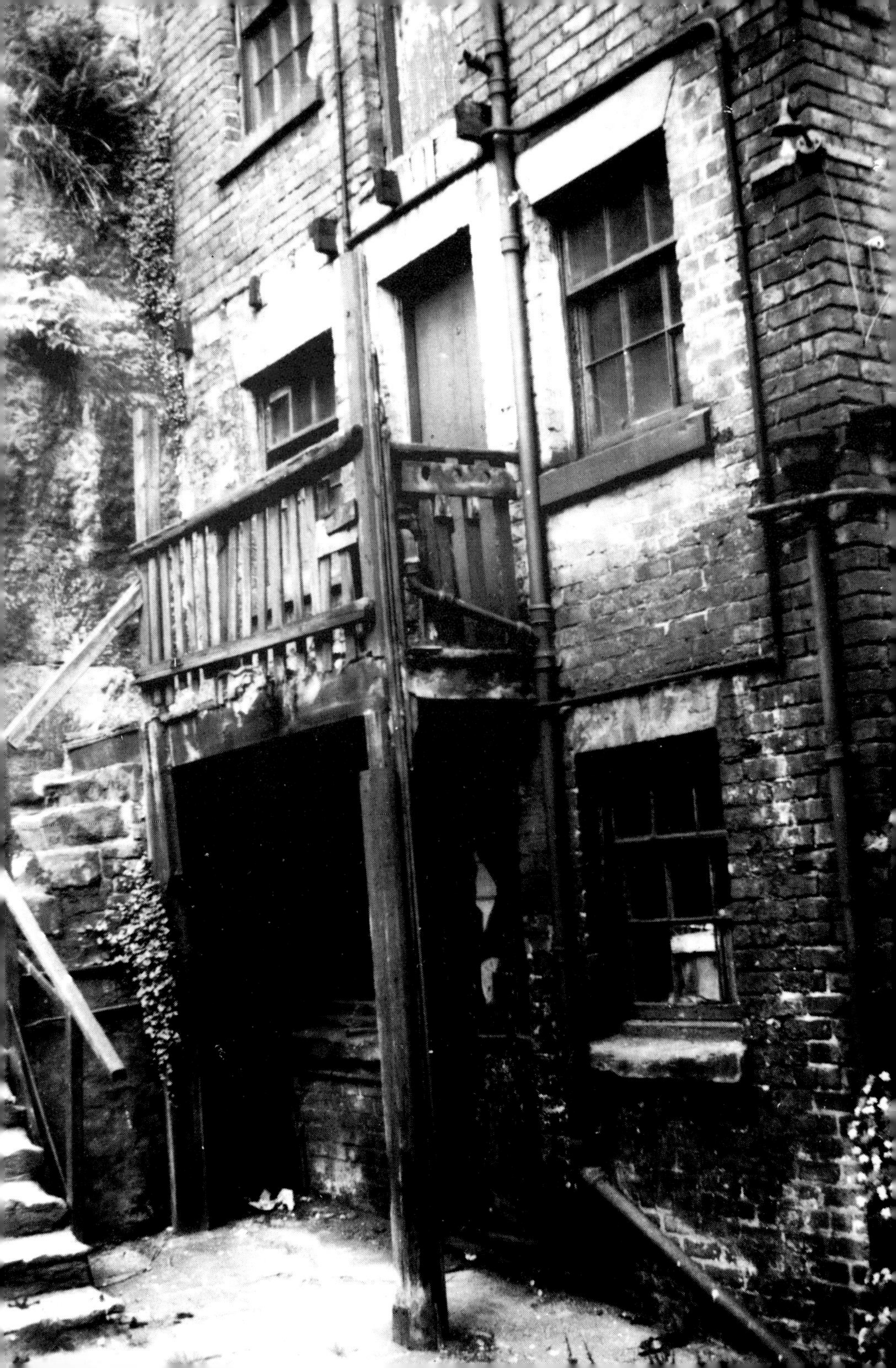

CHAPTER 10

THE TROUBLED YEARS 1883-1891

Henry Freeman's conviction for theft reduced his standing in the community for a time, while that of Henry Bell was enhanced considerably.

In May 1883 four fishermen were needed to represent the port of Whitby at the opening ceremony of the Great International Fisheries Exhibition in South Kensington, London. As lifeboat equipment was on show, Henry Freeman would have been an obvious candidate to represent Whitby, yet he was not chosen. Instead Henry Bell, Thomas Hutchinson, Thomas Langlands and Jamieson Colly went along. Freeman might have wished to stay at home to nurse his sick wife, but it is more likely that he was deliberately excluded because of the fishing lines incident.

This was only the beginning of Henry's problems. Within the next seven years he would encounter difficulties in every quarter of his life. Initially he found himself at the centre of several conflicts with his superiors and his fellow fishermen.

One such conflict was with Chief Officer Smith of the Coastguard. Chief Officer Smith accused Freeman of neglecting his duty by failing to put in an appearance when the lifeboat was launched on the morning of the 4th of April 1884. Robert Austin's coble, the *John and Ann*, was returning to port and appeared to be in danger. The *Robert and Mary Ellis* was launched with a 12 man volunteer crew. It was seen that those in the coble were safe and the lifeboat returned to shore. Robert Gibson was instructed to censure Freeman for not being present.

The trouble between Smith and Freeman may well have been brewing below the surface for some time. Smith was clearly annoyed over the episode. The rift between them must have been of a serious nature for when the Lifeboat Committee announced that they would let the matter stand over, Smith tendered his resignation. The matter was reported in the lifeboat committee minutes for the 24th July 1884.

Another row was provoked by the inclusion of a lifeboat race in the annual Whitby Regatta. It was first run in 1883. Substantial prizes were offered and for the first few years boats from six or seven lifeboat stations regularly competed. The event was always popular as a spectacle but it created great dissatisfaction amongst the crews. The boats varied in size and some were quite heavy. As there was no satisfactory system of handicapping, the lightest boats invariably won. Coxswains of the heavier boats lost interest in the race, but Freeman continued to battle against the odds although his crew began to weary of so hopeless a struggle.

Six boats were entered in the first contest. Henry Freeman had charge of the *Harriott Forteath III*. Thomas Langlands had the *Joseph Sykes* from Upgang. John Storr brought the new *Ephraim and Hannah Fox* from Robin Hood's Bay. Hartlepool,

Crowds line the West Pier as the *Robert and Mary Ellis* is launched into the sea.
(Photograph Courtesy Jeff Morris)

The lifeboat race was held annually as part of the Whitby Regatta. It was a contest in which Freeman regularly participated. As no system of handicapping existed, the lighter boats invariably won. *(Photograph Courtesy Jeff Morris)*

Staithes and Runswick Bay also took part. Objections were raised to the Staithes boat, the *Hannah Somerset,* which had fixed oars, but the race went ahead. It was a close finish. First was the *Hannah Somerset*, followed closely by Langlands in the *Joseph Sykes*. Third was the *Ephraim and Hannah Fox*. The rest were left far behind by the faster and lighter vessels.

Both 1883 and 1884 were quiet years for lifeboat launches, but 1885 saw storms back with a vengeance. The year started with gales and vessels were frequently seeking sanctuary at Whitby. The first call to action happened on the 9th February 1885. There were several vessels lying at anchor in the Whitby Roads. About 4.30 in the morning the wind changed suddenly. This caused them to drag on their anchors and several ships decided to leave. However one schooner called the *Maid of Honor,* laden with coals, looked as if she might strike the rocks. Robert Gibson ordered the *Robert and Mary Ellis* to be launched. Henry Freeman took out the lifeboat with Robinson Pounder as his second coxswain, but his help was not required as another vessel took the *Maid of Honor* in tow. With anchor and chain lost the schooner was assisted to Scarborough.

The coal trade along the east coast of Britain employed many types of vessel. There were the tall masted schooners which carried coal to distant places, and the work horse brigs and barques which kept London supplied. There were also many smaller vessels such as sloops and yawls which ferried lighter cargoes to villages and towns along the seaboard. It was a sloop which ran into difficulties a few months later and which was to involve Freeman in a rescue which almost failed.

The Scarborough registered sloop,*Wear* was owned by West Hartlepool businessmen Messrs Danby and Leonard. At the start of May 1885 she left West Hartlepool with a load of coal destined for Walcott, some three miles south of Mundersley in Norfolk. The sloop had a crew of two: William Brockett, the master, and a mate. On Sunday afternoon, 3rd May, the sloop tried to enter Whitby harbour in heavy seas. Twice she was warned off, but still her master thought he could enter the harbour safely. On the first attempt Brockett brought the vessel close to the piers but the strong wind forced him to veer off. A signal was fired by the Coastguard to warn him to stay away, but Brockett came in for another attempt. Unfortunately he missed the entrance again and was about to turn away a second time when a heavy wave struck the ship damaging her sails and completely disabling her. The sloop began to drift into danger amid heavy breakers north of the West Pier. All Brockett could do was to beach on the sands. Both men on board her then lashed themselves to the rigging.

The firing of the Coastguard mortar was enough to bring a large crowd down to the sea front to observe what was going on. It was also a signal for the lifeboat services to prepare for action.

The yawl *Diamond* of Scarborough pictured here unloading coal into carts on Sandsend beach. A variety of vessels were employed in the local carrying trade, but brigs were most commonly used for this duty. **(Frank Meadow Sutcliffe)**

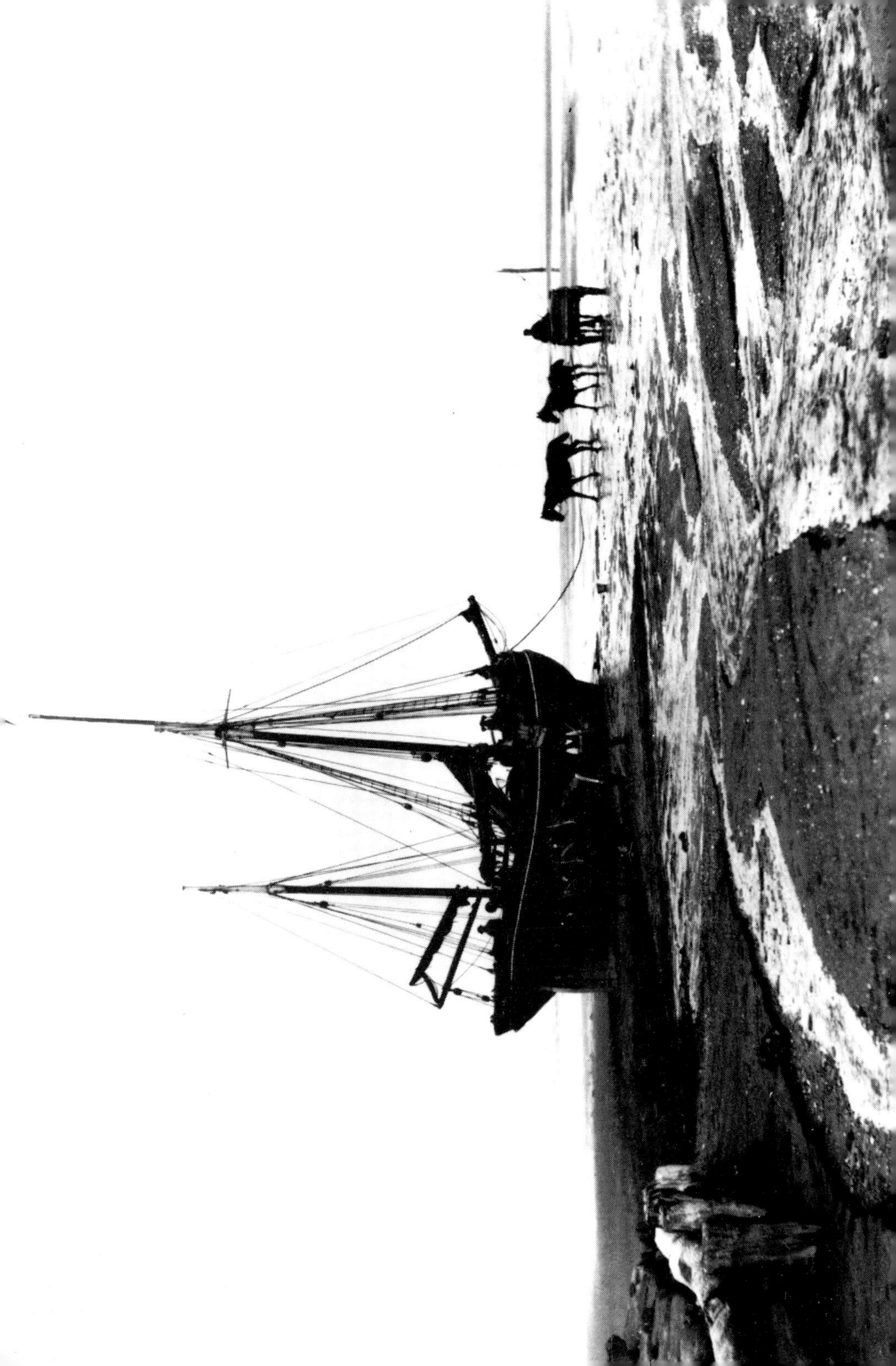

The *Harriott Forteath III* was launched down the slipway and out into the sea. Henry Freeman was coxswain and Richard Robinson the second coxswain. Henry took the lifeboat close to the shore, but after passing the Second Nab, struck on a sandbank. Freeman's crew pushed the lifeboat off with their oars, breaking three in the process. Other oars were lost and spectators waded out to retrieve them and handed them back to the oarsmen.

In spite of the setbacks the *Harriott Forteath* was alongside the wreck within fifteen minutes of launching. The *Wear* lay aground below the West Cliff Saloon. The lifeboat crew soon had grappling hooks on board her and after a couple of attempts both master and mate were safely aboard the Lifeboat and heading for shore.

1885 was a year when several improvements were considered for the town. In May, it was proposed that Baxtergate should be widened by pulling down several Local Board properties and replacing them with new ones set further back. At the same time Robert Pannett provided lamps to light the West Pier. Matthew Wellburn decided to extend his butcher's business from Robin Hood's Bay and Whitby Market Hall. In June he opened a new butchers shop in Sandgate, Whitby.

August was a troublesome month at sea, however. On the 20th. a sudden gale caught fishermen unaware near the harbour mouth. The fishing mules *Daisy* and *Wild Rose* and the coble *Robert and Henry* were all at risk. The master of the *Wild Rose* was thrown from the helm and seriously hurt while the *Daisy* ran into the East Pier and was damaged. Freeman took out the *Harriott Forteath* and rescued the three man crew from the *Robert and Henry*.

The next week the coble *Frolic* was being towed into harbour by the Cleveland tug when the Penzance boat, *Kingfisher*, ran into her. The five man crew were saved but the coble sank along with all her nets, gearing and 25,000 herring on board. This accident illustrates that it was not only the fishermen's lives which were at stake. Chance events could lead to the loss of all their equipment and their livelihoods as well.

Of all the dangers faced by fishermen, perhaps the worst possible situation was when the rescue services could offer no help. Such an occurrence took the lives of Matthew Dryden and Thomas Clarke who had been out in the Whitby coble *Ann Maria* one night in September. They were with Thomas Dryden, about four miles off Robin Hood's Bay. A sudden squall caused the sail to jibe and the coble to upset casting the three men into the water. Only Thomas Dryden made it ashore, a feat which was all the more remarkable since Thomas had a wooden leg!

The brig *Mary and Agnes* is pounded by heavy seas off Whitby Sands. To take this photograph Frank Sutcliffe had to be held by the feet by another man to keep him steady such was the strength of the gale.   (Photograph Frank Meadow Sutcliffe)

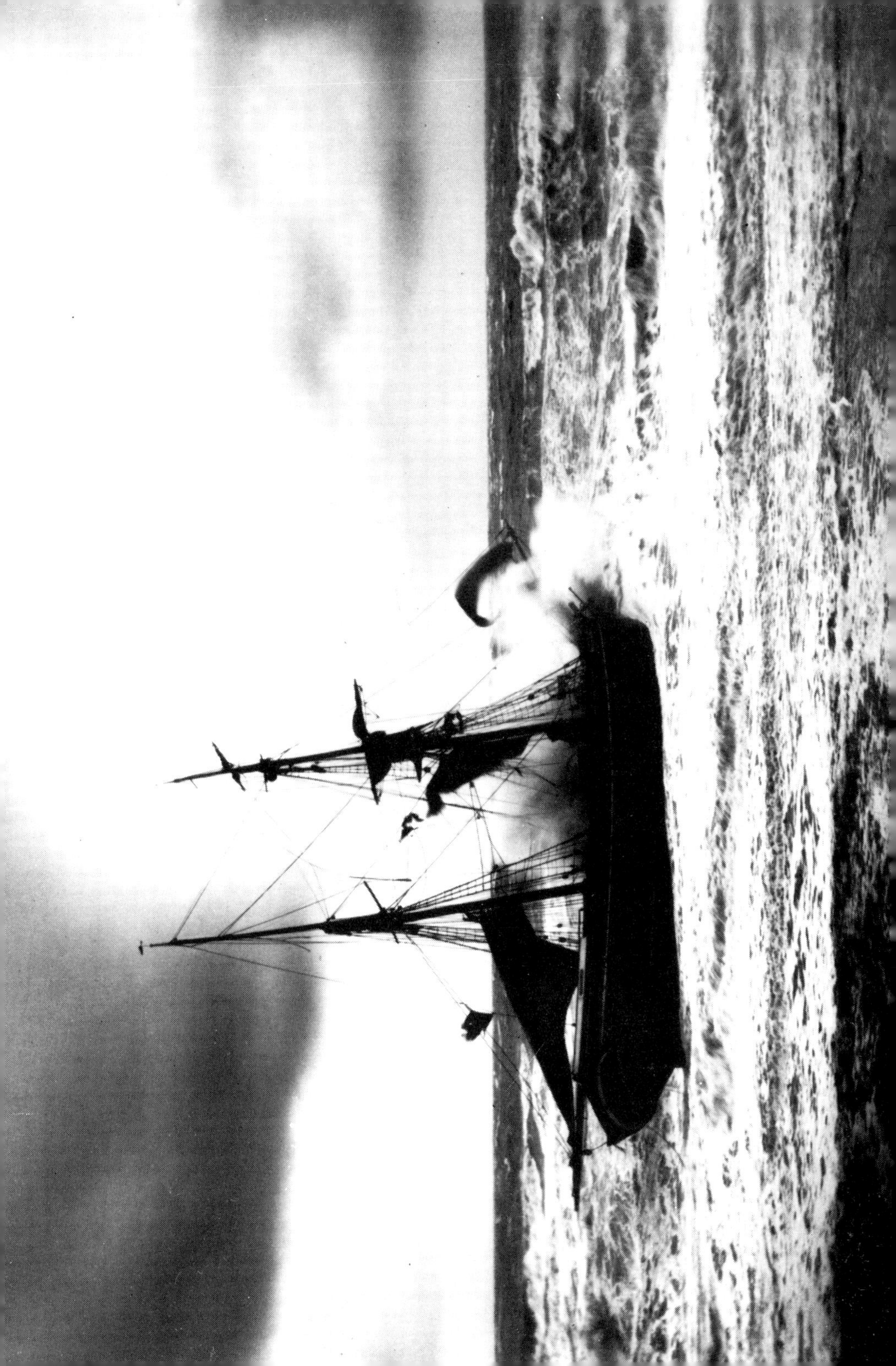

The following month Freeman found himself under fire for his handling of a rescue. The end of October saw heavy gales lashing the Whitby shore. As the weather worsened a look-out was maintained from the Piers and the Coastguard station. Around midday on Saturday 24th October a brigantine was seen to be heading for harbour. The ship proved to be the *Mary and Agnes* of Scarborough in ballast from London to Middlesbrough. The vessel was clearly labouring under the heavy sea. The chief officer of the Coastguard, Mr Brodie-Stein, gave the order for the mortar to be fired. The *Robert and Mary Ellis* was placed in readiness while Freeman and his crew made final preparations for a launch. The Coastguard rocket crew also got ready so that they could be near when the vessel struck. Eventually the brigantine was driven ashore on the sands at the foot of the Saloon, not far from where the *Wear* had grounded.

The lifeboat was launched immediately. A large body of men waded into the water and pulling on the ropes they dragged the *Robert and Mary Ellis* off her carriage. Another rope held by a group of men on the pier kept the lifeboat on course. When this second rope was let go, Freeman hoped the boat would head directly for the stricken vessel. However, the sea was strong and the gale was blowing ESE. The result was that Freeman's lifeboat was blown back onshore to be stranded on the beach a little north of the Second Nab. In what was a repeat of the *Wear* episode, the crew again tried to push the lifeboat off and this time broke two oars. Members of the crowd, who were watching, rushed into the water to get the boat off, but this time the lifeboat held firm and no effort could move her.

The life-saving brigade had more success. A well-placed rocket cast a line over the *Mary and Agnes*. After the crew had made it firm, the first man across was the ship's apprentice who tested the line. The lightest man on board, he braved the raging sea and was followed by the rest of the crew. Exhausted by their ordeal several had to be carried up to the Saloon for medical attention.

The *Whitby Gazette* questioned why the lifeboat was not launched earlier. The newspaper was particularly critical of Freeman's handling of the situation, reviving the memory of the *Wear* rescue where Freeman was said to have been censured for going aground. The *Gazette's* comments appear to have been well founded.

It was the last major rescue Freeman was to handle, and it is sad that after so many successes, it should have been marred by failure. From now on all his lifeboat launches would be to smaller craft. In fact Whitby was to be spared further dramatic episodes at sea for many years.

After the *Mary and Agnes* rescue by the Coastguard another vessel came into sight. She was the schooner, *Dmitry* in ballast from Narva. At first it looked as if she was going to be dashed to pieces on the scaur. Her Russian captain, a man called Sakki, was a skilled navigator. By excellent seamanship he steered the vessel through the rocks along a passage known locally as the Sledway and headed for the harbour mouth. The lifeboat *Harriott Forteath* was made ready, but Captain Sakki managed to guide her safely between the piers. Here he made the mistake of lowering sail and the vessel drifted onto Colliers Hope where the seas reduced the ship to a wreck.

Some five years later the *Dmitry* episode is said to have been used by Bram Stoker in writing his book *Dracula*. Stoker came to Whitby in the summer of 1890 to see if it would be suitable for a family holiday and while there gained inspiration for his novel. Thus, in one chapter, Count Dracula landed in Whitby in the form of a large black dog from a schooner. With all sails set she had sailed into the harbour while a tempest was raging, a corpse lashed to the wheel and no other life aboard her.

Stoker's schooner was a Russian from Varna, named the *Demeter*, carrying a cargo of great wooden boxes filled with mould. Her voyage to Whitby, as described in the Captain's log-book, had been an eerie one, bedevilled by mysterious disappearances among her crew until the captain was the only man left aboard. Entries in the log mention sightings of a 'tall, thin man' on deck. After her miraculous entry into the harbour, the vessel had pitched herself on the beach below the East Cliff. At once an immense dog appeared on deck from below and leapt from the bow on to the sand. Making straight for the steep cliff, it vanished into the darkness, never to be seen again. Only the mutilated body of a local coal merchant's dog, discovered later, left any clue as to the savage nature of the missing beast.

Anxious moments indeed were in store for any vessel which attempted to cross the bar in rough weather. For Captain Sakki, master of the *Dmitry,* it was a task which was accomplished successfully. His good fortune provided inspiration for Bram Stoker's novel *Dracula.* *(Photograph Courtesy P. Pickles)*

Visitors to Whitby today who are of a nervous disposition may rest assured that to venture into the graveyard on the East Cliff involves no danger. Those with a taste for the macabre, meanwhile, will have no difficulty in purchasing a copy of the novel at local bookshops.

The year following the *Dmitry* incident tragedy struck the Freeman family when Henry Freeman's brother was involved in a dreadful accident.

William had carried on the trade of brickmaking in the port. After his wife died in 1881 he was left to bring up the children. By 1886 he had rooms in Jackson's lodging house.

It was there that one Sunday morning in March William Freeman was seated beside a table in front of the fire. In the same room were his two sons, Henry and James, Robert Dawson, a labourer and William Footit, a painter. Robert Dawson had given the boy, Henry, a pair of braces and William had a knife in his hand to make fresh holes so that the braces might fit the lad. James was sewing a button onto Henry's trousers while Henry stood near the table.

William Freeman suggested that the boys peel some potatoes for dinner. Henry began to laugh and his father became angry. William threatened to give Henry a clout around the ear if he did not stop. The boy refused and William stood up to clout him. Unfortunately, Henry ducked and ran straight onto the knife in his father's hand.

Young Henry cried out "Oh dear, you have struck me," and then collapsed. William picked up the boy, carried him across the floor and tried to staunch the bleeding. James dashed out to find his sister, while a local surgeon, Doctor Semple, was sent for. The wound, however, proved to be fatal. When the doctor arrived, Henry was already dead. The boy was only 14 years of age.

The inquest was held at the Black Horse hotel in Church Street, George Buchanan, the coroner, presiding. After hearing evidence from those present the jury decided that the deceased was accidently killed by falling against the point of a knife held in his father's left hand.

In spite of this verdict William Freeman was arrested and brought before the magistrates. After hearing the evidence in court, the magistrates agreed with the coroner and decided to exonerate William Freeman completely. Nevertheless the whole episode was to weigh heavily on William. He moved to the Shambles where he died the next year, a broken man.

By 1886 Henry's own prospects were improving. That summer, he took charge of another herring coble called the *Louie Beckett*. The ownership was a joint one with fellow Lifeboatmen Walter Currie and E. Gash. Freeman registered the boat from 23rd of July just at the start of the herring season.

In 1887 the *Harriott Forteath III* was sold. The old *Whitworth* left Whitby for a new home in August. She was replaced by a new 34 foot lifeboat built by Forrest of Limehouse, carrying ten oars and fitted with all the latest appliances. Named the *Christopher,* Henry used her, shortly after her arrival, in the National Lifeboat race, but his luck did not improve. Of the three boats which competed, the *Christopher* came in third.

During 1888 Henry Freeman lost a valued colleague. John Storr had been his ablest assistant in the lifeboat. Like Freeman he was a fisherman, but unlike Freeman he was a local man, Whitby born and bred. Generations of Storrs had been fishermen before him. He was only a child when his father was drowned in the 1861 lifeboat disaster, but was soon to follow in his father's seafaring ways. As a young man he served as an apprentice on the brig *Prince Albert*. Afterwards he became a fisherman in the port of Whitby, using lines and nets, just as Henry Freeman did.

At the age of twenty-four, John Storr was the master of his first boat, the *Beta* owned by Thomas Storr. It was one of several boats he was either to own or be master of. Three of these were named after stars: *North Star, Star of Peace* and the *Star of Hope.*

But, John Storr is best remembered for his lifeboat work. He was a courageous man willing to put his life at risk to save others. During the 1870's he went out on many rescue missions serving first with Samuel Lacy, then with Freeman. He was one of the *Robert Whitworth's* crew which salvaged the *Svadsfare*. Other rescues included the *Christopher Hansteen, SS Oscar, J.H Lorentzen, Elizabeth Austen, John Snell* and the *Good Intent.* John was second coxswain to Henry Freeman on that fateful January day in 1881 when the lifeboat was taken over the moors to rescue the crew of the *Visiter.* The words of encouragement he gave when many of the lifeboat oars had been broken were never forgotten and the Robin Hood's Bay folk rewarded him by making him coxswain of their new lifeboat. It was a post he was to hold for about two years.

After his spell at Robin Hood's Bay, John Storr remained associated with the Upgang lifeboat. Like the names of the fishing vessels he owned he was a "bright star" in the company of his fellow men. But like all bright stars he burnt himself out quickly and died suddenly on the 28th of June 1888. He was only 38.

Many attended the funeral service conducted by the Reverend Denniss, curate of St. John's, and hundreds of weather-beaten fishermen lined the graveside. It was a moving spectacle which demonstrated how popular John Storr was amongst Whitby folk right up to his death. For Henry it was another blow. He had lost the best of his lifeboatmen. Theirs had been a close friendship and Henry must have been deeply saddened by John Storr's early demise.

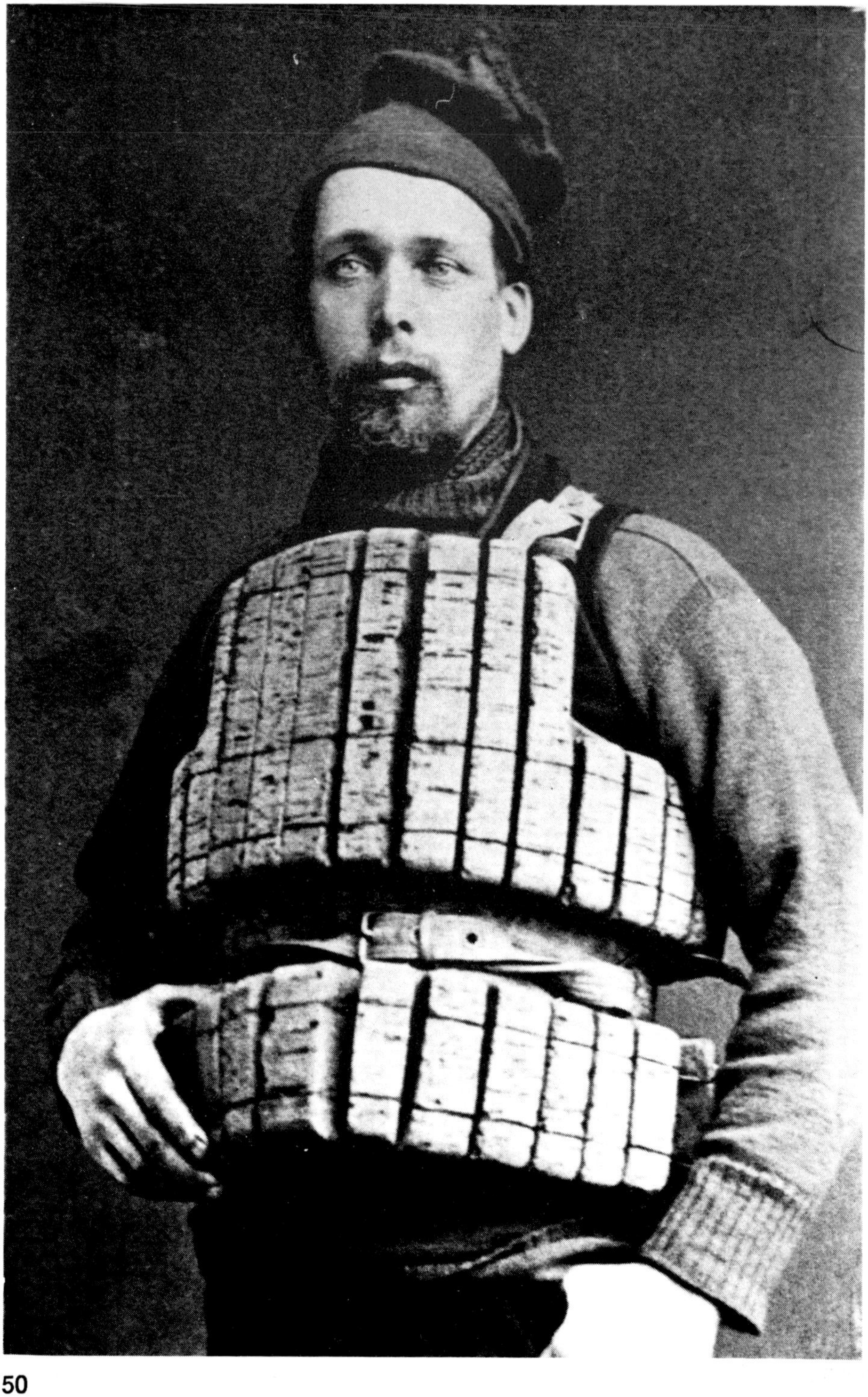

The decade had been a bad one for Henry, but time is a healer and Henry's past troubles were eventually forgotten by the majority of Whitby folk. Henry seems to have mellowed with age. Frank Meadow Sutcliffe has captured the change in the man in his later photographic studies of the veteran fisherman. Yet, Henry was still capable of the occasional outburst as was clear after the 1890 Regatta.

The lifeboat race again was the cause of Henry's anger. On the day of the event seven lifeboats were entered in the race, but only two actually turned up. The Whitby crew had finally tired of the struggle, the *Robert and Mary Ellis* being such a heavy boat. Henry and his crew wanted a handicapping system introduced to make the race fairer. In fact only the Upgang lifeboat, *Joseph Sykes* under Thomas Langlands and the *Free Gardner* from Redcar were there at the start. A third boat, the *Fishermens Friend*, was entered at short notice with a scratch crew. The race went ahead and was won by Langlands, while the ancient *Fishermens Friend* finished last, but still collected third prize.

It was a disappointing race. The *Whitby Times* even suggested that the Whitby crew had persuaded the other crews to stay away. Freeman strongly denied this and had a letter published in the same paper to show his feelings. Being unable to write, Henry must have dictated the essence of the letter which was published as follows:

Sir-Statements being in circulation to the effect that the crew of the *Robert and Mary Ellis* asked the Regatta Committee to guarantee them £1 each to compete in the lifeboat race in the late aquatic sports, and that the Upgang men offered to change boats with them, I, as coxswain of the *Robert and Mary Ellis*, emphatically deny the truth of both assertions, and ask permission to give your readers the true facts of the case. We have, for several years past, taken part in a race, our chance of winning which was - taking the difference in the weight of the Upgang boat and ours into consideration - hopeless. Having been engaged in so many "forlorn hopes" we this year asked the committee for a time allowance of 15 seconds, being less than those who know the relative merits of the boats say we had a right to get. Our reasonable request was refused, and therefore we declined to again follow in the wake of the *Joseph Sykes*. We have hitherto done our best to afford amusement, and uphold the honour of our native town, when fighting against odds, but repeated attempts to achieve the impossible wearied us. It is ungenerous, therefore, in a section of the public to impute to unworthy motives our refusal to again take part in a contest we have not a thousand-to-one chance of winning. Given the start we are justly entitled to, we are able to give a good account of ourselves against all comers.

I am sir, yours, Henry Freeman, Coxswain
Whitby, September 3rd, 1890.

John Storr was the son of the lifeboat coxswain killed in the 1861 lifeboat disaster. John was Robin Hood Bay's first coxswain and second coxswain at Whitby. He died young at the age of 38. *(Photograph Courtesy Tom Wood)*

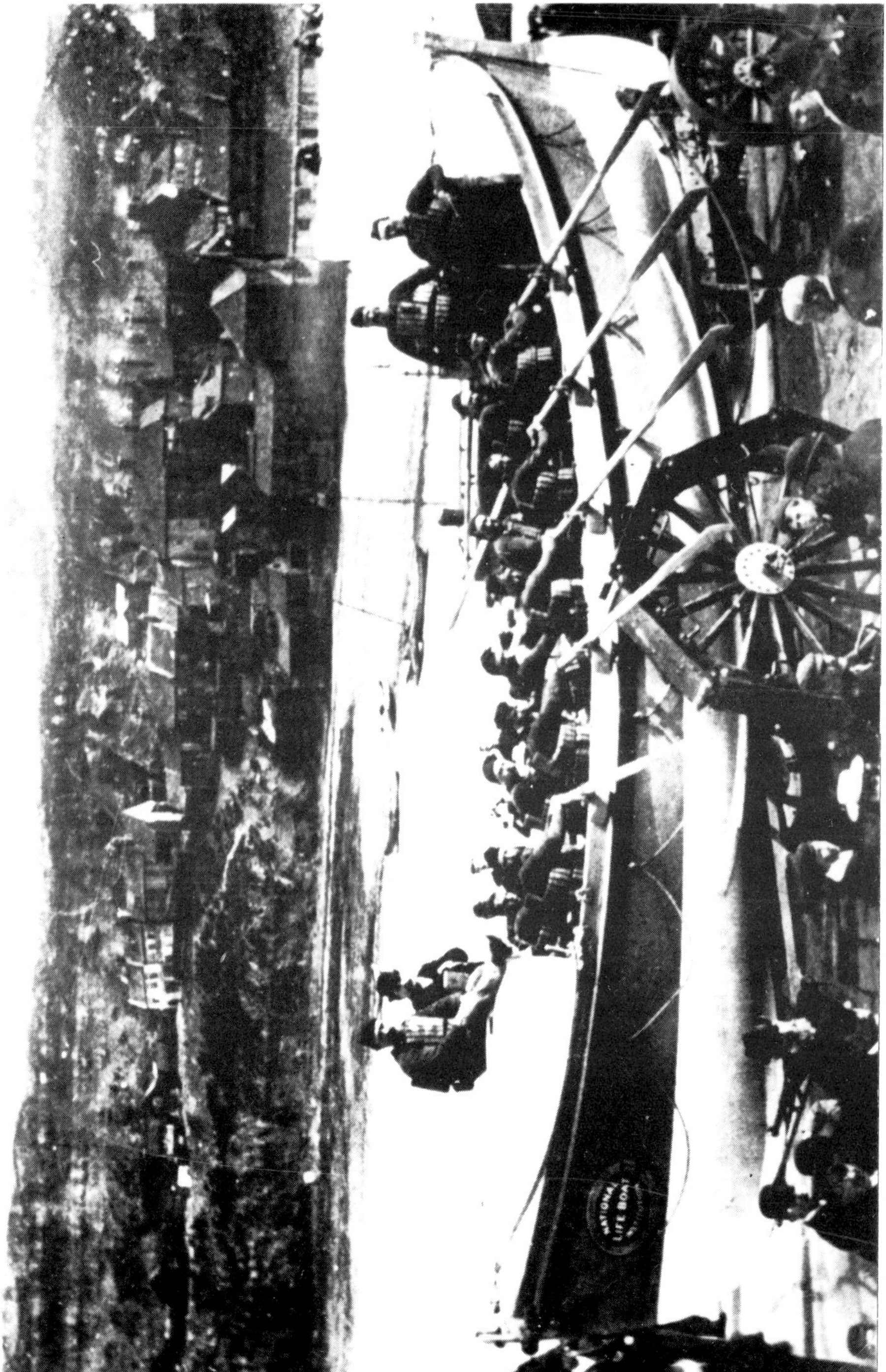
NATIONAL
LIFE BOAT

By now Freeman and his men were no longer satisfied merely to participate. They wanted an opportunity to win a fair race. Winning fairly was something that mattered also to the Upgang coxswain. The next week Thomas Langlands had a letter published in the *Whitby Times* in which he interpreted Freeman's letter as a challenge. He offered to run the race again over the same course using this time the Runswick boat which was of a similar size to the *Robert and Mary Ellis*. In that way Langlands hoped for an equal race.

Freeman apparently did not take up Langlands' offer, at least such a race is not recorded in the local papers. Perhaps Henry Freeman felt he had made his point about handicapping. Certainly the Regatta committee took notice of the events and the lifeboat race was dropped, albeit temporarily, from future programmes.

Not long before this, fate gave Henry a small crumb of satisfaction at seeing an old adversary suffer some bad luck. The architect of his most serious troubles, Henry Bell, found himself on the receiving end of British justice in May 1889. William Smallwood, a blacksmith, sued Henry Bell for money owed to him.

The case was heard at the County Court on the 20th May before M.A. Bedwell. William Smallwood had done some work on two boats then owned by Henry Bell called the *Margaret* and the *Nomad*. The amount came to £3 -6s-2d. Ironically it was a similar figure to the cost of lines lost by Bell in 1883 when Freeman was accused of theft. Much of the case revolved around what work had been done and how much had been paid. Henry Bell challenged all the statements and provided bills and receipts to justify his actions. He showed a lot of skill in his defence, but it became clear that money was owing for work done on the *Nomad*. In Bell's own words the *Nomad* had done 'badly' and he could not pay at the time. Henry Bell claimed to have later 'paid up for the year'.

When Smallwood disagreed, Bell retorted "Don't tell lies". It was a remark which was immediately censured by the judge. "Nice language, that, in a court of justice," he said. "Don't talk like that in a court of justice, for the judge might take a different view as to where the lie is." Bell remained adamant that he had paid, but the judge formed a different opinion and upheld Smallwood's claim. Henry Bell had fourteen days to find the money.

The decade had brought Freeman a succession of traumas and was undoubtedly the worst period of his life. With a sick wife he had endured a difficult court case where his whole future could have been in jeopardy. Later conflicts threatened his position as coxswain. The deaths of his brother William and nephew Henry brought deep personal grief into his life. Yet Henry was able to overcome all these setbacks and carry on. Whatever his innermost feelings he maintained a tough exterior.

The lifeboat *Christopher* with Freeman at the helm.

J. T. Ross *(Courtesy Jeff Morris)*

CHAPTER 11

HENRY FREEMAN AMBASSADOR AND SPOKESMAN

During the 1880s the winds of change were blowing hard at Britain's fishing industry. By the end of the decade moves were afoot with typical Victorian efficiency to organise the industry under a system of regional boards. It was a step which was to benefit the fishermen in some ways but to handicap them in many others.

The 1888 Sea Fishery Act gave County Councils or Municipal Borough Councils powers to set up local fishery districts where British fishermen had the exclusive rights of fishing. Effectively it was to create a three mile limit around the shores of the United Kingdom. Local Committees were empowered to create bye-laws to regulate and control the type of fishing carried on within these limits in order to conserve stocks and protect livelihoods.

At first each district had to be defined and meetings were held involving all the interested parties. From the discussions came all sorts of ideas, but one in particular was favoured by many and that was the creation of a Board whose jurisdiction encompassed the whole of the Yorkshire coast.

Henry Freeman was elected as one of the Whitby Fishermen's representatives. It was a tremendous vote of confidence in him after his recent troubles.

He had been invited in the past to speak on fishing matters. One such occasion had been in March 1881 when the subject of coloured warning lights on fishing trawlers had been under discussion. The issue was one of safety at sea and Freeman was amongst a number of fishermen who gave evidence.

As a spokesman for the Whitby fishing community, Henry Freeman was to work closely with Robert Elliott Pannett, a Whitby Lawyer and County Councillor who had chosen to champion the fishermen's cause. At Mr Pannett's instigation a meeting was held at the West End Room, Whitby, on Saturday 13th April 1889 where the proposed Fishing Board was discussed. The matters of Bye-Laws and jurisdictions were talked over and then the suggestion was broached that the East Riding and North Riding Committees unite to exercise control over the whole Yorkshire coast.

Henry Freeman voiced his dissatisfaction with the idea and insisted that the North Riding should remain separate. In his opinion, Whitby's interests could too easily become subordinate to those of Bridlington. Trawling suited the Bridlington men and he feared that inshore trawling would be endorsed to the detriment of the Whitby men.

Alderman R E Pannett   *(Courtesy of Whitby Literary and Philosophical Society)*

When it came to a vote, there was an overwhelming show of hands against inshore trawling and for a separate North Riding Committee. Further discussions followed including a claim from Thomas Gains that steam trawling was destroying the fish. At the close, Robert Pannett was authorised to take their opinions to a meeting at Scarborough on the following Tuesday.

Unfortunately there was little Robert Pannett could do for the Whitby men during the conference at Scarborough Town Hall. Notable representatives from both North and East Riding Councils were present and others from local fishing organisations, indicating the importance of the debate. It soon became clear that the consensus of opinion was to have the whole of the Yorkshire coast declared as one Sea Fisheries District. Robert Pannett tried unsuccessfully to draw attention to the conflict of interest between the fishermen of the East and North Ridings. Despite his efforts, a motion was proposed to apply to the Board of Trade for the creation of a Fishery District comprising the whole of the Yorkshire Coast. Pannett was not prepared to support the resolution or any amendments made during the debate. Nevertheless, the motion was carried and moves were set in progress to establish the North Eastern Sea Fisheries Committee.

Robert Pannett was appointed to serve on that Committee and Henry Freeman continued in the role of fishermen's representative. Another was Henry Bell, his antagonist in the stolen lines dispute.

At the start of 1890 Henry Freeman went to Beverley to discuss the setting up of the Board and the actual areas it would cover. The Chief Fisheries Inspector of the Board of Trade presided over the inquiry at Beverley's East Riding Session Court. Members from the East and North Riding Councils were there with others from Hull Town Council. During the meeting it transpired that the Board of Trade preferred an even larger authority than first envisaged. They were also opposed to any area finishing in the middle of an estuary as would be the case at the Humber. It was then proposed to extend the fishery district to include the Yorkshire Coast and part of North Lincolnshire, which geographically was defined as being from Redcar south of the Tees to Ingomells in Lincolnshire. The new district would include the large fishing ports of Hull and Grimsby. Matters such as inshore trawling would be dealt with when the Committee was established. Each Council was left to decide whether they went into the district or not, but after the delegates had gone away all voted to join the enlarged district.

The North Eastern Sea Fisheries Committee came into existence at the end of 1890 and the first bye-law they passed prohibited inshore trawling within the district subject to a £20 fine for the first offence and £10 for every day the offence continued.

However, it seems this bye-law was not strictly observed and the practice still went on.

The port of Whitby had become a small cog in the newly organised fishing industry machine. The Whitby men were to rue the day that happened, for very little in the new order was to benefit them. To make matters worse, even the herring was beginning to desert them: the fish was being caught in decreasing numbers. By 1900 the Cornish boats, once regular visitors to the port, had almost ceased to call there in their pursuit of the herring.

Henry Freeman now had two new fishing boats. The *Louie Beckett* was used for herring, while for winter line fishing he had the *Elizabeth Freeman* which was a 6 ton coble fitted with a lug sail. Freeman had bought her in 1888 to replace his old line fishing coble, the *Elizabeth,* which he afterwards sold to John Longster from Staithes.

With reduced catches, Henry and some of his fellows looked to other forms of fishing to supplement their income. In summer the salmon made their way into the River Esk from the sea to spawn. Several Whitby fishermen, Henry Freemen included, took up salmon fishing.

Licences to fish for salmon were granted to the fishermen by the Whitby Esk Board of Conservators. Salmon had become virtually extinct in the Esk, but after the Board had been set up in 1875 the numbers of salmon in the river had increased. Whitby fishermen had taken to netting them at the mouth of the river and along the sands out to sea as far`as Upgang. Weighted nets, often 400 yards in length, were set out to sea. Usually a two man boat was employed at one end while the nets were virtually fixed in one position.

The numbers of salmon being caught in this way became a source of annoyance to the Board of Conservators. They believed the fishermen were endangering the stock by stopping the passage of fish in and out of the harbour. A playground was proposed to restrict the Whitby fishermen as to where they could lay their nets. The Board wanted the use of nets to be prohibited 300 yards from the Pier End. An inquiry was held at the Police Court in Whitby on Tuesday 23rd May 1892.

At this inquiry the Board's proposal was forcibly attacked by Edward Turner who stated that there was no such playground elsewhere. The fishermen in other places were allowed to fish in the public waters. He impressed upon the Inspector that it was totally unnecessary to make a playground. For most of the season it was impossible for the men to fish because of bad weather and there was nothing whatever to stop the fish during that time. Plenty of fish got up the river, so many indeed that it became overcrowded and scores died of disease.

Freeman was one of several fishermen giving evidence. He argued that the fishermen were already restricted as to where they could fish. They could only work from the Pier to Upgang and never went south as the ground was too rocky for deep nets. He thought (sarcastically) the Board might want to make the playground there if they wished. He continued:

> "They are going to spoil our living. We can't get on very well as it is. It cost me £20 in nets last year and I was £5 in debt. Some men have done very well indeed. Last year was my first year in salmon fishing. The river has itself improved in salmon but not in small fish".

It was perhaps John Harland who voiced the opinions of many present. Their conviction was that conservation needs were not the real issue here, but lucrative fishing rights. The owners, they believed, were seeking to discriminate unfairly against the poorer fishermen in favour of the richer anglers. Under questioning Harland said that the making of the playground would have the effect of robbing the poor man of his living. Everything was against the poor man at that time; they were being robbed by the rich everywhere. Such a comment incensed the Inspector from the Board of Trade. The inquiry continued as follows:

The Inspector: "I am afraid if you talk like that I shall not listen to you."
Mr Harland "I must speak the truth."
The Inspector:"The question is how far you object to this bye-law as affecting you as a fisherman. How does it affect you?"
Mr Harland "It affects my fellow men. These poor men should not be robbed of their living for the benefit of the rich men living up the becks."

In spite of the fishermen's objections the playground was brought into being and Whitby fishermen were restricted to fishing from the sands away from the mouth of the harbour.

Further restrictions were imposed on the method by which the fishermen could catch the fish. A strict set of bye-laws gradually came into being which, if strictly enforced, might have deterred most from taking the salmon, but fortunately Mr Luke, the water bailiff, as well as the Board in general chose to turn a "blind eye" to certain practices adopted and fishing for the salmon went on.

At the start of the 1890s there was a concerted nationwide effort to raise funds for the RNLI. In Lancashire, the Lifeboat Saturday movement was created to hold collections, parades and public entertainment whose proceeds went to the RNLI. The idea was adopted by the parent body in London and the various lifeboat committees throughout the country were encouraged to engage in the fund-raising by holding annual Lifeboat Saturdays and Sundays.

At Whitby, the Lifeboat Committee considered the London directive and decided to hold a lifeboat practice to entertain the general public. They would witness the spectacle of the crews preparing for action and launching the lifeboat. Collectors would be present on the pier to receive contributions for the RNLI. The first launch was scheduled to take place at 3.00 p.m. on Saturday 20th August 1892. On the Sunday a sacred concert was to be held in the West Cliff Saloon where money would also be raised. For Henry Freeman, Thomas Langlands and their Lifeboatmen there was a new role to play, that of ambassadors for the Institution.

On the Saturday, the lifeboat was launched into a calm sea with Henry at the helm. The spectacle lacked the drama of a real rescue but still attracted the crowds. On the Sunday the concert went ahead in the West Cliff Saloon. Part of the proceedings were taken up by a lengthy speech made by the Reverend Canon Austen concerning the many memorable rescues made at Whitby. A total of £22-12s-2d was raised by the two day event, hardly enough to finance one rescue, but a start had been made in gaining public support.

In 1893 the *Yorkshire Post* organised an appeal which was to raise over £3000. It came about after the prominent citizens in Leeds noted the success of the Lancashire venture and decided to organise their own Lifeboat Saturday. This event took place on the 10th June 1893 with men from the lifeboat crews of Scarborough and Whitby taking part in the procession.

It was a spectacular parade which required much preparation. There was a small army of 170 people out along the route with their collecting boxes. There were also many fixed collecting boxes placed strategically throughout the city. Two lifeboats named the *Catherine Swift* and the *Worcestershire Cadet*, both now retired from active service, were central to the procession. The nine mile route commenced at Victoria Square outside the Town Hall, wound through the centre of the city and the outskirts and then returned to the Town Hall.

The Scarborough and Whitby lifeboat contingents arrived on the Saturday morning by train, their journeys paid for by the North Eastern Railway Company. They were dressed in their distinctive seafaring apparel. Together, the men and their gaily decked lifeboats made a colourful and memorable scene, described here by the *Yorkshire Post* :

> The two boats spick and span and proud in all the glory of new paint and bright flags were the principal objects in the profuse display of colour upon which the sun shone with undimmed splendour, just as the brave fellows in blue guernseys, cork jackets and red woollen caps were, in the eyes of the tens and hundreds of thousands, who gazed upon them with admiration, the most conspicuous and interesting personages in the demonstration.

The Whitby crew manned the *Catherine Swift*. Those present included Henry Freeman, Coxswain; Thomas Langlands, Upgang Coxswain; R.P.Robinson, 2nd Coxswain; Richard Eglon, 2nd Coxswain at Upgang; William Affleck, Bowman; Thomas Kelly, Bowman, Walter Curry, Edward Gash, Joseph Tomlinson, William Harrison, James Elders and Robert Robinson.

Both Scarborough and Whitby coxswains were introduced to the Mayor and the Mayoress. John Owston, the Scarborough coxswain, handed the Lady Mayoress a bouquet of flowers to mark the occasion. The procession then started with the lifeboats leading the way. Each was drawn on its carriage by six strong railway horses which had been lent by the London and North Western and Great Northern Railway Companies.

Whitby Lifeboat Crew on Leeds Town Hall steps, 1893. *(Courtesy of Whitby Archives)*

Whitby Life-boat crew on the steps of Leeds Town Hall, 1893, in service dress for a Life-boat Saturday procession. Left to right, front row: Thos. McGarry Kelly (bowman) U., Robert Richardson, U., Richard Eglon (2nd cox) U., Harry Freeman (coxswain) W., Thomas Langlands (coxswain) U., James Elder U. Back row: William Harrison, U., Edward Gash, W., Joseph Tomlinson, W., William Affleck (bowman) W., Pounder Robinson (2nd cox), W., Walter Corrie, W. (U. for Upgang Crew, W. for Whitby Crew).

Behind them came the Grimsby crew in a wagonette. Also in the parade was a float designed by the Grand Theatre where an actress played the role of Grace Darling rowing a boat on a painted stormy sea. Fellow members of the theatre, dressed in sailors costumes, travelled in other vehicles carrying purses attached to the end of long poles to aid the fund-raising.

The procession carried on through the industrial district of Hunslet where many engineering works and locomotive firms were established. It passed along East Street and Marsh Lane where the people lived in abject poverty. As the *Yorkshire Post* reports:

> Unwashed and unkempt residents of that locality turned out in thousands and gave their coppers or their approval. At the Workhouse and Industrial Schools special provision was made for the inmates to witness the procession. The women in their white frilled mobcaps and blue aprons and frocks enjoyed the sight immensely, smiling and waving their handkerchiefs vigorously, in strange contrast to the demeanour of the men, who gazed on the scene with a stolidity that indicated amazement rather than indifference.

On they carried past the Infirmary where rows of nurses thronged the balconies and patients stared from the windows. Ultimately they arrived back in Victoria Square, the whole spectacle having taken some four hours. After the procession all who had taken part were invited to tea in the crypt of the Town Hall. In the evening a special concert was arranged to gather further funds for the Lifeboat cause.

The *Yorkshire Post* had approached the Whitby Lifeboat Committee for a photograph of Henry Freeman. However, the Committee was steadfast in their decision not to provide one. No reason was given in their minutes, on that occasion, but when other requests were presented in later years they made it clear that it was not their policy to supply photographs as it might lead to ill-feeling between the coxswains.

Whitby's Lifeboat Saturday and Sunday were held on the 2nd and 3rd of September 1893 and were an exact repeat of those in 1892. A little more money was raised but nothing on the scale of the Leeds demonstration.

In 1894 several lifeboat demonstrations were held in the North East where Whitby was called upon to send its lifeboat crews. In June the Lifeboat Committee minutes record the intention of sending both the Whitby and Upgang crews to Huddersfield. Yet on the day neither crew put in an appearance. Both the lifeboats used in the Leeds demonstration were there; the *Catherine Swift* took part with the Fleetwood lifeboat crew, while the *Worcester Cadet* followed later manned by a crew of "pretty girls". Whitby Lifeboat minutes offer no reason for the non-attendance at the demonstration.

Early in September requests from Hull and Halifax left the Whitby Committee with a difficult decision to make. Being careful not to favour either Coxswain, the Committee sent Freeman and his Whitby crew to Halifax on the 1st September where they took part in the demonstration in Shibden Park. Langlands and his Upgang men were sent to Hull the next Saturday.

This concern for fairness by the Whitby Committee seems a little strange. Hitherto the Upgang Coxswain had always fulfilled a subordinate role to the Whitby Coxswain, but clearly Langlands was now being elevated to the same status. Was it the deliberate policy of the Committee to deflate Freeman's ego? Or were they just paying due recognition to Thomas Langlands?

There were those amongst the Whitby Committee who saw Langlands as Freeman's successor. These gentlemen did not want to have Langlands dissatisfied with his lot and perhaps looked for opportunities to reassure him. It must have been difficult for Langlands to follow in the wake of Henry Freeman whose every trip in the lifeboat found some mention in the local press.

It is understandable that the Committee would wish to appear even-handed. Jealousy and bad feeling between the Coxswains would benefit nobody. Members of the Whitby Committee might even have resented Freeman's popularity. After all the majority of them were wealthy businessmen from the upper class of Whitby society while Freeman was working class. Perhaps they felt Freeman should know his place and not seek a higher station in life.

They must have been in a dilemma. Freeman was the only serving crew member to have gained medals for bravery and so would be a natural focus for public attention at any lifeboat demonstration. For that reason Henry Freeman was Whitby's favourite ambassador to champion the lifeboat cause.

The Lifeboat Saturday at Halifax was a fine one for Henry Freeman and his crew because of the warmth and kindness they received during their brief stay there. They were given rooms in the Trevelyan Hotel in the town. It must have been a rare treat for the fishermen to stay in a hotel and take life a little easier.

On the Saturday the Demonstration took the form of a huge procession through Halifax. For the bystanders witnessing the event, it took fifty minutes to pass. All manner of people and organisations took part in what proved to be a very colourful event. Even the local Fire service were there, the gleaming brass of the fire engines making an impressive sight. Several of the trade societies (as they were known before the term trade union was invented) marched along raising their multi-coloured banners aloft. Superbly groomed horses pulled float after float, each one brilliantly decked out.

⋖ The Lifeboat "Alfred Trower," ⋗

Belonging to the ROYAL NATIONAL LIFEBOAT INSTITUTION, was presented to the Institution by HENRY TROWER, Esq., of St. Mary-at-Hill, London, and by his friends, in memory of Mr. ALFRED TROWER, a well-known Yachtsman. The Boat was stationed at Tramore, Co. Waterford, in 1880.

✥ THIS BOAT ✥

Will be Launched on the Lake at Shibden Park

On SEPTEMBER 1st, after the arrival of the Procession,

BY THE WHITBY LIFEBOAT CREW,

Who will give illustrations of the mode of rescuing those in distress.

THE BOAT WILL AFTERWARDS PLY FOR HIRE ON THE LAKE.

FARES 3d. EACH.

Advertisement included in the 1894 Halifax Lifeboat Saturday Programme price 1d.

> On Sunday, September, 2nd, at 8 p.m.,
> A
> # LIFEBOAT SERVICE
> WILL BE HELD
> ## IN THE NEW PUBLIC HALL.
>
> *Members of the* **Whitby Lifeboat Crew** *will relate their experiences, and Illustrations will be given by the aid of the Lime Light.*
>
> A SILVER COLLECTION WILL BE MADE ON BEHALF OF THE LIFEBOAT SATURDAY FUND.
>
> GEORGE SCARBOROUGH, } Honorary
> ARTHUR TAYLOR, } Secretaries.
> OATES WEBSTER, General Secretary.
>
> Lifeboat Offices: 21a, Silver Street, Halifax.

Reproduced from the 1894 Halifax Lifeboat Saturday Programme.

At the heart of the procession came the *Mary Stamford* lifeboat with Henry Freeman and his crew aboard. The parade ended in Shibden Park where an entrance fee was charged to assist the Lifeboat funds. Various events were organised within the Park, but the highlight was the launching of another lifeboat the *Alfred Trower*, into the lake. Freeman and his crew rowed around the lake and even performed a staged rescue of a drowning man before returning to the shore.

The Whitby Crew were then taken back into town aboard a char-a-banc. That evening they attended a show at the Royal Theatre. Between the acts all the lifeboatmen were taken onto the stage and introduced to the audience which responded with hearty cheering. Henry Freeman then came forward to thank everyone for the warm reception they had received.

On the Sunday the Whitby Lifeboat Crew were given a conducted tour of the Fire Station and were then driven over the moor in a wagonette. A lifeboat service was held in the New Public Hall on Sunday evening. It was due to start at 8.15 p.m., but by 7.30p.m. the Hall was full. During the proceedings Henry Freeman was again called upon to speak. As he rose to his feet, people in the hall cheered. The silver medal he won was proudly displayed on his chest. Henry admitted he was not a talker but went on to describe the events of the 1881 rescue when the crew of the brig *Visiter* were saved.

The Halifax demonstration was a great success which raised £519 for the Lifeboat cause. It also provided many happy memories for the Whitby Lifeboatmen, and Henry and his crew made a return visit there in 1899.

In Whitby, the 1894 Public Lifeboat Practice was confined to the Saturday. The Sunday concert had to be abandoned. It was discovered that it was illegal to hold a concert in the West Cliff Saloon owing to the rigid observance of the Sabbath.

Meanwhile Henry Freeman continued to act as a spokesman on fishing matters as bureaucracy threatened the livelihoods of his fellow fishermen. At the December 1893 meeting of the North Eastern Sea Fisheries Committee, restrictions were considered on the use of certain types of fishing nets. In particular the Offal, Seine, Sand Eel and Trammel nets all came under close scrutiny after Mr Ashford reported these nets destroyed immature fish. Several members of the Committee then proposed that a ban be imposed on the nets except for the purpose of taking bait.

Robert Pannett was concerned that such a ban would affect the Whitby fishermen who used sand eel nets. The sand eels were caught for bait between May and July. It was a cheap form of bait for long line fishing and if Whitby men were prevented from using the net they would suffer hardship. He persuaded the Committee to have their inspector, Mr Ashford, examine the matter further. After his inquiries at Whitby and Scarborough, Mr Ashford reported very little hardship would occur if their use was prohibited. Mr Pannett managed to stall a final decision on the issue by suggesting a special sub-committee be appointed to investigate the problem further.

The inquiry was held at the Crown Hotel, Whitby on Saturday 3rd March 1894. The Chairman of the NESFC, W.H.St.Quintin presided. Robert Pannett first presented the case for retaining the sand eel net. His first witness was Thomas Langlands who explained the use of the nets which were employed between Whitby and Sandsend. He stated that mussels were normally used for bait but these cost as much as 3s a day while the sand eel cost nothing. Several men had a share in a sand eel net and all they caught were the eels. There was often a water bailiff present and he would notice if any immature fish were caught. Thomas Langlands' testimony was supported by Henry Freeman, Henry Bell, John James Storr and Robert Pounder Robinson. The case having been made for the use of the net, Henry Freeman was then called upon to describe the limits within which the fishermen would like the nets to be used. These limits were then agreed and incorporated into the NESFC Bye-Laws.

There was a rather amusing incident involving the Sea Fisheries Committee inspector, Mr W.Ashford, when he embarked on a purge of Crab and Lobster fishing. Certain minimum sizes were laid down in the Bye-Laws and Mr Ashford made surprise visits to different seaports during April 1894. At Bridlington he examined barrels of crabs ready for despatch and returned nearly a hundred crabs to the sea. Several catches at Filey and Flamborough were seized and immature crabs were returned to the water. On arrival at Whitby he found not one undersize crab on the boats or along the shore. In his report to the Committee he wondered if word had preceded him. More likely the subtle hand of Robert Pannett was at work here.

Several of Whitby's fishermen were called to give evidence on the 19th October 1895 concerning the mininum sizes of crabs and lobsters which could be caught. The NESFC were seeking to increase the minimum size permitted and were testing out the fishermen's reactions. Meetings were held in different ports to gain an overall picture. Mr Pannett was present at the Whitby meeting as well as a large body of fishermen. The proportion of Whitby fishermen who carried out this trade was small compared to the line and herring men. Henry Bell was the chief witness though Thomas Langlands and Richard Eglon were also called.

At the start of 1896 Robert Pannett was involved with the NESFC Shellfish Sub-Committee. For some time they had been considering ways of culturing mussels to supplement the line fishermen's supply of bait. On the 6th of March Mr Ashford and the expert conducting the survey arrived in Whitby to examine the Esk for sites suitable for mussel culture. Freeman and Robinson were on hand to take them around the river in their coble. After examining several sites a portion of the Colliers Hope was set aside to grow mussels as a test area.

Despite the Bye-Laws, inshore trawling continued to make inroads into the Whitby fishermen's living. Calls were made for the Fisheries Committee to purchase a boat to patrol the Three-Mile Limit in order to safeguard the fishermen's interests. Robert Pannett argued against this course of action. He believed this would be an unnecessary expense particularly as the coble fishermen were vigilant enough. In any case, he felt one boat would not be enough to root out the practice.

Matters were not helped by the man responsible for policing these Bye-Laws, W.H. Ashford. Mr Ashford was given the post of Fisheries Officer during August 1893 at the age of 41. Previously he had been for six years manager of the Port of Hull Trawl Fishermens Society! Whilst he held his new post very few prosecutions were brought and then the fines were pitifully small for those convicted.

Eventually it was decided to purchase a fishing vessel to patrol the district, but the damage had been done. For Whitby's fishermen now found it even harder to make a living.

Early in 1897 there was widespread concern in Whitby about the lack of fish. This concern is reflected in a newspaper interview the following year with a Whitby fisherman. It is quite possible that this was Henry Freeman for the man was referred to as a well-known veteran fisherman. Few held stronger views against inshore trawling than Henry, himself. The interview makes clear that the fishermen were reluctant to inform on those breaking the Bye-Laws and had very little desire to testify in court even though the matter directly affected them. Part of the text is given below:

Extract from the *Whitby Gazette* 25th November 1898

When our representative went to the well known fisherman alluded to for the purpose of having a short chat with him, he found the veteran occupant sat over a cosy fire in a well-lighted and ventilated room. Upon entering and being well acquainted with him, the hardy fisherman exclaimed :-

"Now, what are you after this time?"

"Oh", said our reporter, "I've just come to have a short conversation with you, as you appear to be a good authority, as to whether it is a fact that the fishing trade at this port is retrograding?"

"Oh, fearfully", was the reply; "it's been going from bad to worse for some time now, but more particularly during the past two or three years. Several fishermen have gone away to sea, and others have gone to Hartlepool, Middlesbrough, Stockton, and other places in search of employment; for they cannot live here. What, there's nobody going to sea now, compared with what there was at this period of the year a few years ago!"

"What do you attribute this falling off to, then?" enquired the reporter.

"Why, them trawlers."

"I thought their operations were debarred within the limit of three miles from shore?" observed the reporter.

"Aye, but they come within a mile from shore; you can see that very often. The scarcity of fish is almost entirely due to the mauling and maiming by the trawlers."

"Then what do your catches average?"

"Well, if you get a box (about twenty) you do very well indeed. If you get two score haddocks, or small codlings, it is considered a very big catch; in fact, people want to know where you have been to get them. There was a time when you used to get twenty score in a day, but you can go to the same place now and can't get one score. In fact, I don't know what's going to become of us. I know if I'd been a bit younger I should have gone away myself."

"Well, you seem to make plenty for a subsistence."

"Aye, it's all right talking, but you can go to sea and come back out of pocket. I was off two days last week, and realised about 8s. for the catch, and my expenses came to more than that. In fact, I was off one day, and got 4s.3d. for the catch and the expenses alone amounted to 6s.3d."

"Could you suggest any remedy?"

"Oh, there's nothing but stopping the trawlers. We might manage to get a bit of bread if they were kept outside the limit, but it's a difficult job keeping them out. What, even in Staithes there's ever so many houses been vacated on account of the fishermen having had to go away to gain a livelihood. In fact, this year there's only about half the number of boats fishing."

Henry Freeman could speak passionately about matters which concerned him. His role as spokesman for the Whitby fishermen revolved around what he knew and what affected his living. He was vehemently against inshore trawling and was also interested in the preservation of bait. The restriction of the sand eel net's use affected him personally as did the supply of mussels. He spoke out against the restrictions in salmon fishing because that affected him likewise.

His voice carried conviction and his name carried weight because of his heroic deeds as Coxswain of the lifeboat. With his fellow representatives he helped the Whitby folk to defend their own interests against the policies of the North Eastern Sea Fisheries Organisation which was concerned more with the interests of Hull and Grimsby than of Whitby. In the event what was achieved was somewhat less than what was desired.

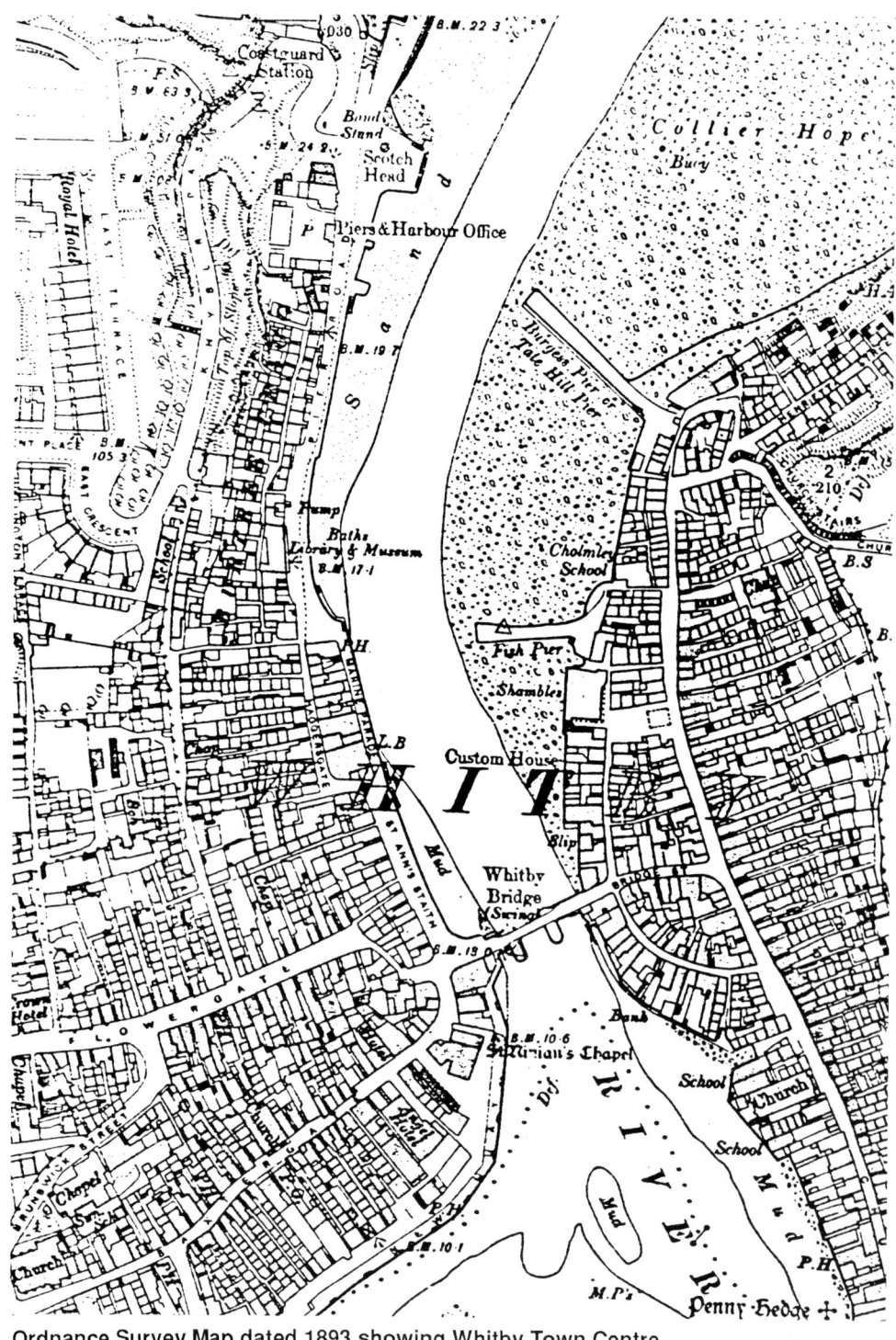

Ordnance Survey Map dated 1893 showing Whitby Town Centre.

CHAPTER 12

THE FREEMANS IN WHITBY

Only a brief walk separated the homes of Robert Pannett and Henry Freeman but their lives were set worlds apart. Robert Pannett resided on the West Cliff at 14, Normanby Terrace, among Whitby's wealthy and influential elite. Henry Freeman, however, lived in one of the town's many tenements. Huddled together up narrow yards, these overcrowded buildings were the cramped and primitive living quarters of Whitby's working classes.

The contrast was stark. Robert Pannett's house was quite a fashionable residence. Behind the white Yorkshire stone facade and walls thick enough to deaden the strongest wind were splendid rooms containing delicate friezework around the walls. Across the ceilings and over the hallways was elaborate artwork. The upper floors held the servants' quarters where the housekeeper and the other domestics were accommodated. The house in which Freeman lived was spartan by comparison. A few basic rooms was all he could afford on his income as a fisherman.

When Henry came to Whitby, one of his early addresses was at Boltons Buildings, Cliff Street. Built of durable stone its three storeys housed at one time twenty-one residents.

Sometime after his marriage to Elizabeth Busfield he moved to live in a yard behind Church Street. This was one of Whitby's longest roads. From the base of St Mary's steps it ran along the east side of the port to Spital Bridge. On one side of the street lay the River Esk and on the other a steep slope rose to the East Cliffs. Because of the lack of land houses were built wherever possible. They crowded the waterfront reaching down to the sand itself. On the opposite side an almost unbroken line of buildings faced Church Street and behind them tenements were constructed.

Most of the houses on Church Street had a row of tenements behind them. Here the poorer classes dwelled often paying rent to the landlord who lived in the house on Church Street. Each yard was in reality a small community where the Jet workers slaved at their polishing wheels, the fishermen mended their nets and the artisans eked out a meagre existence.

These yards had a certain atmosphere about them which has been captured so vividly through the lens of Frank Meadow Sutcliffe, the Whitby Photographer. His portraits in black and white almost come alive such is their clarity and content. In his photographs the tenements are shown to be built of handmade bricks whose uneven surfaces stand out against the mortar binding them. Doors and windows are functional and lack often the vaguest trace of decoration. Huge wooden shutters hang beside the multi-paned windows to keep out the worst of the elements. The only ornaments are the fishermen's tackle and wicker baskets.

Pannett House, 14 Normanby Terrace, was once the home of the distinguished solicitor, Robert Pannett. Emma Freeman, Henry's second wife, was housekeeper here, in 1881. Today Pannett House is a guest house. *(Photograph Ray Shill)*

Stricklands Yard, the Cragg. This portrait by Sutcliffe shows how close some of the houses were built to the Cliff face, and how cramped were the living conditions.
(Photograph Frank Meadow Sutcliffe)

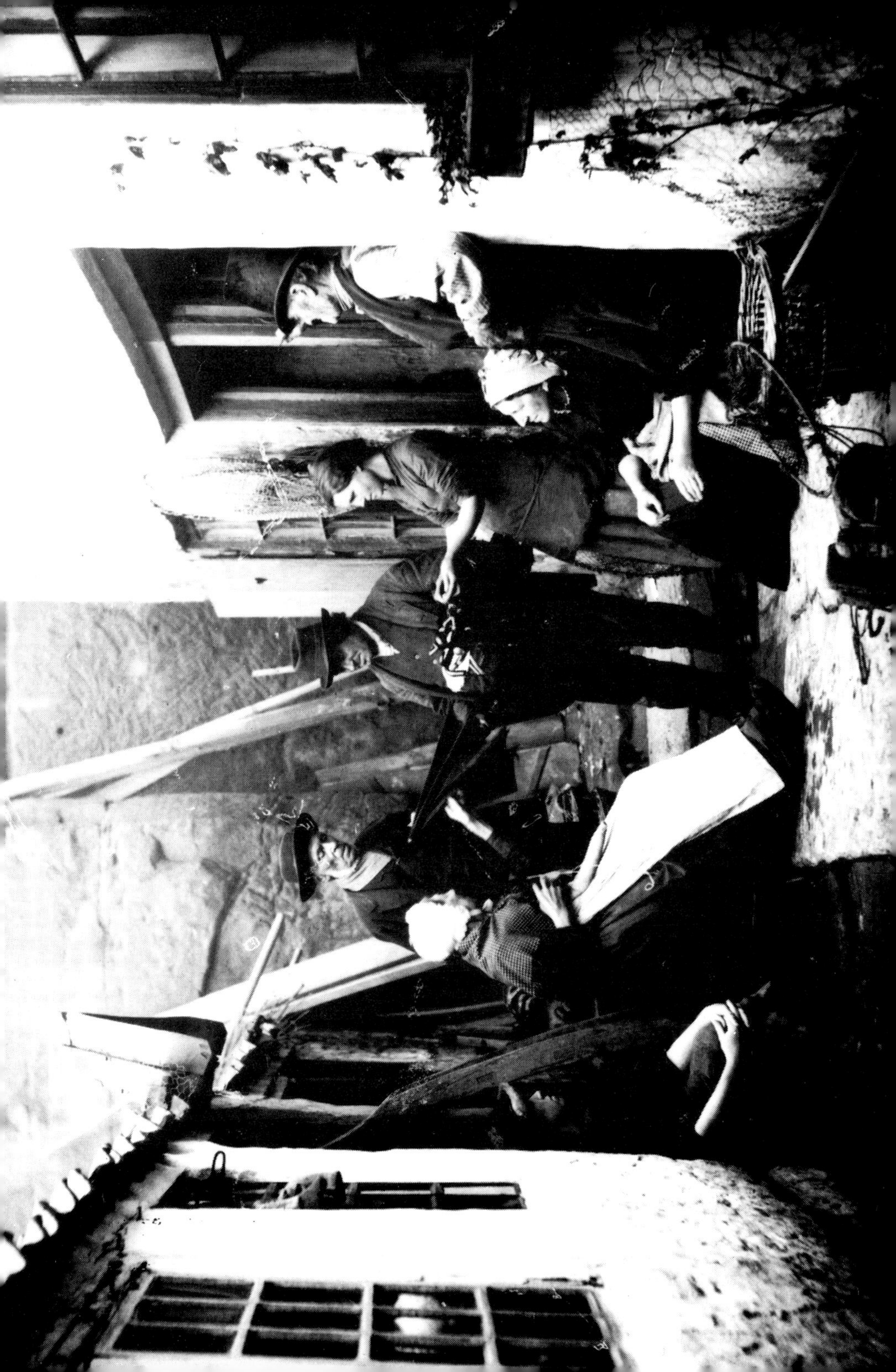

Frank Sutcliffe's studies are alive with human detail. Women abound in long dark dresses and aprons. Headscarves often cover their hair or shawls their shoulders. Usually the groups are posed as they sit around bent on some discourse. Sometimes they work busily skaning mussels and baiting lines. At other times they merely sit to pass the time of day. Perhaps they talk about their husbands away in their boats shooting their lines or exchange gossip about each other.

The men appear in different guises. The fishermen carrying their lines wear guernseys, wide-brimmed hats and tall boots. The Jet workers are identified by their waistcoats and collarless shirts. Some "gaffer" might appear with jacket and neckerchief, and sometimes to complete the picture small children in smocks and frocks mingle with the adult groups.

In one such yard was the home of Thomas Busfield when he had become successful in the Jet Trade. Here Elizabeth Busfield had spent her youth and later was to live with her new husband Henry Freeman. No doubt Henry and Elizabeth stayed with Thomas Busfield at first but soon they had their own dwelling in the yard, near to Elizabeth's parents.

According to the 1871 and 1881 census the name of this yard was Kilvington's Yard. This name is derived from John Kilvington who carried on the business of hairdresser and perfumer at No.85 Church Street with his son Benjamin. Both ladies' and gentlemen's hair was cut on the premises often in private booths.

Kilvington's Yard was also known as Clark's Yard, presumably after another local worthy, and it is this second name which has survived to the present. Today, a sign reading Clark's Yard appears on the wall in the entry between 85 and 84 Church Street, and most town directories commonly refer to the place by this name.

Each yard was a little world in its own right. The residents included quite a cross section of people besides the Jet workers and the fishermen. This will be readily apparent from the table below:

THE RESIDENTS OF KILVINGTONS YARD 1881

Francis Frankland	Jet Manufacturer
James Speedy	Tailor
Samuel Davenport	Painter
Henry Freeman	Fisherman
William Wustell	Jet Manufacturer
Henry Kitching	Painter
Thomas Nicholson	Ironworker
Elizabeth Busfield	Wife of Jet Manufacturer
Charles Fryer	Tinsmith

......details as per 1881 census.

84/85 Church Street. No. 85 was the home of the Kilvington family. In 1882, the house was offered for sale and Benjamin Kilvington moved to Flowergate.

Modern view of Clark's Yard (centre left) looking down on Church Street from the East Cliff. The houses in this part have altered little since Freeman's time.

(Photograph Ray Shill)

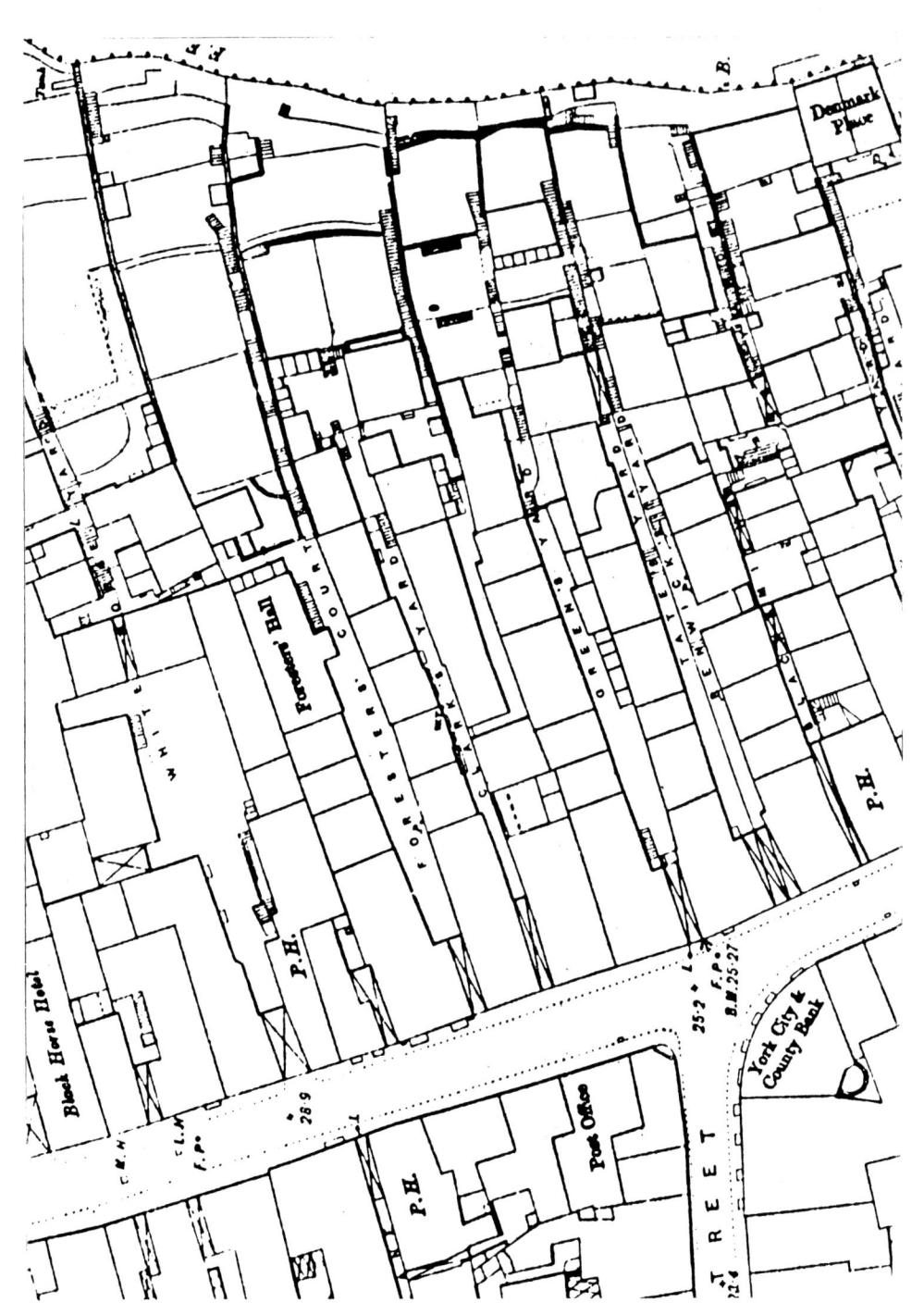

Ordnance Survey Map dated 1893 showing the yards off Upper Church Street. Clark's Yard, formerly known as Kilvington's Yard can be seen centre right.

174

A 1955 view of Clark's Yard from street level.
(Courtesy of Whitby Literary and Philosophical Society)

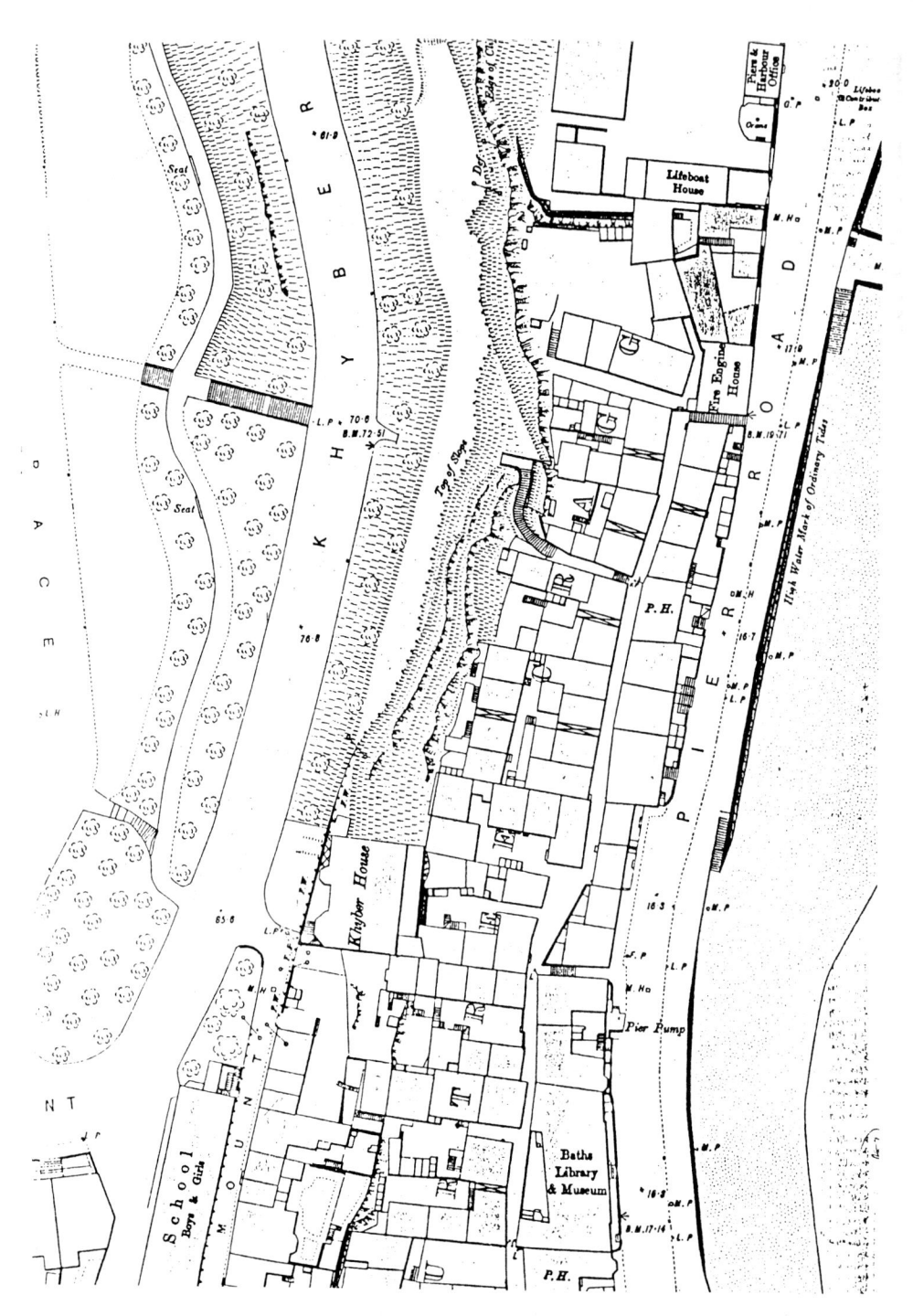

Ordnance Survey Map dated 1893 of the Cragg. This was a long narrow passage behind Pier Road with many yards leading off it.

176

This view of Barry's Square (1955) conveys well the dilapidated conditions in which residents of the Cragg were expected to live.
(Courtesy of Whitby Literary and Philosophical Society)

A view of The Cragg as it appears today *(Photograph Ray Shill)*

A large proportion of Whitby folk lived in the yards. In Church Street alone there were at one time over fifty of them each with families ranging in numbers from three to twenty-three. If the adjoining Tate Hill and Henrietta Street were considered as well, the number of people living just in these yards was well over a thousand.

Sometime in the early 1880s, Henry and his wife left Clarks Yard and moved to the Cragg, which was an area where many of the fishermen lived but which was considered a poorer district. Placed in the shadow of the West Cliff the dwellings were packed tightly behind the Pier Road. Here landlords were said to charge high rents for inferior accommodation.

Why Henry moved to the Cragg is not known. After the death of his mother-in-law perhaps he felt there was no need to remain in Church Street and at the Cragg he was nearer to the Lifeboat station. But there is a strong possibility that financial troubles prompted his move, despite income from several lifeboat rescues. He had sold his big coble, the *Garland* in April 1881 and for a couple of years he relied mainly on his line coble the *Elizabeth* to earn his living. For those occasions when a larger boat was needed Henry borrowed one. For example, in 1883, he had the use of the *Alexandra* through his friend Thomas Mennell. The cost of the court case and the trouble over cutting other fishermen's lines must only have made matters worse.

Exactly when they moved is also unknown. Freeman was certainly at the Cragg by late 1885 because the electoral roll proves this, but they could have changed addresses at any time after 1881. Elizabeth's illness at the time of the court case may have been a consequence of poorer living conditions. If so, this would point to their having taken up residence at the Cragg as early as the winter of 1882/1883. If not, the heavy fine imposed on Henry at the end of the trial could well have precipitated the move in the months that followed.

The money paid in rents for Whitby tenements varied somewhat, depending on the size of the accommodation and the location within the port. From the sales notices published in the *Whitby Gazette* and *Whitby Times,* it is possible to calculate the average yearly rent a tenant might have paid. For example in 1883 in Church Street there was a solid stone building divided into 15 dwellings, receiving a rent of £88 per annum. If divided equally each apartment would realise £5-17s-4d each. Similarly, the tenement occupied by Henry's sister-in-law Rebecca Whitton in Millers Yard was part of a lot of thirteen tenements offered for public auction in November 1892. The yearly rents for them amounted to £77-19s-4d, or an average of £5-19s-11d each.

In other parts of Whitby yearly rents could drop to £4 or £3. In May 1905 three tenements at Boulby Bank, Church Street produced a rent of £12-5s, while Langdale Buildings above Station Square fetched £45-1s-8d from the twelve dwellings there. Unlike house prices of today, the rents were slow to rise and when they did it was in pennies rather than pounds. In Kilvingtons Yard the rents would have been comparable to those charged in Millers Yard and it would be reasonable to expect Freeman to be faced with a rent approaching £6 per year, or a little more than 2 shillings per week. At the Cragg rents were cheaper.

Little is known of Elizabeth Freeman, during her marriage to Henry. She never bore any children, yet it was said of Henry that he loved children. He must have been a friendly uncle to his brother William's family as well as to the sons of Emma Watson, Elizabeth's sister. In fact, John Henry Watson, Henry's nephew, is recorded as staying at their home in Kilvingtons Yard in 1881.

By 1889 Freeman's financial situation must have improved as he was able to take a house in Bakehouse Yard which leads off Haggersgate and connects with Cliff

A number of yards disappeared during the 1950's and 1960's particularly in the Church Street area. The two illustrations shown below are examples of yards now gone:

Elbow Yard, at the lower end of Church Street

Street at the top. Today these houses are quite respectable dwellings in a picturesque setting. Living here, Elizabeth Freeman would have been near her sister Rebecca Whitton who by this time appears to have been residing in Millers Yard.

According to Harold Brown, their house was No 6 and was to be found at the top behind the Presbyterian Chapel which faced Cliff Street. It was an old house, older in fact than the chapel. It was pulled down some years ago and the site is now a vacant piece of ground.

Henry's brother William spent many years living in a tenement near the railway station, during which time he carried on the trade of brickmaker. A brickmaker's life was just as precarious as a fisherman's and Threadneedle Yard where William's house stood contained some of the worst accommodation to be found in the port. Threadneedle Yard was almost obliterated later by the making of a new street, Wellington Road. After then access to what remained was made through Dark Entry Yard. Today, the old yard slums have been replaced by newer buildings but Dark Entry Yard remains. It is possible to imagine the Freeman children playing on the steps of Dark Entry Yard leading down into the gloom where William and his family lived.

Ann Freeman died in 1881 leaving William to look after his now adolescent children. He is described as a caring man and a good father, but like his brother Henry he had his bouts of temper, which his children came to respect. Yet he seems nevertheless to have allowed them more freedom than perhaps he should have done. In 1881 after his wife's death he was called before the magistrates because his youngest son was not attending school. The sad events of 1886 truly shattered his life. By then the family had taken rooms in Mrs Jackson's lodging house in the Market Place opposite the Shambles. Even though acquitted of any blame for the death of his son Henry, William took the accident to heart and died the following year.

Of William's children the following is known: Sarah Freeman went into service for Margaret Stancliffe who lived in Baxtergate. She married William Tyreman, a Whitby jetworker, in 1877 and set up home in Threadneedle Yard near her father. George Freeman became a Jet worker and later married Anne Robinson, an innkeeper's daughter. In 1881 George was a jet ornament manufacturer living in Langdale Buildings. Julia Freeman married another jet worker, William Booth. They lived for a while in Baxtergate where Julia carried on a greengrocers business. Mary Freeman took employment with Edward Watson and worked as a general servant at the Plough Inn.

William Freeman Junior seems to have been a bit of a rogue. It appears that this son became a groom then a cab driver in Whitby. He, too, must have taken his brother's death to heart as a William Freeman, groom, was found drunk one summer's day in 1886 on the Pier at Whitby. He was brought before the magistrates and fined for being drunk. Drunkenness was not uncommon among Whitby fishermen

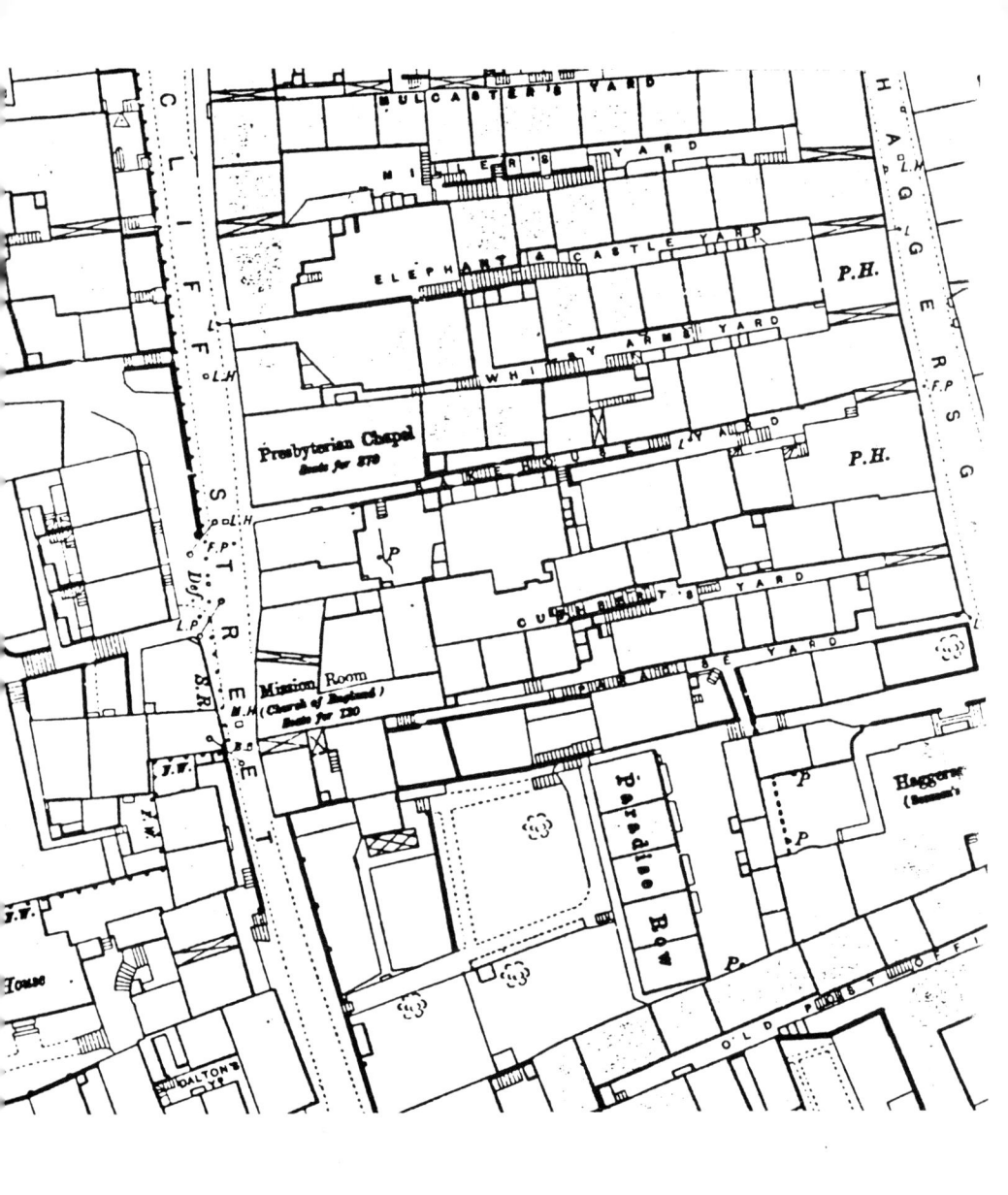

Ordnance Survey Map dated 1893 showing the Yards between Cliff Street and Haggersgate, including Bakehouse Yard. Henry Freeman lived in the building adjacent to the Presbyterian Chapel.

182

Modern view of Bakehouse Yard, looking from Haggersgate to Cliff Street. This was Freeman's last address. His house, now demolished, stood near the top, on the right.
(Photograph Ray Shill)

but very few cab drivers dared to overindulge as their occupation demanded a certain sobriety. This experience did not deter the young William Freeman who the next year was found drunk in charge of his cab on the Hawsker Road. Again he was brought before the magistrates who increased the penalty for his offence.

By now William should have been more careful as it was evident that the local police had their eye on him. Yet, a year later he found himself before the magistrates again. This time he was sober, but an umbrella left in his cab had not been handed into the Sanitary Authority as the local Bye-Laws demanded. William had taken some visitors at the Royal Hotel for a drive, but afterwards Susannah Coates left her umbrella in the cab. William found it afterwards but did not return it to the owner. Instead he left it with a Mrs Mason at Dock End. Even though William had no intention of theft he was severely dealt with, being fined £1-9s-6d as well as the 10s 6d costs. Half of the fine was awarded to the aggrieved owner and the other half to the poor. Clearly the magistrates did not welcome repeated appearances before them.

William Freeman the younger moved to Hartlepool, presumably because of his harrassment in Whitby and took up labouring. Later this William Freeman married Elizabeth Ord there.

Modern view, showing Arthur Sawdon's showroom. Threadneedle Yard was situated behind this building. *(Photograph Ray Shill)*

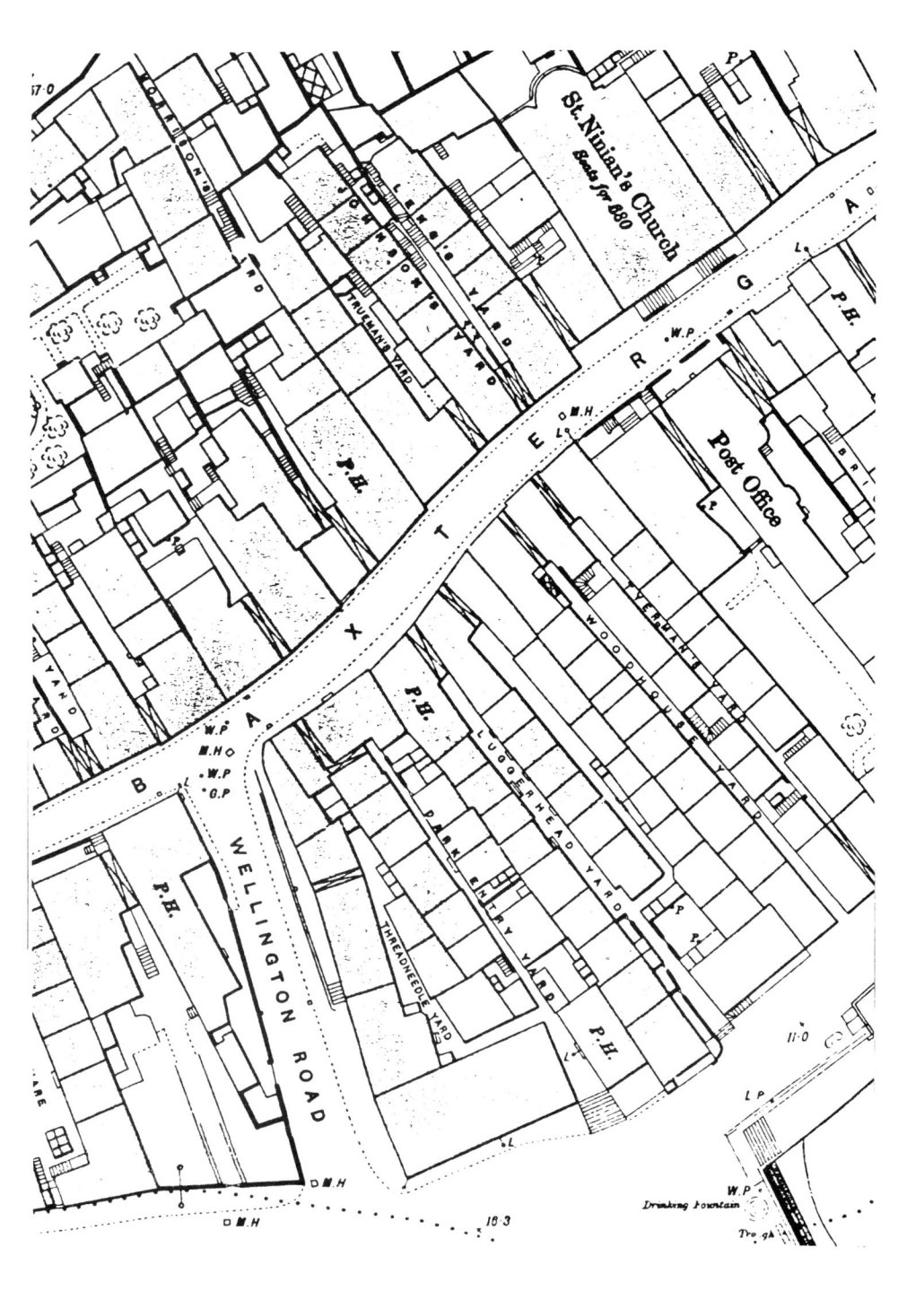

Ordnance Survey Map 1893 showing the Yards connecting with Baxtergate. Threadneedle Yard can be seen between Wellington Road and Dark Entry Yard.

185

Francis, younger William's brother, later lived in Guisborough, where he became a deputy overman. He died there in 1899, aged only 29. Of Henry Freeman's other nephews from Whitby, James and John Thomas, little is known, though either may have been connected with the firm of J Freeman and Co, watchmakers, jewellers and silversmiths who were trading in the early 1890's from 21a Skinner Street.

The fate of Henry Freeman's sister, Sarah, is a complete mystery. It is known that after her marriage to William Wherrit she bore him a daughter when they lived in Baxtergate. Later William Wherrit moved to Hartlepool and remarried at Greatham, County Durham. His new bride was Mary Thompson. It is interesting to note that William is recorded as a Bachelor on the marriage certificate. Sarah seems to have left him, but the daughter, Margaret Elizabeth, remained with the father. No record appears to exist of Sarah's death at that time or of her remarrying later. No trace of her later life has been uncovered.

Henry's father and mother also came to live in Whitby. They took a tenement in Cappleman's Yard and lived there until William died in 1876. Now a widow, Margaret stayed with her son William in Threadneedle Yard before she too died, aged 85, in 1878.

The impression has been given in other texts dealing with Henry Freeman that few people in Whitby, if any, could justly claim to be related to Henry Freeman, but this is clearly not the case. Several of his nephews and nieces by William his brother became established in the port. Though Henry, himself, did not have any children by his marriage to Elizabeth there were many who were related to him.

Elizabeth Freeman died on the 5th of June 1898 in Bakehouse Yard. She was 62 years of age. Her death certificate records the cause of death as liver disease. It would seem that Henry would now never have any direct issue. Yet life has a habit of creating strange twists and for Henry a new chapter was still to unfold.

OLD WHITBY, CAPPLEMAN'S YARD.

Cappleman's Yard was home to Henry's father William during his final years
(Photograph J. T. Ross. Courtesy of Pat Pickles)

CHAPTER 13

THE WATSON FAMILY

Henry Freeman's whole life underwent a considerable upheaval during 1898. Not only did he lose his wife Elizabeth, but just months after her death, the local lifeboat Committee began discussing his retirement from the service. Now that he was 63, he was entitled to his pension of twelve pounds a year. If he wished to resign, he was free to go.

The choice, however, was not left up to him. At the Annual Meeting of the Local Committee in January 1899, it was unanimously resolved that he should retire on the 1st October 1899, some months after his 64th birthday. The resolution was presented to him in writing after the meeting.

In less than eighteen months, therefore, two major parts of Freeman's life were taken from him: Elizabeth his partner in marriage for the past 36 years, and his job as Coxswain at Whitby which he had held for 22 years. This untimely combination of circumstances must have left him feeling extraordinarily powerless and painfully aware that he was now in his declining years. What was left was just his fishing, and the grim prospect of a lonely old age.

It is perhaps a measure of Freeman's resilience that within less than three years he had married again. The wedding took place on 5th February 1901, at the Primitive Methodist Chapel at Hartlepool, and his bride was Emma Watson, the widowed sister of his deceased wife, Elizabeth.

For a man of Freeman's age to re-marry would be somewhat unusual even in our day, and no doubt it was rather unconventional for his own times. But in marrying his deceased wife's sister, he was breaking more than just a trivial social convention. He was, in fact, breaking the law. Without doubt, it was for this reason that the wedding ceremony was conducted well away from Whitby. In Hartlepool the civil and ecclesiastical impediments to their union would not be known.

It had long been the Church's position that marriage with a deceased wife's sister was prohibited by Holy scripture. Not only Canon law but also the English civil law on the subject were derived from the prohibitions laid down in the book of Leviticus. The Biblical rules concerning matrimony between blood relatives were not so restrictive, however, as were the later extensions of these rules. For the premise that marriage makes man and woman one flesh led to the conviction that if it was wrong to marry one's sister, it must be equally wrong to marry one's wife's sister.

This particular extension to the Old Testament rules was responsible for widespread hardship. If a wife died and left her husband with young children to rear on his own, often the only help available to the widower was from his sister-in-law.

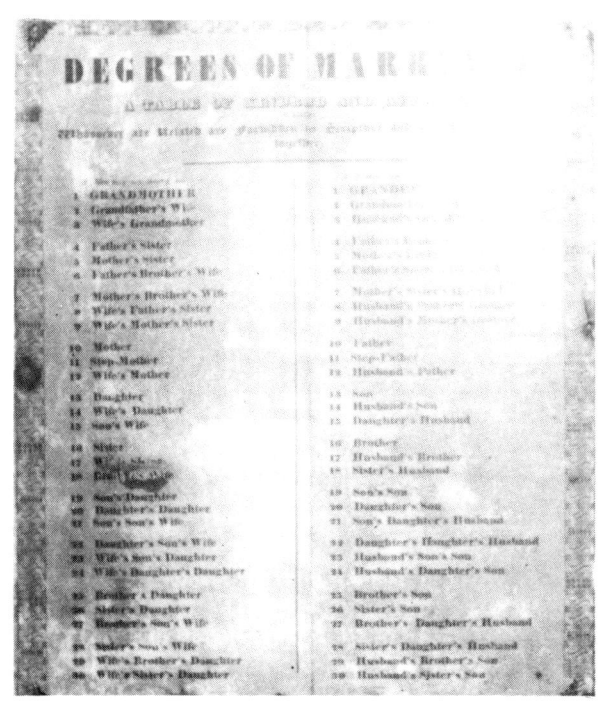

This notice which is still to be seen today in St Mary's Parish Church, Whitby, shows the illegality of Freeman's marriage to his sister-in-law Emma Watson.

(Photograph Ray Shill)

Emotional involvement frequently grew between them from their closer association. Yet the law prohibited the natural expression of that involvement in marriage.

Since 1835 when Lord Lyndhurst's Act was passed, which declared such a marriage to be void, there had been a long campaign to legalise marriage between a man and his deceased wife's sister. But this did not succeed in securing a change in the law until August of 1907, with the passing of the Deceased Wife's Sisters Marriage Act.

When Henry Freeman married Emma Watson in 1901, therefore, he did so in certain knowledge that he was breaking the law. What could have prompted him to take such a risk? And what were the circumstances which led to his relationship with Emma?

Certainly there were no children by his first marriage which necessitated Emma's taking over the mothering role in the Freeman household. Yet there was one factor in Freeman's first marriage where Emma's help might have been needed urgently from time to time, and that was Elizabeth's poor state of health, owing to a liver disease. If her illness had been a protracted one- and it is known she was ill at the time of the court case against Freeman in 1883- there would have been sufficient opportunity for a strong bond to have developed between Henry and Emma.

The controversy over the marriage laws had been prolonged and bitter, and to some extent, the public disquiet over these unjust restrictions must have brought the law into disrepute by the turn of the century. With no immediate prospect of legal reform, Henry and Emma clearly decided that there was no harm involved to anyone in their marrying. Their decision was a lucky one. They were able to share what remained of Freeman's life as a married couple. The law did not alter until nearly three years after Freeman had died, so in the event, it proved to be a case of fortune favouring the brave.

Emma had been a widow for more than 30 years following Kirby Watson's death in America. By her former marriage, Emma had borne three sons: William Thomas Watson, John Henry Watson, and Kirby Watson Jnr. When their father was killed in 1869, William had been just four years old, John Henry was two, and Kirby, the youngest had not yet been born. At the time of Emma's marriage in 1901, her sons were well into adult life: William the eldest would have been 36, John Henry 34 and Kirby 32. All three now became Henry Freeman's stepsons. Both William and John Henry had been married for more than ten years. Kirby Junior was still unmarried, and remained so throughout his life.

Kirby Watson, Emma's first husband had been born on 2nd December 1839 at Pocklington. His father, William Watson who was a farm labourer, had married Bessey Skinn in Dember 1837 at Sculcoates, Hull. Kirby was their second child; an elder brother Peter had died two days after birth. In the 1841 Census the Watsons were living at Chapelgate, Pocklington. William Watson was then aged 20, Bessey, Kirby's mother also 20 and Kirby, just 1 year old.

By 1851, the Chapelgate census entry has Bessey Watson as the head of the family. Kirby was by this time 11. His father seems to have died young, when the boy was just 10 years old, leaving Kirby's mother to rear a family of four children on her own. Bessey Watson is described in the census record as a pauper, and in her care were Kirby and three younger children, William, Mary Ann and Elizabeth, a baby of just five months.

Exactly how Kirby Watson met Emma prior to their marriage in October 1863 is a mystery. It has not proved possible to discover where he was living after 1851, or to ascertain when he began work on the railways. All that is known is that he was residing in Pocklington in 1863, and that by then he was working as a railway porter.

Kirby and Emma frequently changed addresses as Kirby strove to further his career. Each of his children were born at different places and in quite different circumstances. After Kirby's death all three were farmed off separately to relations and friends as Emma was forced to take employment to feed herself and pay something for their upkeep. Life as a widow cannot have been easy for Emma Watson despite the rallying round of her relations. How much she saw of her sons during their formative years is not clear.

1901. Marriage solemnized at Primitive Methodist Chapel, Hartlepool in the District of Hartlepool in the County of Durham

No.	When Married	Name and Surname	Age	Condition	Rank or Profession	Residence at the time of Marriage	Father's Name and Surname	Rank or Profession of Father
89	Fifth February 1901	Henry Freeman	65 years	Widower	Fisherman	Cliff St Whitby	William Freeman (deceased)	Fisherman (master)
		Emma Watson	55 years	Widow	—	30 Potter St West Hartlepool	Herman Neufield (deceased)	Ft Master (master)

Married in the Primitive Methodist Chapel according to the Rites and Ceremonies of the Primitive Methodists by Licence by me, William Thorner, Minister.

This Marriage was solemnized between us, { Henry Freeman / Emma Watson } In the Presence of us, { William Thomas Watson / Mary Matilda Baldry }

A. Watson deputy Registrar

Hartlepool
14th April 56

Emma Freeman was Henry's second wife. This portrait was taken in her later years.
(Photograph Courtesy David Watson)

Undoubtedly Emma's mother Mrs. Busfield played her part, but help might well have come from Kirby's younger brother William. A man answering his description appears on the 1881 census. Living then in Whitby Street, Hartlepool, the 38 year old William earned his living as a Hay and Corn Merchant. A native of Fridaythorpe, near Pocklington, where parents William and Bessey Watson had him baptised on 19th March 1843, William was living in Hartlepool in the 1860's at about the same time as Kirby and Emma. Then a carrier by trade, he married Ann Elizabeth Simmons from Stockton and had a daughter Laura by her.

The 1881 census mentions both Ann Elizabeth and Laura as living with William, but also gives a son George then ten years old who was born in New York, America. It is possible, therefore, that Kirby Watson did not journey to America alone, but that brother William was there for part of the trip. Unlike Kirby, William returned, and established a successful business in Hartlepool, one that at least paid enough for him to employ a servant girl.

The first of Kirby's sons by Emma was William Thomas, and he, too, was born in Hartlepool. Little is known of his childhood except that part of it was spent in Middlesbrough.

William Thomas was married on July 26, 1890 at Christ Church, West Hartlepool to an Alice Mary Foster, the daughter of Thomas Foster, a mariner. William was a ships plumber by trade. They had at least five children, of which three grew to maturity: May, William and Thomas Busfield. William Thomas Watson spent most his life in West Hartlepool and died there in January 1942, at the age of 76. His wife, Alice Mary, died two years before him in May 1940, at the age of 77 years.

In the Pannett Park Museum today is a whistle that once belonged to Henry Freeman. This item was donated by William, the son of William Thomas whilst he was living in Birmingham. David Watson, his son, still possesses a photograph of Emma Watson and a sermon thought to be written by his great-grandfather Kirby Watson.

Emma and Kirby Watson's second son John Henry was married in September 1889 at Stockton-on-Tees to Ann Elizabeth Sample, the daughter of George Sample, a gardener. Both were then 22 years old. John Henry's occupation at the time of his marriage was that of ships carpenter. His grand-daughter Ellen Holcroft recalls that he had ten children, her mother being the third child. Among the ten children, there was one named Henry Freeman Watson. In 1931, when Emma Freeman died, John Henry Watson was living at "Fairhaven", Maltby, near Middlesbrough in Cleveland. Today this is the home Doreen Simpson who kindly assisted in this research. Ellen Holcroft recalls, however, that for many years John Henry Watson had lived with his wife and children at 5 Wellington Street, Norton-on-Tees. John Henry Watson died at Maltby in 1941 and his widow, Ann Elizabeth Watson, remained alone at "Fairhaven", Maltby until her death in 1946.

William Thomas Watson, Henry Freeman's eldest stepson

(Photograph Courtesy of Mrs K. Walker)

Of particular interest was the fate of Kirby and Emma Watson's youngest son, Kirby Watson Jnr, who had been born on 1st July 1870 at Church Street, Whitby, just eight months after his father's untimely death in Illinois, America.

Almost nothing is known of him from 1871, when he was just 9 months old, right up to his death in 1954. The 1871 census describes the baby as a boarder in the house of Thomas Walker, a miller, at 34 Church Street. From that time until his death at the age of 83 his life is a blank. Ellen Holcroft recalls that he was a "Gentleman of the road" and that he "roamed the world and the seven seas." He was quite educated and could converse on many subjects, but never married, and was considered the "Black Sheep" of the family.

If his life remains shrouded in mystery, fate at least allowed Kirby a memorable death. The circumstances of his passing are recorded in the pages of the *Whitby Gazette* for 1954.

> **ELDERLY MAN'S INJURIES**
>
> **Whitby Inquest Adjourned**

Headline from Whitby Gazette, 26 March 1954.

The first report headed "Elderly man's Injuries: Whitby Inquest Adjourned" appeared in the *Whitby Gazette* of Friday March 26, 1954, and concerned the death of Mr Kirby Watson, aged 83, an inmate of St Hilda's Hospital, Whitby, as a result of pneumonia, associated with a fractured breast bone and ribs.

A male attendant at St Hilda's Hospital, Clifford Robert Dunn, said the deceased was of no fixed address and had been a patient at the hospital since before Christmas. Until then "he had more or less tramped the road. He had talked about being at sea and being in prison for fourteen years. He knocked about the countryside, and as far as he knew, was a retired labourer." Dunn had seen Watson alive at 9 p.m. on 17th March, when he checked the patients at night. He understood the deceased died at the hospital on the 19th March.

Dr Stanley Wray, a senior pathologist, gave details of his postmortem examination, conducted on 20th March. The case was adjourned for three weeks so that further inquiries could be made.

The next report appears in the *Gazette* of April 15th 1954, under the headline, "Open Verdict at Whitby Inquiry: Inquest into Hospital Patient's death."

> **OPEN VERDICT AT WHITBY INQUIRY**
>
> **Inquest into Hospital Patient's Death**
>
> **Coroner's Comment**

A number of witnesses gave evidence at the Inquest held on April 14th: Ethel Foster, acting matron at the Hospital, Dr Wilson, Clifford Dunn, male orderly, Harold Brown, ward orderly, Fred McNeil, and Mr Harry Holbrook, orderly.

Much concern focused on the circumstances surrounding Kirby Watson's death. Asked by the Coroner whether the fracture to the breast bone and ribs could have been caused by a blow from a fist, Dr Wray said they could. But in reply to a second question, he agreed the injuries could have been caused by a fall against some particular object.

Ethel Foster, the acting matron, described Watson as "a most difficult man". She referred to an incident where one of the orderlies, Mr Holbrook, had been shaving Mr Watson when the patient jerked back and knocked the razor out of his hand, causing a small cut on Watson's arm. She gave instructions for Watson to be taken to her, and he was brought by Mr Holbrook and Orderly Brown. He was left with her and he made a certain complaint whilst she was dressing his arm.

The Coroner commented that he did not think they should have the nature of that complaint, as there was no one else there to concur. Mrs Foster added she did not take much notice of it as Watson was rather given to exaggeration.

The Coroner corrected an impression given at the earlier hearing that Watson had a criminal record. He understood from the Police that there was no truth in that. Matron Foster testified that the cut on Watson's arm was the only injury she had seen; there was no indication of any other injury. On the 18th March Watson had taken a turn for the worse and she had put him to bed. When she examined his chest she had found a very extensive bruise. She left a message for Dr. Wilson with the secretary, to inform him of Watson's marked change of condition.

Dr Wilson said that he had seen Watson on the 16th March in the male sick ward, but Watson had refused to let him examine him, saying he wanted to see an outside doctor, but made no complaint to him. Dr Wilson took this as the kind of insult Watson was used to handing out and was not offended. He explained that Watson was not a sick patient in the Hospital, but a Part III patient and as such was presumably fit and well. There was nothing to stop him going out and seeing another doctor if he wanted to. When he examined Watson on the 19th, the man was obviously dying from pneumonia. Dr Wilson put him on penicillin treatment, but it was quite hopeless. When Watson died he informed the Coroner.

Witness Clifford Dunn said Watson was wandering about at Glen Esk on March 14th. Watson was "one of the most erratic and abusive men one could meet. There was a pantomime with him every time he was shaved or bathed." Dunn testified that when he bathed Watson with Mr Holbrook on the 17th March there was no mark on him. He "got in and out himself" and complained only about his arm.

Harold Brown testified that on March 16th he was told by Matron to go to the bathroom to bring up Kirby Watson, and found him inside with Mr Holbrook. There was a triangular cut on Watson's left arm. Watson seemed "rather excited" but made no complaint. He and Holbrook took Watson to the Matron who bandaged his arm. He did not see him again until 2pm on the 18th, when he noticed a large bruise on his chest.

Fred McNeil said he was in the day room. He heard Watson's shouts when Holbrook and Watson were in the bathroom and could hear Watson say "Leave me alone." Watson came out with a cut on his arm.

According to Harry Holbrook's statement which had been taken by Police Inspector Claude Walker Thompson under caution, Holbrook said that on March 16th he went to attend to Watson at 10 a.m. Watson was in bed expecting a visit from the doctor. He asked Watson to get out to wash while he made his bed. Watson was his "usual aggressive self" and used obscene language to him. Watson got up unaided and went to the bathroom. Later when shaving him, Watson had struck his hand while he had hold of the razor. As it fell he grabbed it and it caught Watson's left fore-arm. The arm was bleeding so he went for the Matron to dress it. Watson later went back to his bedroom and on the following day was his "usual self." When he returned to duty on March 18th Watson told him he had fallen out of bed twice the previous night.

In his summing up, the Coroner made it clear that there was real difficulty in ascertaining how Watson had sustained his injury. They had very little evidence at all. They had heard from more than one witness that the man was awkward to deal with, and continually made complaints. Sometimes, he said, it happened that when a man who was always complaining had a real complaint, or something real to be complained about, he did not get the attention he deserved. It was "the old story of crying wolf."

Mr Wilkinson, the Coroner, said the evidence was insufficient to warrant anyone being put on trial, and there was no admissible evidence against any individual. He thought the Jury must say there was insufficient evidence to show how Watson came by this injury. Nobody wanted to try and hide or white-wash anyone. In accordance with the Coroner's directive, the Jury returned a verdict that there was insufficient evidence to show how the fractures came about.

In this inquiry clearly the ward orderly Harry Holbrook had been under some suspicion, but the Jury was unable to find any clear evidence to warrant proceedings being taken against him or any other individual.

Looking back on the the case recently, Mr Harold Brown, now an archivist with the Whitby Literary and Philosophical Society, remembers well the hospital where he used to work. Formerly the Whitby Union Workhouse, the building had undergone major alterations in 1948 when it was redesignated as St. Hilda's Hospital. The old workhouse had been gutted. New floors were laid, and walls were newly plastered, to cover over the whitewash and doom-laden Biblical texts which had previously adorned them. (The admonition "Prepare to Meet Thy God" painted in huge letters, would hardly have been the most sensitive or comforting of messages with which to greet elderly sick admissions to the hospital, as Harold points out!)

The hospital was in two parts: upstairs were the Mulgrave and the Abbey Wards (male and female) which cared for the chronic sick or geriatrics. Each ward had its own day room. On this floor Harold Brown worked as a Ward Orderly attached to the Mulgrave Ward. Downstairs, meanwhile, was the Part III accommodation for ambulatory residents, both men and women, housed in separate wings, where Harry Holbrook worked as a male attendant. Clifford Dunn, a porter, helped Holbrook to bath the patients and used to take over on Mr. Holbrook's days off.

Harold Brown only really knew Kirby Watson during the last few days of his life when he was brought up into the Mulgrave Ward after his accident. He believes Watson was known as a datal man: that is, a man who worked on farms by the day, and who travelled from farm to farm seeking work. He spent the winter in the Part III accommodation within the hospital (as it was termed after the workhouses were made into hospitals after 1948.) Patients such as Watson were called ambulatory residents as they were allowed out of the premises during the day. From the inquiries Mr. Brown has made, it appears that he never had any visitors during his fateful stay at St. Hilda's.

Kirby Watson was the last of the Watson sons to die. It appears that at his death he had no family or close relatives and that no one knew him, or his connection with Henry Freeman. Virtually from his birth to his death, Kirby's life remains essentially a closed book. Like his father before him, Kirby Watson died apart from family and loved ones.

He was buried in an unmarked grave on 23rd March 1954, in Whitby's Larpool Cemetery. Whether or not he ever really knew his famous step-father or whether he even met him, is unknown. Today he is buried not far from the grave where his mother, and Henry Freeman, and Elizabeth Freeman are at rest.

CHAPTER 14

HENRY FREEMAN, VETERAN LIFEBOATMAN

During October 1892 the lifeboat was launched to a coble *Palm Branch* which was in trouble. Freeman, Langlands, Robinson and Eglon all being out fishing the role of Coxswain fell to William Moat. He took out the *Robert and Mary Ellis* with a young crew. They raced through the rough seas and rescued the coblemen. That same month Robert Coulson, one of the fishermen accused with Henry Freeman of cutting lines, was washed overboard and drowned off Saltburn whilst out fishing.

Early the next year, other cobles found themselves in danger. On Wednesday, 11th January the wind was blowing hard from the North East. There were heavy showers and a rough sea on the bar. Four cobles were out in the afternoon. One coble chose to land her catch in Robin Hood's Bay, but the other three decided to head for Whitby. As they returned to the harbour they faced a considerable danger. The coastguard made ready the life-saving apparatus while the *Robert and Mary Ellis* was got out of her boat-house, placed on her carriage and taken down to the West Pier. The first coble to come into sight was the *Star of Peace*, John Storr's old boat, now skippered by William Hawkesfield. She lowered her sail and her crew managed to row her across the bar even though heavy waves crashed down upon them.

The lifeboat was launched with Henry Freeman at the helm and her crew pulled through the heavy sea to the other cobles, the *Rose Marion* and *William*. Their passage across the bar, however, was not as lucky as that of the *Star of Peace*. All the fishermen were rescued and landed safely on the beach, but their cobles were wrecked after being driven ashore.

The loss of the cobles was a savage blow to their crews. The fishermen of Whitby were falling on hard times. Their livelihood had been threatened by inshore trawling and poor catches. In the winter some families had become destitute. Soup kitchens were beginning to appear and free coal was being handed out to some of the poor. For Henry and his fellow fishermen this last decade of the nineteenth century was to be a testing one.

On the 2nd March another coble, the *Mary Alice* was in danger as she approached the bar with a load of mussels gathered from the Tees. The recent rains and snow had brought a lot of water down the river and the sea on the bar was very choppy. Freeman and other fishermen warned Captain Gibson of the coble's predicament and against his better judgement he ordered that the *Robert and Mary Ellis* be launched. The launch proved unnecessary. As the lifeboat was rowing out to the coble, the *Mary Alice* safely crossed the bar with the aid of lines thrown from the East pier.

During the winter of 1893 the lifeboatmen of Whitby were called out in the most appalling weather conditions. On the 18th November there was a severe gale and the seas were mountainous. Driving showers of sleet, snow and hail had reduced visibility to a minimum. Many of the Whitby folk were at home, for it was not safe even to walk the streets. Amid the blinding hail, tiles and chimney pots were crashing down into the road from the roof tops threatening life and limb. That morning William Douglas was on duty as signalman for the Coastguard when he saw a steamship battling through the maelstrom. As she passed Whitby Rock it was clear that the ship would run aground on the sands. Robert Gibson was informed and he had the lifeboat *Robert and Mary Ellis* brought out onto the slipway. Henry Freeman held his men in readiness.

The vessel was the SS *Southwark* in ballast from London to Sunderland. Thirteen souls were in peril that morning aboard the 335 ton iron ship. It was soon clear to Gibson that the vessel would strand half a mile along the sands and it would be hopeless to expect Freeman and his crew to row through such a sea. Thomas Langlands was ordered to the Upgang station and together with a large body of men he had the *Upgang* lifeboat brought out on her carriage onto her slipway and his crew got into the boat ready to launch. Through the force of the wind gigantic waves were being swept right up the slipway to within a few yards of the lifeboat house. As one wave crashed down, Langlands, with incredible coolness, gave the order to launch and the lifeboat was borne away on the crest of the terrible sea. The wave then crashed down on the carriage sweeping it up and turning it over and over again. The launchers scattered as the sea bent and broke the lifeboat carriage.

The *Southwark* had run aground near the Volunteer Battery. Brodie Stein the Chief Officer of the Coastguard arrived on the cliffs above with the rocket apparatus and managed to get a line aboard the vessel and her crew were taken ashore. Meanwhile Langlands and his men gallantly struggled through the waves to reach the ship. After pulling for an hour the *Upgang* reached the *Southwark* only to find that after all their labours their assistance was not required. She slipped back to the cliffs where she was hauled up to a place of safety.

That day visited chaos and destruction upon shipping along the coast. Most lifeboats saw action including the Robin Hood's Bay lifeboat which went out to rescue the crew of the brig *Romulus*. On land the gales wreaked havoc. On the West Cliff at Whitby, the Iron Church was blown down, while in the Esk Valley not a miner's cottage escaped some form of damage. Perhaps most remarkable was the fate of the Windmill at Boldon near Sunderland. The wind drove the sails round so fast that the friction set fire to the wood and the mill burnt down! No small wonder that this day was later christened "Hurricane Saturday".

In May 1894 both Coxswains, Langlands and Freeman, were summoned before the Lifeboat Committee at the request of Captain Holmes, an inspector from

Henry Freeman in his later years. In this study, the stern features have mellowed somewhat. *(Photograph Frank Meadow Sutcliffe)*

the parent institution. Some of Freeman's crew had written to Mr Holmes complaining about an incident when Mr Gibson had refused to despatch the lifeboat. On this occasion there had been calls for the lifeboat to be launched but Gibson declined to give his authority. Instead he had given permission for Freeman to go ahead providing Freeman took the responsibility, thereby ensuring the launch would be made at no cost to the Institution. Henry Freeman would not oblige and so the lifeboat remained in her house.

Gibson's caution is not surprising. The costs incurred just in launching two lifeboats to the *Southwark* came to over £60. His funds were not unlimited and in circumstances such as those in May 1894 Robert Gibson had difficult decisions to make. First and foremost was whether or not to launch the lifeboat. That involved assessing the danger to those in difficulty. It also called for an examination of what alternative action could be taken to achieve the same result. The fishermen, themselves, understandably had pressing needs to make a little money on the side during the difficult times which then existed for them. No doubt they pressured Gibson to launch the lifeboat when the opportunity arose. Balancing these competing demands must have been an unenviable task.

On this occasion Gibson evidently resisted these pressures, hence the complaint to Captain Holmes. Nevertheless, Robert Gibson received a unanimous vote of confidence from the committee and Henry Freeman was instructed to keep his crew under better control in future. Like the *Svadsfare* inquiry years before Henry had fallen prey to local Lifeboat politics.

During 1894 there was talk of making another lifeboat house between Upgang and Whitby but these ideas were shelved for a new lifeboat house to replace the existing wooden sheds at Whitby. A purpose-built brick building to house both lifeboats was the result which was completed in 1895 by local builders J. Langdale and Son.

This sketch shows the Harbour Master's House and the two RNLI Boathouses as they were prior to 1895.

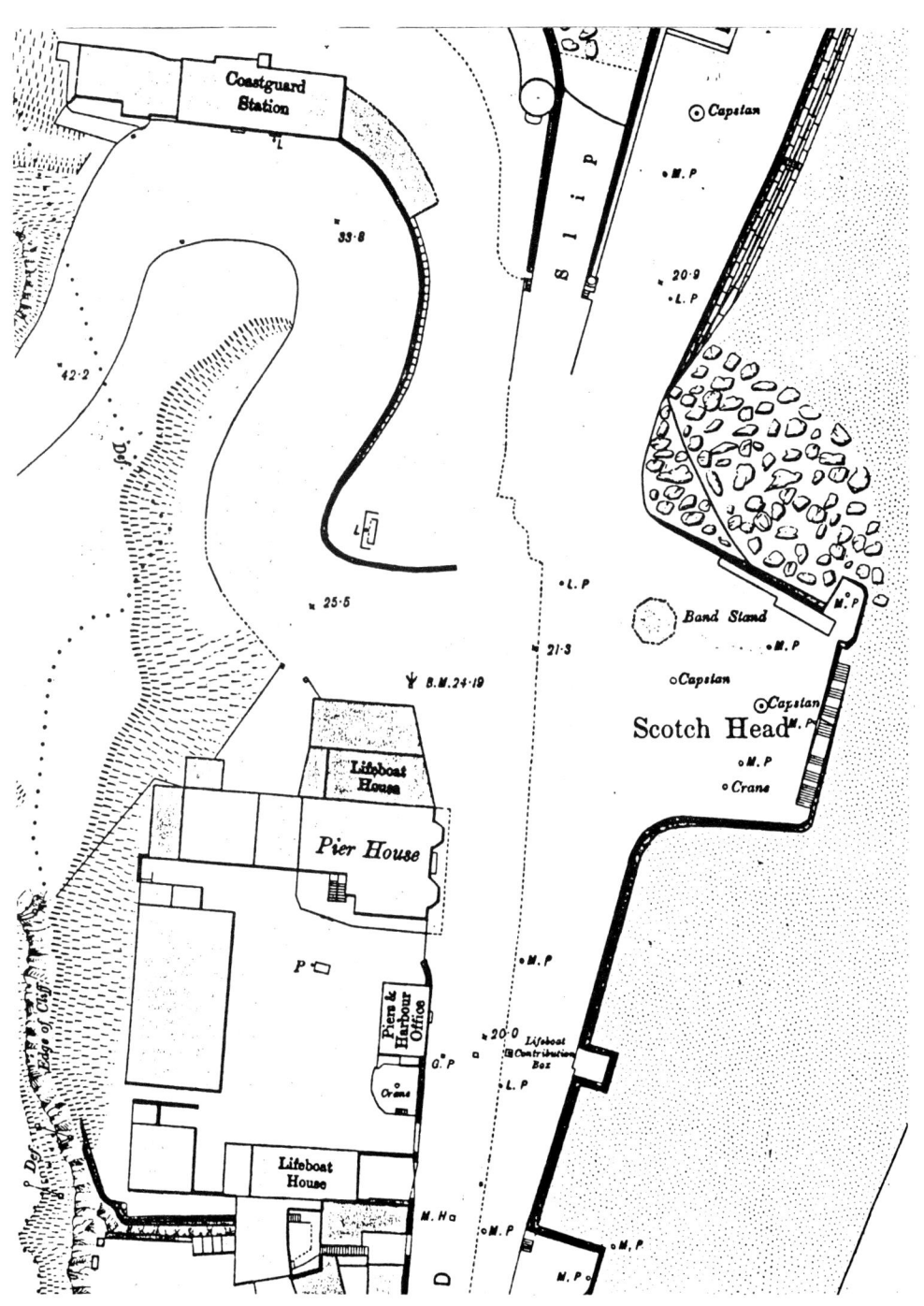

Ordnance Survey Map 1893 showing Pier Road, and the location of the two lifeboat houses. The one adjacent to the Pier House was a wooden shed which housed the No. 2 lifeboat. The other houses the No. 1 lifeboat.

ROYAL NATIONAL LIFE-BOAT INSTITUTION
LIFE BOAT
SUPPORTED BY VOLUNTARY CONTRIBUTIONS
ROYAL NATIONAL LIFE-BOAT INSTITUTION
LIFE BOAT

WHITBY
YACHT CLUB
ROYAL NATIONAL LIFE-BOAT INSTITUTION
LIFE-BOAT
SUPPORTED ENTIRELY BY VOLUNTARY CONTRIBUTIONS
ROYAL NATIONAL LIFE-BOAT INSTITUTION
LIFE-BOAT
SUPPORTED ENTIRELY BY VOLUNTARY CONTRIBUTIONS
LIFEBOAT
MUSEUM
One way

As soon as the lifeboat house was completed a new lifeboat was delivered to the port. Called the *John Fielden,* this was to be the No.2 station boat replacing a reserve boat previously on loan. The *John Fielden* arrived by train in November and was launched direct from the railway truck into the harbour with Henry Freeman at the helm. She was rowed out of the harbour around to the rocks where her crew were much impressed by her handling.

Henry Freeman's last years spent in the port were relatively trouble-free. Old age had mellowed him but with age came a greater astuteness. Henry remained quite capable of "breaking the rules" from time to time, but was no longer inclined to do so overtly. He seems at last to have realised that to be left in peace demanded a certain discretion.

In 1898 Henry Freeman was still Coxswain of the lifeboat. Some twenty-one years had passed since his stormy appointment. Though approaching his sixty-third birthday he still rose to the call and took the lifeboat out when needed. In February and April there were several launches to fishing cobles in distress.

One Sunday in February, on a fine morning, several fishermen went out to rebait their crab and lobster pots. There were fourteen cobles out to sea about a mile and a half from the shore. Some were returning to the harbour at noon when a heavy squall blew up. It was cold and snow lashed the coblemen's faces. As the seas rose heavily over the bar, the dangers of the situation became clear. If any boat were upset, the likelihood of survival for any man cast into the freezing waters would be small. Yet as they approached the bar the anxiety on their faces changed to relief as Harry Freeman hove into view at the helm of the *John Fielden* lifeboat to watch over their passage into the harbour.

As the winds whipped up the seas and the wind rose to gale force the men aboard the remaining seven cobles thought it would be too risky to head for Whitby. Two sheltered at Saltwick while the other five went to Robin Hood's Bay to beach their boats.

On the Monday an improvement in the weather led the fishermen to return to their craft and all seven set out again for Whitby. The two from Saltwick safely made the harbour, but those who had stayed at the Bay had a longer distance to travel and the sea again turned rough. One of the five cobles returned to Robin Hood's Bay, while the other four came on. The seas were now too rough to land at Saltwick and the four

The 1895 Lifeboat house replaced the existing two buildings on the pier. Henry Freeman had charge of this new building from its opening until his retirement.
(Photograph Courtesy of Jeff Morris)

Modern view of the 1895 Lifeboat house, which is today the RNLI Museum on Pier Road.
(Photograph Ray Shill)

crews decided to head for Whitby. The lifeboat was launched. This time Freeman took out the *Robert and Mary Ellis* to aid the fishermen.

The tide was ebbing and it was becoming increasingly dangerous to cross the bar into Whitby Harbour, but R. Dryden's coble, the *Wasp* made it safely across. Behind him was the *Ralph Ward Jackson* containing Walter Curry, Thomas Hutchinson and W. Harland. This coble had once been owned by Henry Freeman, but now was owned and mastered by fellow lifeboatman and friend, Walter Curry.

When crossing the bar the heavy sea crashed down on the coble washing away her tiller and spinning her right round. It was a miracle the vessel was not capsized. Freeman, however, was soon close enough to assist his friend. Lines were thrown from both the lifeboat and the pier and by this means the coble was hauled up the harbour even though it was half full of water.

Having secured the safety of Curry and his crewmates, Freeman then turned his attention to the other two cobles, the *Martha Dryden* and *Tranquil*, now half a mile from shore. He took out the lifeboat to them and took both crews aboard. With the five fishermen safely rescued the lifeboat returned to shore and their cobles were moored for the night. Unfortunately they broke away and were wrecked, leaving the men without a livelihood.

For Henry big ship rescues were now rather a thing of the past. Instead lifeboat practices and protecting his fellow coblemen occupied a considerable amount of his time. Moreover there was a new concern. With the increasing number of visitors coming to the port during the summer, there was the added danger of inexperienced bathers and boatmen getting into trouble.

To help remedy this problem the purchase of a beach lifeboat was sanctioned. She was called the *Balcarras* and was delivered to Whitby in June. Her builder was W. Farmer of Boulogne and at the time the press expressed their dissatisfaction with the decision to employ a French builder instead of a local one. She had a small carriage and could be launched by a horse or six men. Normally four or five would be enough to man the boat. Her master became Joseph Kay while Thomas Welham was appointed one of the boatmen in charge.

At that time the beach at Whitby presented a quite different sight from the one we know today. Arranged along the sands were lines of cumbersome bathing machines which could be hired by the visitors who wished to bathe in the sea. In accordance with the strict Victorian morality they were segregated and the gentlemen's machines were placed at a discreet distance from the women's. The new beach lifeboat had been set up near the men's bathing machines because the men were usually more adventurous and therefore more likely to get into difficulties.

Argument's bathing machines line the water's edge at Whitby.

(Photograph Courtesy of Pat Pickles)

On Friday 15th July, the sea was choppy. Kay and Welham decided the sea was too rough to launch the boat, but stayed on the beach to provide assistance and advice. About seven in the morning the bathing machines were unlocked and several gentlemen bathers arrived to make use of them including one E.de Kretschmar a banker from Richmond in Surrey.

On previous days, this particular gentleman had preferred to swim from the beach, but on this day he had hired a machine because of the rough sea. Once inside it his machine was hauled out into the water. Welham warned him not to go far out but the advice was ignored. While bathing Mr de Kretschmar strayed into a patch of rough water, got into difficulties and soon found himself swept out to sea. Welham saw this and, being a strong swimmer, swam out wearing a cork jacket in an attempt to save the man and succeeded in reaching him.

All this had been observed by Henry Freeman who was out at sea with Walter Curry and a young boy fishing for salmon. Weighing anchor Henry and Walter headed for Welham but were careful how they entered the rough water in their coble. Henry soon reached Welham who had by now gained a hold of de Kretschmar. Both were hauled up into the boat and brought ashore. Unfortunately, however, de Kretschmar was already dead.

At the inquest the effectiveness of the new bather's lifeboat was called into question and Henry Freeman was asked to give evidence about the day's events. Henry confirmed that it would not have been possible to launch the boat, but was still critical of the *Balcarras*. In his opinion it was a boat unsuitable for its purpose. She had to be turned around to be launched unlike a lifeboat which could go into the sea directly. The rowlocks were in the wrong place so that the oars might not touch the water in rough weather. Her carriage, too, was poorly designed causing difficulties with launching her.

The magistrates took note of all Freeman said and recommended further investigation. Thomas Welham was commended by them for his act of bravery. Freeman himself paid tribute to Welham's courage in his reply to a question by the magistrate:

" Had the character of this boat been different, do you think it would have had any effect in saving the life of this poor man?"
Henry replied, " I don't think so, Welham did all he could. Welham behaved like a man, there is no mistake about it."

De Kretschmar was found to have accidently drowned. Only two other bathers had met a similar fate on Whitby beach, but his death caused a clamour to improve things. The concern was echoed in a letter published in the *Whitby Times* a couple of weeks later. Its contents make quite clear that Henry Freeman was a personality well known far beyond Whitby, even as far away as London.

Sir- A friend in your district has sent me a copy of your journal dated 22nd inst and I am agreeably surprised to learn therefrom that bathing at Whitby is not so dangerous as I had been led to believe. My holiday arrangements this summer are completed, but I hope to be able to take my family to your town next year without fear of funerals before my eyes. As regards Mr Freeman's evidence at the recent inquest, I may perhaps, be allowed to remark that in the matter of selecting the type of beach boat, the prophet is still without honour in his own country. Many people in the south have heard of Mr Freeman, and it seems to me that the opinion of the chief of the local "StormWarriors" would have been worth having as to the kind of boat required before it was ordered.
I remain, Sir, Yours Truly, Paterfamilias
Hampstead, July 26th

In August the lifeboat race was again held as part of the Whitby Regatta and involved all three Whitby lifeboats, the *Upgang, John Fielden* and the *Robert and Mary Ellis*. Henry skippered the *Robert and Mary Ellis* and as on previous occasions he saw Thomas Langlands romp home first with the Upgang lifeboat.

On this occasion there were compensations. Lady Sarah Elliot treated the lifeboatmen to a dinner at the Talbot Hotel. Mr Horne presided with Henry Freeman as vice-chairman. Her ladyship's health was toasted and that of Henry Freeman and a good time was had by all. Another toast wished Henry many more years as Whitby Coxswain.

But it was not to be. 1899 proved to be his last year in the post. At the end of the year the parent institution in London informed the Whitby Committee that Henry Freeman became eligible for a pension when he reached the age of 63.

During their January 1899 meeting the retirement of Henry Freeman came on the agenda and after a discussion amongst the members present it was decided that Henry Freeman should retire at the start of October. Robert Gibson was instructed to inform Henry Freeman in writing.

After all the service he had given, Freeman was effectively told to retire. All his life he had been battling not only against the elements but frequently too against authority. Henry must surely have been angered by this decision. Certainly he, himself, believed that he had many more years to serve.

Henry's term as Coxswain can never be described as smooth. It was a combination of dramatic rescues and controversy. On the rescue missions in which he participated one hundred and fifty-two lives were saved. It was a record few RNLI Coxswains past or present could match. His quarrelsome and single-minded disposition had in earlier times led him into conflict with his superiors. Two members of the lifeboat committee resigned because of him. His age now gave the committee the opportunity to let Freeman go and make way for a younger man. In Thomas Langlands, they had a most able replacement.

Langlands was universally popular with the committee. He proved a worthy successor distinguishing himself particularly during the sinking of the *Rohilla* in 1914. Thomas had a much more fortunate term as Coxwain and unlike Freeman, when he came to retire he was able to pick the date himself. Langlands retired in 1920 after the Great War. Just a little more than twenty years separated their retirements, yet the contrast in their treatment is remarkable.

It was a mild winter for Henry Freeman in his final year as Coxswain. In fact, the lifeboat never actually left the slipway, being held in readiness on only two occasions. When James Wood's pleasure coble *Robert* fell into difficulties in heavy seas that August Henry was called to duty for the last time. He took out the *Robert and Mary Ellis* onto the bar and remained there until the *Robert* was safely past.

The next week was the Regatta and Henry Freeman contested for the last time. Freeman came in first, well ahead of the rest. After so many defeats in this contest one cannot help thinking the event was staged, but, even if this was the case, it was a nice gesture by the other crews.

Freeman retired as Coxswain on 1st October 1899 and collected a well-earned pension leaving Thomas Smith Langlands to take his place. Langlands was much younger than Freeman. Born in 1853, he would have been only two when Freeman came to Whitby. Yet he had almost put in as many years as Freeman in the Lifeboats.

If Freeman was bitter about his forced retirement, he did not show it. With stoical acceptance he withdrew from the Lifeboat scene. From then on the Lifeboat Committee minutes are silent about Henry. When he finally died not even a condolence for his widow is recorded.

Henry Freeman retired from the RNLI in 1899. To commemorate his long service a photo supplement was produced to accompany the Whitby Gazette of Friday, October 13th 1899. *(Photograph Courtesy of Whitby Gazette)*

CHAPTER 15

A QUESTION OF LEGALITY

Financially Henry Freeman was better off than his fellow fishermen. He had a pension from the RNLI and money from a testimonial raised on his behalf. All through November and December of 1899 and January and February 1900 the Whitby newspapers record payments being made into the testimonial fund. The generous contributions made by the public clearly reflected the respect and feeling the people had for the man at the end of his years as Coxswain. But this income was not sufficient to support him and his wife alone. Thus even in "retirement" he remained a fisherman and is recorded as having made large catches of salmon from time to time.

In the few short years which they shared together, Henry and Emma were deeply involved in the affairs of the Primitive Methodist Church in Whitby. One of Whitby's older residents, Eileen Leadley recalled in 1987 that both were strong Primitive Methodists and presumed that they met at church. She remembered in particular Emma Freeman's efforts to raise money for the "new" Primitive Methodist Church in Whitby which was opened in Church Street in 1903. The newspaper account of the opening ceremony includes Henry Freeman's name as among those present. Obituaries at the time of Freeman's death record that he was a regular attender at Church Street Primitive Methodist Church.

In these later years Henry spent his leisure hours in a variety of ways. Part of his time was given to the Conservative Club in Whitby where he was a member of the Committee. Henry attended various Party functions sometimes acting as a steward.

Life for Henry was much calmer now and there was little to trouble him. All the controversies and arguments of the past had been forgotten. Retirement had become sweet. He had a caring wife and had gained a family. What more could a man ask for?

But in the dark eddies of fate more ill fortune lay in store for Henry. The next summer, amongst the visitors to the port were two men whose home lay by the Tweed. They had been invited down to Whitby by Francis Ley a member of the Esk Fishery Board.

Peter Mackintosh and Thomas Malcolm stepped off the train at Whitby one day in June mingling with the holiday makers and joining their carefree progress into the town. They had no thoughts of pleasure on their minds, they simply had a job to do. At home they were employed by the Tweed Commissioners and had a vast experience in fishing for salmon. Now they were at Whitby at Mr Ley's personal request.

The Primitive Methodist Chapel, Church Street, as it appears today, although it is no longer used for worship. Opened in 1903, it replaced an earlier chapel frequented by members of the Busfield family. Emma Freeman remained one of the congregation until her death. *(Photograph Ray Shill)*

On June 15th 1904 Henry Freeman went out in the morning to fish for salmon with two others. Mackintosh, Malcolm and another man, John Kirkwood, were on the West Cliff looking down on Freeman. With a powerful telescope they were able to observe everything he did. Of particular interest to them was the way he went about setting his nets.

Later that month, Thomas Langlands and William Richardson were observed. In July, Robert Allen and then William Corner were studied from the same vantage point. Satisfied with their labours the men from the Tweed reported back to Ley.

The result of this clandestine investigation brought Henry Freeman before the magistrates again. Along with Thomas Langlands, William Richardson, Robert Allen and William Corner, he stood accused of illegal salmon fishing. It was not a case brought by the local fishery board, but by the Worshipful Company of Fishmongers in London. The lawyer, Herbert G. Muskett, came up to conduct the prosecution on their behalf, while Percy Middleton from Leeds acted for the defence of the fishermen. The case was tried in a tense atmosphere charged with public feelings for the accused.

The whole case centred around nets which were fixed instead of free floating. Whitby salmon fishermen adopted the practice of fixing their nets at one end to the sand and at the other to their boats which lay at anchor. This contravened a Bye-Law that no "fixed engines" should be used to catch the salmon.

The local Esk Fisheries Board had chosen not to enforce the law as all the accused held licences. No doubt the fishermen would have happily gone on in the same manner but for Ley's intervention. He had persistently argued with his fellow conservators about the matter and finally despairing of their ever taking action had sought outside help to spy on the fishermen.

The case was conducted on Tuesday 26th July 1904 before W Pyman, W.N. Walker, C. Murwood and Robert Elliot Pannett. Mr Muskett's opening address was both lengthy and technical, but concerned itself with the illegality of the way the men set their nets and of the type of nets they used. It was explained that the only legal way for licenced fishermen to catch salmon was with a draught or sweep net which was to be kept in motion during the whole time.

The Whitby men had been warned the previous August about using nets fixed by stones at the buoy end. They had discontinued this practice but had now begun to fish with the buoy end in shallow water, the lead of the nets then effectively fixing the one end to the sands.

Peter Mackintosh was then called to give evidence on the ways in which the defendants had contravened the Sea Fisheries Act, describing each infringement he had observed. Freeman's offence was slightly different for he fished further out and the buoy end of his net was not resting on the bottom, though it was fixed to his boat at the other end by a rope and his boat was anchored. Thus the nets were fixed at one end only. In the other cases, the nets were fixed at both.

During his cross-examination Mr Middleton was curious as to why Mackintosh had not warned the fishermen about the offences they were committing:

Mr Middleton " Do you know that as a matter of fact these cases were reported to the local Fishery Board?"
Peter Mackintosh "I don't know".
"You didn't report them, of course?"
"Not to the Board, I reported them to Mr Ley."
"And do you know that he reported them to the local Fishery Board?"
"I don't know."
"And do you know that they refused to take any proceedings in the matter?"
"I don't know."
"Have you heard so?"
"I have heard nothing."
"So your observations against the various men took over a month?"
"Yes."
"You had every opportunity of warning them and telling them what you had seen?"
"Oh, yes."
"And that they had done wrong?"
"Yes."
"Did you ever do so?"
"No."
"Why?"
"I wanted to keep the matter to myself."
"You were there as a guardian of the law?"
"Yes."
"And you were waiting until you thought they had committed sufficient breaches of the law?"
"I didn't think I was justified in warning them."
"Oh! Why?"
"I reported the offence to Mr Ley when it occurred."
"But when you saw Freeman come in and knew he had been doing wrong why didn't you tell him at once you were going to report him?"
"I reported the matter to the person I was told to do so." (sic)
"But why not warn him?"
"Because he would have gone away and warned the others"

There was laughter in the court.

Mr Middleton "That was your object then, to get these people to commit further breaches of the law?"
"They knew perfectly well what they were doing."
"Was that your object: to let as many men commit breaches of the law as possible before you made a report?"
"I let them do what they liked."
"Were you paid on commission for the number of cases you reported?"
"No."
"Are you sure?"
"Yes, certainly."
"Do you know that the very first indication any of the defendants had was when they got the summons?"
"That may be."
"Don't you think it would have been better and wiser to have warned the men?"
"I had no instructions to do so."
Mr Muskett: "Your duty would only be to report what you saw they had done?"
"Yes."

Thomas Malcolm repeated the evidence of his colleague and was subjected to the same line of questioning from Mr Middleton. Both men remained steadfast: their duty had been to report only to Mr Ley and to give nothing away to anybody else.

Mr Brown, Clerk to the Esk Fisheries Board then faced questioning and confirmed that the Board was aware of the malpractice by the fishermen, but had not done anything to prevent it.

Mr Middleton then proceeded with the defence. He complimented his legal adversary, Mr Muskett on the manner in which he had dealt with the case. Henry Freeman was his first witness. He denied having his nets fastened to his boat, or using stones or weights, or committing any infringement which contravened the terms of his licence. His method of fishing was to shoot the nets, let go of the anchor and ride by the nets, which were always loose in the water. Freeman admitted having the buoy end in shallow water but it was impossible to fish in any other way. Furthermore, the buoy end of his nets always lay in 3 or 4 fathoms of water.

Mr Pyman: "How is your net fastened to the boat?"
Freeman "When we shoot our nets we cast them adrift."
Mr Pannett "How is the net kept floating at the sea end?"
Freeman "By corks. We have buoys at the end and corked all along."

But Mr Muskett spotted a flaw in Henry Freeman's testimony to help his argument. Freeman had admitted the nets had remained stationary and Muskett concluded that therefore every inch of the nets must lie on the bottom. If this was not the case then the fish could not be caught. Since they lay on the bottom then the method of fishing was illegal.

Mr Middleton countered this argument by noting there were no restrictions in Freeman's licence as to the depth of water he should fish in, but Muskett's point of law had been demonstrated.

All the other fishermen gave similar evidence about the way they fished. Questions were raised about tides, depths of water and the need for leaded nets. At one point it was even stated that the nets still drifted even though they were rigid. William Luke, the water bailiff, considered the method of fishing was in order and James Handley, the Chief Officer of the Coastguard, corroborated what Luke had said.

The magistrates retired and for over forty-five minutes considered the facts. On returning they had to conclude that the defendants by their own admission had made their nets stationary and therefore fixed. In law, they had broken the statutes and the bench felt bound to convict them. Under the circumstances, however, the magistrates chose to impose a nominal penalty of one shilling for each defendant and to remit the costs.

The ruling must have been made reluctantly by the justices as they spent a long time discussing the matter. It is surprising that the case ever came to court, especially as the local Board or their agents believed no offence had been committed.

Surely the prosecution must have been engineered by Ley on behalf of powerful private interests, those nameless owners of fishing rights beside the Esk, who stood to lose by the fishermen's activities. Not content with their victory in establishing a playground in the Esk estuary, they had sought to restrict and hamper the salmon fishermen in every way possible to maximise on their profits from those rights.

In August 1904 the *Whitby Times* announced that there was little doing in sea salmon and herring fishing, the catches being most meagre. With the herring in decline and bottom feeding fish decimated by indiscriminate inshore trawling and now rigid rules about the catching of salmon, many Whitby fishermen must have despaired of the prospects for the future.

CHAPTER 16

A PEACEFUL END

Henry must have despaired, for he fell ill in December and for two weeks he could hardly sleep. His great personal strength ebbed away and he died peacefully in his sleep from heart failure. In our modern society Henry would perhaps have survived, but after a lifetime of battling and struggling, he may have lost his determination. The sea had become his life, the very fibre of his being, but each year had brought some new problem and yet more harassment.

After a short illness, he died at noon on Tuesday 13th December 1904 while the sea boiled and foamed. Whipped up by a strong wind, huge waves crashed down on Whitby pier. It was as if the sea had anticipated Henry's passing from this life and was beating out its own salute against the harbour walls.

For Emma, this was another tragic moment in her life. Her three years of marriage with Henry were briefer even than her time with her first husband, Kirby Watson. Henry's sudden death must have been a terrible shock for her. Henry was far too robust a man to quit this life without putting up a fight. Emma's faith sustained her, however, and carried her through the difficult times ahead.

Present at his death was the pastor of the Church Street Primitive Methodist Chapel, the Reverend Challenger, who came to administer the last rights. Henry had been a familiar sight to the Reverend as he went about his business in the port, Henry's towering frame almost a landmark itself. Seeing Henry in his final hours was quite a surprise as he remarked afterwards. He thought of Henry as strength personified but as he raised the giant man's arm that day it fell back, weak and limp.

Also present at his death was Julia Booth, his niece. There was a closeness between Julia and Henry which seems to have been of long standing. Perhaps Freeman looked upon her as the daughter he never had.

The funeral took place on the following Friday. It was well attended, many relatives and friends having come to witness the ceremony which consigned the honoured lifeboatman to his last resting place on the hill high above the Esk Valley at Larpool Cemetery.

Henry was a big man. He stood over six feet tall and even at death weighed 17 stone. His large coffin was specially made of pitch pine with heavy brass mountings. It was borne out of the house in Bakehouse Yard up into Cliff Street by his fellow lifeboatmen. Dressed in their blue guernseys and red caps they placed it in the hearse. Among their number was Walter Curry, his friend and longstanding fishing companion. The Union Jack was draped across the coffin and several floral wreaths in the shape of an anchor, cross and star were placed around it.

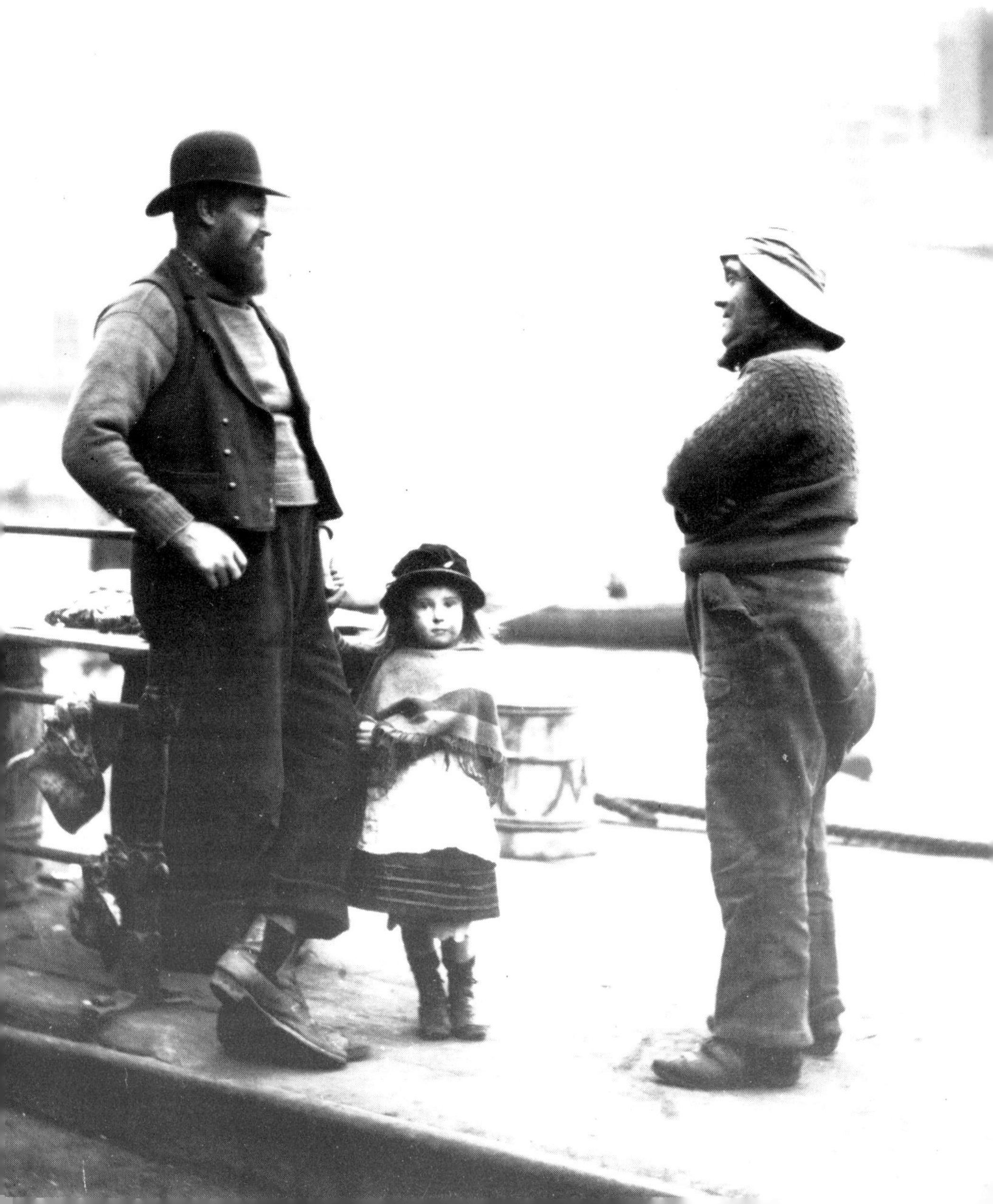

At one-thirty in the afternoon, the cortege moved slowly away along Cliff Street. Marching in step behind the hearse were fourteen of Henry's lifeboat colleagues. Next came the cariages containing the friends and relatives and behind them was a large crowd who followed on foot.

The procession wound its way down the Khyber Pass and along the pier. For the last time Henry was conveyed past the Lifeboat House then acros the bridge over the River Esk into Church Street. Along the route the blinds of the houses - mostly those of fishermen - were drawn. In the harbour many of the cobles had flags flying at half-mast as a sign of respect, not only for Freeman, but also for Robbie Patton, another veteran fisherman being buried that day.

Finally the cortege halted outside the new Primitive Methodist Chapel in Church Street for the first part of the burial service. The solemn proceedings were conducted in a crowded church by the Reverend E.W.Challenger.

The service opened with the singing of two verses of the hymn "Rock of Ages". Mr Challenger emphasised its appropriateness by saying that in the closing hours of Mr Freeman's life he had repeated to Freeman the words of that hymn. Although only semi-conscious, Mr Freeman had followed the words and the hymn was therefore the last words he heard him speak.

The Reverend Challenger's eulogy dwelt on Freeman's generosity, heroism, kindness and his giant strength. He knew no fear in the presence of danger. Freeman had a brave heart and was yet as gentle as a child. How the little ones loved and clung to him! His strength was his finest gentleness, and his gentleness his finest strength - and he combined them wonderfully. Those associated with the town had been recounting during the past few days his heroism - they had been looking those years in the face which had for ever gone from them, when they had heard his stentorian voice ring out; and in his presence strength had grown stronger.

The previous Saturday night he had sat beside his bedside and they talked over many things. Freeman seemed to fall back into reminiscence of one day when they were out with the boat. He said that some of them seemed to be almost without hope, yet he felt he had to be strong. He said that he knew that from every heart in the boat there went up a prayer to God; and he prayed, too. "Oh God take us back to land again". When the end came it was the quiet sleep of an innocent babe - not a struggle, but a calm and gentle sleep. With the rest of humanity, he had his faults, but he was generous to a fault.

Henry Freeman, pictured here on the New Quay at Whitby with a small girl. Though childless himself Henry's fondness for children was well-known.
(Photograph Frank Meadow Sutcliffe)

After the service in Church Street the coffin was conveyed up to the cemetery for the burial service. Upon the coffin lid was the simple inscription:

HENRY FREEMAN
Died Dec 13 1904
Aged 69 Years
Trusting in Jesus

When Henry Freeman died, the Busfield family were present in strength to pay their respects and provide support for Emma. At the funeral were Mr and Mrs J.N.Frankland, Mr M and Miss Groves (West Hartlepool) Miss E and Miss K. Whitton, Mr T. Busfield(Scarborough), Mr H.Busfield, Mr and Mrs A. Whitton, and Emma's own son, Mr H.Watson (Stockton) with his wife.

There were wreaths from Julia Booth, from his 'little friends' Evra, Rita, and Fiona and from E. Whitton. A handsome wreath, which arrived too late for the funeral, was also received from the Hon. and Rev. Augustus Byron, of Kirkby Mallory, Leicestershire, a constant visitor to Whitby, with whom the deceased had long been acquainted.

A great number of letters of sympathy for Emma Freeman were forwarded from all over the country from friends and well-wishers.

Emma was to outlive her second husband by some 26 years. She died on 7th March 1931, at the age of 85 years, at 12 Middle Hospital Yard. Present at her death was John Henry Watson, her second son. In a period spanning 68 years between 1863 and 1931, from her first marriage to Kirby Watson, to her death, Emma had been married for no more than ten years altogether. Clearly of all five sisters, Emma was the unluckiest in love.

Eileen Leadley recalled how once she was taken as a child by her grandmother to see Emma Freeman, "this tiny old lady who lived up one of Church Street's many yards. I was told that she was the widow of Henry Freeman, and that she was one of the women who worked very hard to raise the money for the 'New' Primitive Methodist Chapel, a very attractive building..." Eileen remembers that she was a very small old lady, dressed in black, wearing a bonnet and cape, who attended the Church Street Primitive Methodist Chapel until she was too frail to leave her home. Emma's home was in the Seamen's Hospital, a block of Almshouses in Church Street, which still exist, let at a peppercorn rent to retired seamen or their widows. Presumably she was granted one of these cottages after her husband died. When Centenary celebrations were held in Whitby in 1921 to mark the birth of Primitive Methodism in the town, Emma Freeman was evidently in good enough health to serve at the many meals that were a feature of that occasion.

The Seaman's Hospital in Lower Church Street. Emma Freeman lived in Middle Hospital Yard in her later years, and died here in 1931. *(Photograph Ray Shill)*

Emma Freeman was buried on 9th March 1931 in the same grave as Henry Freeman, her second husband, and her sister, Elizabeth, Henry's first wife. Today, the grave is marked by a headstone which acknowledges only the name of Henry Freeman. No mention is made of the two Busfield sisters whose care and devotion sustained the man through his life.

Henry Freeman was a unique man. For an illiterate son of a brickmaker he had risen to a position of eminence. His determination and stubbornness had shaped his future. The younger son in a brickmaking family, he had little to look forward to in Bridlington. There he would always be subservient to his elder brothers. By going to Whitby he was able to establish himself in the trade in his own right. But on achieving this goal he found no lasting satisfaction in it and took to fishing. In this he discovered an interest which remained with him to the day he died.

Some say that one has to be born into a fishing family to understand the sea and make a good fisherman, but Henry soon acquired the necessary skills to succeed in his new occupation. His native intelligence equipped him well for the transition.

His feeling for his fellow man led him into the lifeboat service, but his powerful strength and rigid determination kept him there. He was a natural choice for coxswain and justly proved the faith placed in him.

Though sometimes argumentative, he had a way with his fellow lifeboatmen which instilled courage into them and some spectacular rescues were pulled off as a result. Many mariners owed their lives and their families' futures to Henry Freeman.

In a different age with wider educational opportunities no doubt he could have progressed even further. But in these Victorian times, Henry achieved as much as he was able. Few of his contemporaries received country-wide acclaim as he did.

Yet since his death most of his deeds have been forgotten. Whitby today is remembered for Caedmon, Captain Cook, Dracula, the novelist Mary Linskill, Scoresby and Saint Hilda. Apart from the Frank Meadow Sutcliffe studies of the veteran lifeboatman which adorn the Sutcliffe Gallery's Flowergate window display, the man might have been forgotten.

For over eighty years his grave even lacked a headstone. It took the fund raising abilities of a group of school children to find the money for one. In 1986 they walked the six miles from Whitby to Robin Hood's Bay along a route which followed closely the path of the *Robert Whitworth* in 1881 to the brig *Visiter*. At last there was a permanent monument to the memory of a man who gave his all to save others.

Many things can be said of Henry Freeman. He had both good and bad in him but what set him apart was his great courage and his ability to give courage to others. These qualities are uncommon in every age but were never more needed than in the era of the rowing lifeboat.

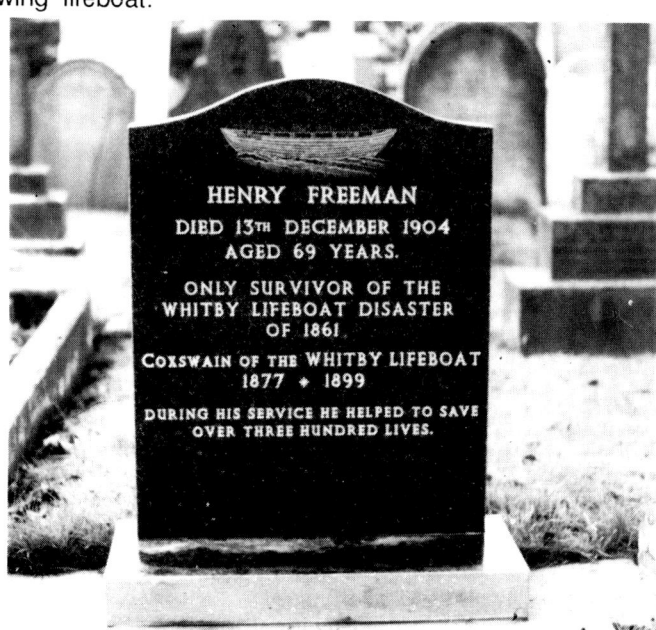

The headstone as it appears on Freeman's grave today bears no mention of his two wives who are buried with him.   *(Photograph Ray Shill)*

Pupils of Whitby School who helped raise money for a headstone for Freeman's grave are seen here in the company of the present lifeboat coxwain Peter Thomson in May 1986. *(Photograph Courtesy of Whitby Gazette)*

POSTSCRIPT

The publication of this biography brings to a close some six years of research that began in the late summer of 1985.

During that period we have consulted a wide range of sources but ultimately we have had to depend heavily on newspaper accounts, official records and archive material. The information thus gathered, while extremely valuable, inevitably has its limitations: it provides a detailed picture of Freeman as a public figure, but sketches only in vague outline his nature as a private individual.

Questions therefore are left as to the more personal details of Henry Freeman's life. The quality of his relationships with family, wives, in-laws, stepsons and those among whom he lived and worked cannot be stated with any certainty. All those who knew him are long since dead. Memories of him which have survived are few and may well have become distorted with time.

The type of source material which, more than any other, could help to construct a more rounded picture of the man was not available to us. Yet, there is every likelihood that in some dusty attic there may exist some written record of one who might have made Freeman's acquaintance, perhaps whilst on holiday, or when he was a visitor in their town. A diary, or some letters, or even a postcard could add immeasurably to our knowledge of the man. By this means we might learn about his habits and pastimes, his likes and dislikes, and about his feelings and behaviour towards family and friends. Until such evidence emerges, however, we can only speculate about such matters as why Freeman had no children, how caring a husband he was, or how he related to parents, sisters and brothers.

During our research we were lucky enough to make contact with descendants of the Watson family, such as David Watson of Bexhill and Mrs Ann Hill of Halesowen, who kindly supplied us with important family documents. Indeed, we met Mrs Hill only a short time before going to print, and it was she who allowed us access to Henry Freeman's silver medal which had been in the care of her mother for many years. Thanks to her, we have been able to include a photograph of the medal in this edition. Until then, its whereabouts had been one of our unsolved mysteries.

A number of mysteries however still remain unsolved. Some of these gaps in our knowledge have been alluded to in the text. Where, for example, was Kirby Watson (Senior) in 1861, before he married Emma Busfield? He seems to have been living outside Whitby. If so, how then did he meet Emma? And what of his sons by Emma? We know little about who raised them, and where: in particular, Kirby, the youngest just seems to vanish after the age of nine months and the rest of his life is a virtual blank, until his death. Where was his mother, widow Emma Watson, between 1881 and her marriage to Henry Freeman in 1901? Just how long did she remain in the service of Robert Pannett? And how long had she been living in Hartlepool when she married Henry?

Then there is the matter of Henry's sisters, Ann, Mary, Jane and Sarah. All our attempts to discover what became of them in later life proved fruitless. Sarah's disappearance is without doubt the most interesting. Did she die in some peculiar circumstances, or did she simply leave her husband? Did she remarry? Could she have moved to another part of the country, or even have emigrated? No trace of her has been discovered after 1859.

Other puzzles were not mentioned specifically in the text. In the account of Henry Freeman's funeral which appeared in the Whitby Times, a Mrs Hunter is listed among those who were at the head of the funeral procession alongside Emma Freeman. Her inclusion among the names of close family members suggests strongly that she may herself have been a close relative. If so, who was she? Could she perhaps have been one of Freeman's missing sisters, returning to pay her last respects to her famous brother? Or was she perhaps just a close friend at Emma's side to provide moral support to the grieving widow?

Finally, we were unable to find a photograph which we needed to illustrate one of our chapters. It proved impossible to find a photograph of Captain Gibson, the harbourmaster of Whitby.

The jig-saw therefore is not yet complete. Perhaps in time it will be completed as readers who find themselves in possession of some of the missing pieces bring them out of their present seclusion into the public domain.

Ian Minter and Ray Shill
Birmingham
November 1991

Harold Brown seen here admiring Heny Freeman's medal. *(Photograph Ray Shill)*

Margaret Thatcher being presented with portrait of Henry Freeman when she opened Supreme Plastics offices in London. *(Courtesy Supreme Plastics Ltd)*

APPENDIX 1

THE FAMILY TREE OF HENRY FREEMAN

```
John Freeman...................
                   :                     William Priestley...Dorothy Collins
                   :                                              :
...................:.........................................    :..........
   :        :           :           :            :           :    :
 John      Nanny     WILLIAM      Mary        Susanna      Sarah  :
                        :...............................MARGARET PRIESTLEY
                        :
........................:................:...................................
 :       :       :       :       :           :         :      :
Ann      :       :       :       :       Charlotte:    :      :        James
b.1822   :       :       :       :         b.1832.:    :      :        b.1841
 :       :       :       :       :           :        :       :
 :     Mary      :       :     George= Jane            :      :
Emily  b 1823    :       :     b.1830  Stephenson :    : Jane = Henry
Alice    :       :       :           :             :   : b1837  Varley
Ada    Eliza     :       :        Ward             :   :        :
(all ileg.)      :       :        Clara            :   :        :
                 :       :        Louisa           :   :     Thomas
                 :       :        Anne Elizabeth   :   :
                 :       :        Tom              :   :
                 :       :        Mary             :   :
Patience = John  :       :        Eliza            : Sarah= William
Gutherleys b.1825:       :        Margaret         : b.1837 Wherrit
  :              :       :        John William     :        :
Charles    Ann= William  :        George Robert    :     Margaret
Mary    Langton b1827    :        Henry            :
Agnes      :             :        Ada              :
Tom       Margaret(ileg.):
John      Elizabeth(ileg.) :
William   George             :
Zillah    Julia              :
Sarah     Mary         : Elizabeth Busfield=HENRY   Emma  =   Kirby
Henry     Ada          :                    b1835   Busfield  Watson
Henry     William            :                        :      :      :
Fred      Francis            :                        :      :      :
Ward      Henry       Thomas= Bethalina               :      :      :
          James      b1829   Cowling                  :      :      :
          John           :         :......George      :      :      :
          Charles      Elizabeth   :      Cowling     :      :      :
                       William     :                  :      :      :
                       Margaret  Mary               :..Emma Watson....:
                                                      (Busfield)     :
                                                ........................:
                                                :          :        :
                                         William Thomas    :        :
                                         WATSON b.1865     :        :
                                                  :     Kirby
                                               John Henry  WATSON
                                               WATSON b.1867 b.1870
```

228

APPENDIX 2

HENRY FREEMAN'S FISHING COBLES

The following is extracted from the Whitby Customs House register of fishing boats and is a list of those vessels Henry Freeman is recorded as being master of:

Port No.	Name of Vessel	Type of Vesel	Form of Fishing	No of Men	Tonnage	Length over Keel	Period of Mastership	Registered Owner
370	Alexandra	Coble	Herring	4	10	30ft.	14.06.1870 -14.07.1875	Thomas Mennell
375	William & Margaret	Coble	Long Line	2	2.5	19.5	18.11.1870 -18.09.1872	Henry Freeman
398	Quartelle	Mule	Herring	4	7	33	29.08.1871 -17.05.1872	Thomas Turner
418	Elizabeth	Coble	Long Line	3	2.5	19.5	19.12.1872 -12.03.1888	Henry Freeman
429	Wings of the Morning	Mule	Herring	4	8	32	11.05.1876 -01.01.1877	Henry Freeman
496	Garland	Keel Boat	Herring	5	14	37	09.10.1876 -28.04.1881	Henry Freeman

Boat registered owners Henry Freeman and Thomas Mitchell until 07.06.1877, then Henry Freeman sole owner

57	Janes	Mule	Herring	4	10	33	02.10.1883 -18.07.1886	James Graham
53	Louie Beckett	Coble	Herring	3	3	22	23.07.1886 -1910	H Freeman W Currie E.Gash

From 30.07.1896, W.Currie and H. Freeman owners
H.Freeman registered master until boat sold 1910!

127	Elizabeth Freeman	Coble	Nets & Lines	3	6	29.6	15.02.1888 -02.10.1906	H.Freeman

229

APPENDIX 3
THE RESCUES IN WHICH HENRY FREEMAN PARTICIPATED

Date	Vessel in danger Name	Type	Lifeboat or other vessel used	Lives saved
09.02.1861	John and Ann	Brig	Staithes Fishing Coble	5
09.02.1861	Gamma	Schooner	Whitby No1 Lifeboat	4
09.02.1861	Clara	Barque	Whitby No1 Lifeboat	11
09.02.1861	Utility	Brig	Whitby No1 Lifeboat	4
09.02.1861	Roe	Schooner	Whitby No1 Lifeboat	6
09.02.1861	Merchant	Schooner	Whitby No1 Lifeboat Lifeboat sunk	-
15.10.1864			Whitby Coble	1
19.10.1865	Elizabeth?	Schooner	Lucy	-
08.01.1866	Lena	Coble	Whitby Coble, Jane Ann	3
08.01.1866	Maria	Coble	Whitby Coble, Jane Ann	3
31.12.1866	Lion	Schooner	Lucy	5
24.05.1876		Coble	Robert Whitworth	3
01.03.1877	Christopher Hansteen	Brig	Robert Whitworth	8
05.01.1878	Oscar	Steamship	Robert Whitworth	22
08.05.1878	Eliza	Fishing	Robert Whitworth	2
08.05.1878	James & Sarah	Boats	Robert Whitworth	2
12.09.1878	Welcome	Fishing B	Robert Whitworth	2
13.03.1879	J.H.Lorentzen	Steamship	Robert Whitworth	17
28.10.1880	Elizabeth Austin	Schooner	Hariott Forteath	5
28.10.1880	Reaper	Schooner	Robert Whitworth	4
28.10.1880	Good Intent	Yawl	Robert Whitworth	8
28.10.1880	John Snell	Brig	Robert Whitworth	5
15.01.1881	Lumley	Snow	Robert Whitworth	-
19.01.1881	Visiter	Brig	Robert Whitworth	6
06.12.1882	Star of Hope	Brig	Robert and Mary Ellis	6
03.05.1885	Wear	Sloop	Harriott Forteath III	2
20.08.1885	Robert and Henry	Coble	Harriott Forteath III	3
24.10.1885	Mary and Agnes	Brigantine	Robert and Mary Ellis	-
11.01.1893	Rose Marion	Coble	Robert and Mary Ellis	3
11.01.1893	William	Coble	Robert and Mary Ellis	3
02.03.1893	Mary Alice	Coble	Robert and Mary Ellis	-
21.02.1898	R.W.Jackson	Coble	Robert and Mary Ellis	3
21.02.1898	Tranquil	Coble	Robert and Mary Ellis	3
21.02.1898	Martha Dryden	Coble	Robert and Mary Ellis	2
				152

This list is compiled from reports in the Whitby press and RNLI returns. No doubt Henry Freeman may have gone out on other rescues but the nature of these are not presently known.

ASSISTANCE GIVEN TO FISHING COBLES

Date	Craft	Lifeboat
02.12.1879	Four Fishing Cobles	Harriott Forteath II
15.04.1880	Lady Morris	Harriott Forteath II
15.04.1880	Star of Peace	Harriott Forteath II
20.04.1883	3 fishing cobles, 1 pilot coble.	Robert and Mary Ellis
06.02.1895	Several Cobles	Christopher
15.01.1896	Secret	John Fielden
13.02.1896	Several Cobles	John Fielden
27.07.1896	Star of Peace	John Fielden
12.03.1897	30 fishing cobles	John Fielden
20.02.1898	Several cobles	John Fielden
28.04.1898	Several cobles	John Fielden
19.08.1898	Robert, pleasure coble.	Robert and Mary Ellis

Bibliography

In compiling this work the following sources have been consulted:

Newspaper Material :
Bridlington Free Press
Halifax Courier.
Halifax Guardian.
Manchester City News
Manchester Examiner.
Northern Echo.
Preston Pilot & County Advertiser.
Scarborough Gazette
Shields Daily Gazette & Shipping Telegraph.
South Shields Daily Standard.
The Times.
Whitby Gazette.
Whitby Times
Yorkshire Post.

Printed Sources :
J. Harvey Bloom, Robin Hood's Bay: A Retrospect circa 1927.
Halifax Lifeboat Saturday Official Program 01/09/1894.
P.Howarth. Lifeboat Story 1957.
A.F.Humble. The Rowing Lifeboats of Whitby 1974.
Lewis. The Lifeboat and its Work 1874.
Jeff Morris. The Story of the Whitby Lifeboats.1982
Eric Rodway. Whitby in 1851.
Richard Weatherill. Ancient Port of Whitby 1908.
Rev George Young, A Picture of Whitby 1840.

Archive Material :
Bridlington Priory Church Parish Registers. Humberside CRO.
Eastrington Parish Register. Humberside CRO.
Hartlepool Parish Registers. Cleveland CRO
North Eastern Sea Fisheries Committee Minutes, Humberside CRO.
Stranton Methodist Records. Cleveland CRO.
Ships logs for the brig Visiter various dates 1830 -1881
- Public Record Office, Kew; Maritime History Archive, Memorial University of Newfoundland, Canada.
Sunderland Shipping Registers. Tyne and Wear CRO.
Whitby Shipping Registers. Whitby Library courtesy National Maritime Museum.

Whitby Fishing Boat Registers, North Yorkshire CRO.
Whitby Parish Registers, North Yorkshire CRO.

Other sources.:
Percy Burnett files, Whitby Literary & Philosophical Society.
1841- 1881 Census material for Bridlington, Flamborough, Filey, Hartlepool, Pocklington, Scarborough and Whitby.
RNLI Returns of Services for Whitby and Upgang Lifeboats 1865-1900.
Whitby Lifeboat Committee Minute books up to 1900.
The original Manchester Lifeboat Committee Minute book.
Ordnance survey of 1891 for Whitby.
Larpool Cemetery Burial Records.
The Dalesman Sept 1981
The Lifeboat.
The Engineer.
St.Catherines House Indexes of Birth, Marriages and Deaths.
Lloyds Shipping Registers.
National Maritime Museum Greenwich (Department of Printed Books and Manuscripts).
City of London, Guildhall Library, Aldermanbury.
Sutcliffe Gallery, Flowergate, Whitby.

We would also like to thank the following people and organisations
for their help:

Birmingham Reference Library.
Harold Brown, B.E.M. S.B.St. J. , Whitby.
British Library, National Newspaper Library, Colindale.
British Library, Census Office, Portugal St, London
British Library, Map Dept.
Calderdale Public Libraries.
Cleveland County Archives Dept, Middlesbrough.
Hilary Daley.
Fleet Fotos, London (J. E. Ballard).
The Francis Frith Collection, Andover, Hants. (Thanks to Michelle Turner).
Mrs Muriel Freeman, Bridlington.
The Fylingdales Local History Group.
Carole Gaute, Lymington Marina, Hants.
Daisy Hardy, Robin Hood's Bay.
Hartlepool Central Library.
Mrs Ann Hill, Halesowen.
Les Heath, Editor, Whitby Gazette.
Ellen Holcroft, Bramhope, Leeds.
The University of Hull (with thanks to Miss J. M. Smith and to Joyce M. Bellamy).

Humberside Record Office, Beverley (thanks to K. D. Holt, County Archivist)
The Illustrated London News, Picture Library, London
(thanks to Elaine Hart).
Information Service, Danish Embassy, London.
Information Service, Embassy of the United States of America, London.
Revd. Ray Jones, Nantwich, Cheshire.
Mr Frederick Lane, Sevenoaks, Kent.
Eileen Leadley, Whitby.
Revd. J. Christopher Ledgard, Brunswick Methodist Church, Whitby.
Mr John Marsland, Robin Hood's Bay.
Mr David Oliver May, FRINA, Lymington Marina, Hants.
McClean County Historical Society, Bloomington, Illinois, USA
(with thanks to Greg Koos).
Memorial University of Newfoundland, Maritime History Archive
(with thanks to Roberta Thomas, Heather Wareham and Mary Bridson).
Methodist Church Archives, Manchester
(with thanks to the Revd. William Leary).
Jeff Morris, Archivist, Lifeboat Enthusiast Society.
The National Maritime Museum, Greenwich
(with thanks to Joan Horsley and to Mrs Gervaise Vaz)
Rev Edwin Newlyn, Rural Dean of Whitby.
North Yorkshire County Library Divisional Headquarters, Scarborough.
North Yorkshire County Records Office, Northallerton.
Mr Richard P. Pennock, Robin Hood's Bay.
N.W.Pepper, Bridlington.
Mrs Pat Pickles, Wakefield.
Mr Stewart Pottas, Supreme Plastics Limited, Whitby
Public Records Office, Chancery Lane.
Public Records Office, Kew.
Doctor R. W. H. Roeder, Supreme Plastics Limited, London.
The Royal Library, Copenhagen, Denmark.
RNLI, Manchester.
RNLI, Poole, Dorset.
RNLI, Whitby Museum.
Scarborough Borough Council Cemeteries and Crematorium Office, Scarborough.
Scarborough Borough Council Technical Services Department
(thanks to Mr D. Green, Whitby Office).
Michael J. Shaw, Whitby.
Mr R. C. Shayler, Solihull.
Doreen Simpson, Maltby, Cleveland
Stockton Reference Library, Mrs J. Chesney.
The Sutcliffe Gallery, Whitby (with thanks to Bill Shaw).
Mr E. Thomson, former RNLI Secretary to Whitby Lifeboats.
Peter Thomson Coxswain of the Whitby Lifeboats.

Tyne and Wear Record Office, Newcastle.
United Methodist Church Commission on Archives and History, Illinois, USA (with thanks to Mr Richard A. Chrisman).
Frank and Kathleen Walker, Middlesbrough.
David Watson, Bexhill.
Whitby Archives (with thanks to Colin Waters, Director).
Whitby Conservative Club (with thanks to Max Thomas).
Whitby Gazette (with thanks to Mr Les Heath, Editor).
Whitby Literary and Philosophical Society (with thanks to Alan Berends and Harold Brown).
Whitby Library (with special thanks to Sandra Turner)
Whitby Registry Office (with thanks to Mrs Ruth Whitehead, Supt. Registrar)
Margaret Whitworth, Whitby.
T.H.Wood, Whitby.

Finally we are indebted to:

Chris and Rosemary Clegg
Alan Dalton
Robin Elliott
Mrs Dorothy Minter
Mrs. Johanna Shill
John D. Shon

INDEX

B
Bait 58, 60, 63, 66
Balkholme 18
Barton-on-Humber 18
Bloomington, Illinois USA 41
Boynton 23
Beverley 156
Brickmaking Trade 16, 18, 20, 22, 23, 25
Bridlington 15, 18, 20, 22, 24,25
    Bempton Lane 25
    Brickyards 22,25
    Ings Lane 23
    Lifeboats 86,87
    Old Town 18
    Priory Church, 18-20
    Quay 18
    St John's Street 20
    Union Workhouse 25
    Westgate 25
Burlington 18

C
Crab and lobster fishing 60,62
Cod fishing 60, 71
Cork life jackets 10,12, 59

D
Dan 60
Dracula 147
Duncoats 18

E
Eastrington 16
Enclosure Acts 16
Esk Board of Conservators 157

F
Family relations
    Elizabeth Busfield
    /Elizabeth Freeman (wife) 31-33, 35, 179, 186, 188
    Elizabeth Busfield (Craven) (Mother-in-law) 35, 172
    Eliza Mary Busfield 35,44
    /Eliza Mary Thistle 44, 46
    /Eliza Mary Frankland 46, 48
    Emma Busfield 35
    /Emma Watson 40-41, 43-44, 179
    /Emma Freeman (2nd wife), 188-90, 217, 220, 221
    Jane Busfield 35
    /Jane Groves 39-40
    Rebecca Busfield 32,35
    /Rebecca Whitton 40, 179, 181
    Thomas Busfield (Father-in-law) 31,34-35, 36, 38, 172
    Thomas Craven Busfield 35, 48
    Ann Freeman (Sister) 18, 24-25
    Charlotte Freeman (Sister) 18
    Francis Freeman (Nephew) 186
    George Freeman (Brother) 18, 24-5
    George Freeman (Nephew) 181
    Henry Freeman (Nephew) 148
    James Freeman (Brother) 23
    James Freeman (Nephew) 148, 186
    Jane Freeman (Sister)
    /Jane Varley 20,25
    John Freeman (Brother) 18, 23, 25
    John Freeman (Uncle) 16
    Julia Freeman (Niece) 181
    /Julia Booth 217
    Mary Freeman (Niece) 181
    Mary Freeman (Sister) 18, 24-25
    Sarah Freeman (Niece) 181
    Sarah Freeman (Sister) 20, 25
    Sarah Wherrit 181, 186
    Thomas Freeman (Brother) 18, 24
    William Freeman (Father) 15, 16,18, 25
    William Freeman (Brother) 18, 23, 24, 148
    William Freeman (Nephew) 181, 184
    Patience Freeman (Gutherleys) 23, 25
    Ann Freeman (Langton) 23, 181
    Margaret Priestley (Mother)
    /Margaret Freeman 18
    Jane Freeman (Stephenson) 24
    Margaret Elizabeth Wherrit (Niece) 25, 186
    John Henry Watson (Stepson) 41, 43, 179, 190, 193
    Kirby Watson (Stepson) 43, 190, 194-198
    William Thomas Watson (Stepson) 41, 190, 193
Filey 24
Fishing Industry 20-21, 58-72

Flamborough 20
    Lighthouse 21, 23
    Lighthouse Farm 23
    National School 23
    North Landing 20
    South Landing 20
Flamborough Head 21-24
Frederickshaven 44

G
Gilberdyke 16

Great Exhibition 1851 36
Great Intl. Fisheries Exhibition 140
Great Storm (The) of 1861 6

H

Hartlepool 25,27,40 44,49, 188
Herring Fishing 62,65 71-72
Howden 15,17

J

Jet Ornaments 35-36
Jet Trade 17,35-39

K

Kit 60-62, 65
Kronstadt 44

L

Laeso Island 44
Lifeboat Demonstration (Lifeboat Saturday)
    Halifax 78-79
    Huddersfield 78
    Leeds 159-161
    Whitby 78, 79, 158, 161
Lifeboatmen:
    William Afflek 159
    John Batchelor 92
    George Boyes 57
    John Cass 52
    John Clarkson 92
    Christopher Collins 8, 12, 13
    William Cummings 92-93
    Walter Curry 67, 92, 93, 159, 207, 217
    John Davidson 92
    John Dixon 6, 13
    Isaac Dobson 9, 12
    John Dryden 92, 93
    William Dryden 6
    Richard Eglon 159, 165
    James Elders 159
    William Fletcher 57
    F. Foster 92
    Thomas Gains 54, 57, 84, 90, 93, 124
    Matthew Gales 92
    Edward Gash 77, 92,159
    Richard Gatenby 85
    Robert Harland 9
    William Harland 57, 73
    William Harrison 159
    Thomas Hartley 78, 82-86
    G. Hodgson 92
    Henry Hodgson 92
    John Hodgson 92
    William Holmes 57
    Samuel Hutchins 36, 79
    Thomas Kelly 159
    Samuel Lacy 54-57, 71, 74, 78, 82, 85
    Peter Langlands 56
    Thomas Langlands 77, 84, 87-91, 97, 151, 153, 158-161, 165, 200, 209, 213
    Matthew Leadley 8, 11, 13
    Robert Leadley 6
    George Martin 6
    William Moat 199
    Francis Osborne 57
    John Palmer 83
    William Patterson 83
    Joseph Patten 56, 57
    John Philpot 8, 11, 13
    John Pickering 50-57, 74, 81
    James Pounder 86, 90-93, 98, 117-118
    Robinson Pounder 92, 142
    William Richardson 92
    Pounder Robinson 159
    Robert Robinson 159
    Richard Stainthorp 8, 57
    John Skelton 109, 111, 113
    John Storr (1861 Whitby Coxswain) 6-13
    John Storr (son of above) 83, 84, 85, 86, 109-113
    Thomas Storr 8, 9
    William Storr 8, 10
    John Thompson 83, 85
    Joseph Tomlinson 159
    William Tyreman 6, 12, 13
    Luke Walker 85
    William Walker 9
    John Waters 92
    William Waters 93
    William Winspear 92, 93
Lifeboat Race 151
Lifeboats
    Balcarras 206, 208
    Christopher 149, 152
    Robert and Mary Ellis I 118, 119, 120, 121, 141, 142, 146, 151, 153, 199, 200, 206, 208, 209
    Ephraim and Hannah Fox 117, 140, 142
    John Fielden 205, 208
    Fishermen's Friend 52, 54, 57, 79, 80
    Free Gardner 151
    Hannah Somerset 142

Harbinger 87
Harriott Forteath I 78-86
Harriot Forteath II 52, 85, 90, 92, 93
(Old) Green Boat 50, 51, 52
Lucy (1) 50-57
Lucy (2) 87
   Robert Whitworth 74, 78-93, 98, 103, 108-109
   Harriott Forteath III 119, 140, 144, 149
Petrel 52, 57, 86
Robert Whitworth I (Bridlington) 86
Robert Whitworth II (Bridlington) 87
Mary Stanford 163
Catherine Swift 159, 161
Joseph Sykes 97, 98, 119, 140
Alfred Trower 163
Upgang 200
William Watson 55, 74
Worcestershire Cadet 159, 161
Long Line Fishing 58, 62

M

Market Weighton Canal 16, 17

N

North Eastern Railway 26, 52, 65, 96
North Eastern Sea Fisheries Committee 71, 156, 164, 165
Northumberland Dock, Newcastle 96

O

Offal net 164
Over 56, 124, 126

P

Pannet Park Museum 193
People and Personages:
   Robert Simpson Adamson 101
   Robert Allen 213
   William Todd Anderson 101, 113
   W. H. Ashford 164, 168
   Rev Canon Austen 159
   Robert Austin 140
   Charles Bagnall 123, 124, 135
   William Barrett 123
   John Barry 113
   Henry Bell 72, 123-127, 136-137, 153, 165
   Thomas Bell 124
   William Bell 101, 103
   William Booth 181
   William Brockett 142
   Harold Brown 181, 186
   Captain Butler 8, 11, 12
   Rev E.W. Challenger 217, 219
   Susannah Coates 184
   Robert Cooper 108
   Rev Robert Jermyn Cooper 103, 106, 113
   William Corner 213
   Robert Coulson 123, 131, 136
   Robert Crosby 59, 60, 62, 124, 129, 131, 137
   Robert Dawson 148
   Dean of York 118, 119
   Rev Denniss 149
   Thomas Dobson 87
   Algernon Dodd 103
   John Douglas 78, 80
   Clifford Dunn 196, 197
   George Elliot MP, Sir 90
   W. R. Fawcett 123, 126-127, 131-135
   Alice Mary Foster 193
   Ethel Foster 197
   William Frank 65
   John Ness Frankland 46
   Richard Frankland 46
   Charles Jackson 25
   Captain James 88
   Robert Gibson 83, 90, 92, 93, 97-99, 103, 107, 142, 200, 201, 209
   William Griers 82
   Matthew Groves 39-40
   John Harland 158
   William Hawkesfield 199
   Harry Holbrook 196, 197
   Joseph Kay 206
   Benjamin Kilvington 172
   John Kilvington 172
   Christopher King 23
   E. de Kretschmar 207, 208
   Richard Lewis 118
   Francis Ley 211
   Peter Mackintosh 211/3/4/5
   Thomas Malcolm 211, 214, 215
   Thomas Mennell 72, 128-129, 133, 179
   Percy Middleton 213-216
   James Midwood 83
   Edward Musgrave 87
   Herbert Muskett 213, 215, 216
   Commander Napean 99, 118
   George Ord 27
   Ann Oxley 128
   William Clark Oxley 62, 129

Robert Elliot Pannett 44, 144, 154-156, 164, 165, 169, 213
James Philpot 123
William Richardson 213
George Robinson 101
Captain Richard Robinson 103, 113
Trueman Robinson 101
Superintendent Ryder 124
Ann Elizabeth Sample 193
Dr Semple 148
Richard Sheppey 73
Thomas Shimings 92
Charles Smales 119
George Wakefield Smales 55, 77-82, 86-88, 90, 119
Richard Smith 46, 65, 83, 84, 87
Margaret Snowden 29
Matthew Snowden 54
George Splayfoot 24, 25
Margaret Stancliffe 181
Brodie Stein 200
Frank Meadow Sutcliffe 169
Matthew Thistle 44-47
Claude Thompson 197
Mary Thompson 25
William Tose 9, 10, 12, 83
William Tyreman 181
Frank Unthank 124
Henry Varley 25
George Vasey Junior 26
George Vasey Senior 26
Thomas Walker 43
Captain Ward R.N. 79, 81
Bessey Watson 190
Kirby Watson (1st husband, Emma Busfield) 40, 41, 43, 190
William Watson (father of Kirby, above) 40, 190
William Watson (brother of Kirby, above) 190, 193
Matthew Wellburn 108, 113, 144
Thomas Wellham 206-208
Mark Winn 52, 54, 71
Captain Wharton 85
William Wherrit 25
Joseph Brown Whitton 32, 40
Jonathan Whitton 40
Robert Whitworth 86, 87
John Woodhouse 96-97
Woodcock family 23
Pocklington 40
Portington 15, 16

R

Robin Hood's Bay 101-103, 200, 205

Bay Bank 108, 111, 112
Laurel Inn 109, 110
Rocket Brigade 103
Wayfoot 103
RNLI 32, 50, 55, 85, 93-95, 158
Runswick Bay 78
River Humber 15-17

S

Salmon Fishing 213
Saltwick 205
Sand Eels 60
Sand Eel Net 167
Scarborough 39, 48, 57, 155-156
Sea Fishery Act 71, 154
Seine net 164
Sewerby 25
Shields 27
Ship Owners
    Marwood and Co 44
    Smales Brothers 81
Ships and Vessels:
    Cruiser 27
    George Bentinck 27
Barque: Clara 8, 9
    Godstadt Minde 79
    Royal Rose 51, 52
    Svadsfare 78-81, 149
Brigs: John and Ann 6
    Christopher Hansteen 88, 149
    Otterburn 90
    Maria Soames 54
    Medora 101
    Prince Albert 149
    Romulus 200
    Star of Hope 120
    Trebizond 44-47
    Tribune 13
    Utility 9
    Visiter 100-116
Brigantine: Mary and Agnes 145, 146
Cobles: Alexandra 72, 127, 137, 179
    Ann Maria 144
    Ann and Elizabeth 87
    Beta 149
    James and Sarah 90
    Jane Ann 55-57
    Eliza 90
    Elizabeth 73, 179
    Frolic 144
    John and Ann 140
    Garland 88, 179
    Lady Morris 90
    Lena 56

Lily 124
Louie Beckett 148
Margaret 153
Maria 57
Martha Dryden 206
Mary Alice 199
Nomad 153
North Star 149
Palm Branch 199
Quartelle 72
Ralph Ward Jackson 206
Robert 209
Robert and Henry 144
Rose Marion 199
Samuel and Sarah 54
Star of Hope 149
Star of Peace 90, 149, 199
Thomas and James 88
Tranquil 206
Wasp 206
Water Lily 88
William 199
William and Margaret 72-73
Wings of the Morning 82
Fishing Yawl: Good Intent 70, 92
Mules: Daisy 144
Wild Rose 144
Schooners: Agenoria 83
Dmitry 146-148
Elizabeth 55
Elizabeth Austen 70, 92
Gamma 8
Flora 10
John Snell 93, 149
Lion 57
Maid of Honor 142
Merchant 10-12
Reaper 92
Roe 9
Wiliam 119
Sloop: Wear 142, 144
Snow: Lumley 96-100
Steamships: Alice 54
King Arthur 122
Beatrice 122
James Gray 122
J. H. Lorentzen 90-91, 149
Ocean Queen 54
Oscar 90, 149
Southwark 200
Wykeham 122
Steam Tug: Admiral 119
Emu 88
Hilda 54
Stainsacre 108

T
Trammel net 164
Tyne Dock, Newcastle 101

U
Upgang 97
Upgang LIfeboat Station 55-57, 74, 77, 97

W
West Hartlepool 40, 41, 49
Whitby
    Bakehouse Yard 40, 179, 181, 217
    Baxtergate 25, 144
    Boltons Buildings 27, 169
    Brickyards 25, 26
    Cappleman's Yard 186
    Church Street 35, 48, 178, 179
    Church Street Primitive Methodist Chapel 211, 217, 219
    Clarks Yard 172, 178
    Cliff St 40, 217
    Coastguard 51, 83, 88
    Colliers Hope 90
    Colliers Ghaut 65
    Conservative Club 211
    Cragg 71, 178
    Dock End 50, 53, 65, 69
    East Cliff 60, 63, 88
    Fishbum Park 26, 44
    Fishburn Park Primitive Methodist Chapel 41, 42
    Franklands Coffee House 48
    Grape Lane 35
    Khyber Pass 51, 219
    Kilvingtons Yard 39, 43, 44, 172, 179
    Langdale Buildings 181
    Larpool Cemetery 198, 220
    Millers Yard 179, 181
    Police Court 123, 125, 135, 157
    Regatta 72, 140, 209
    Rocket Brigade 51, 83, 87
    Seamans Hospital 220
    Spital Bridge 130, 131, 169
    St Hilda's Hospital 197, 198
    St Marys Church 13, 26, 31, 33, 40
    Tate Hill Pier 10
    Threadneedle Yard 181, 186
    West Cliff 26, 83
    West Cliff Saloon 98, 144, 158

Y
York 35, 118